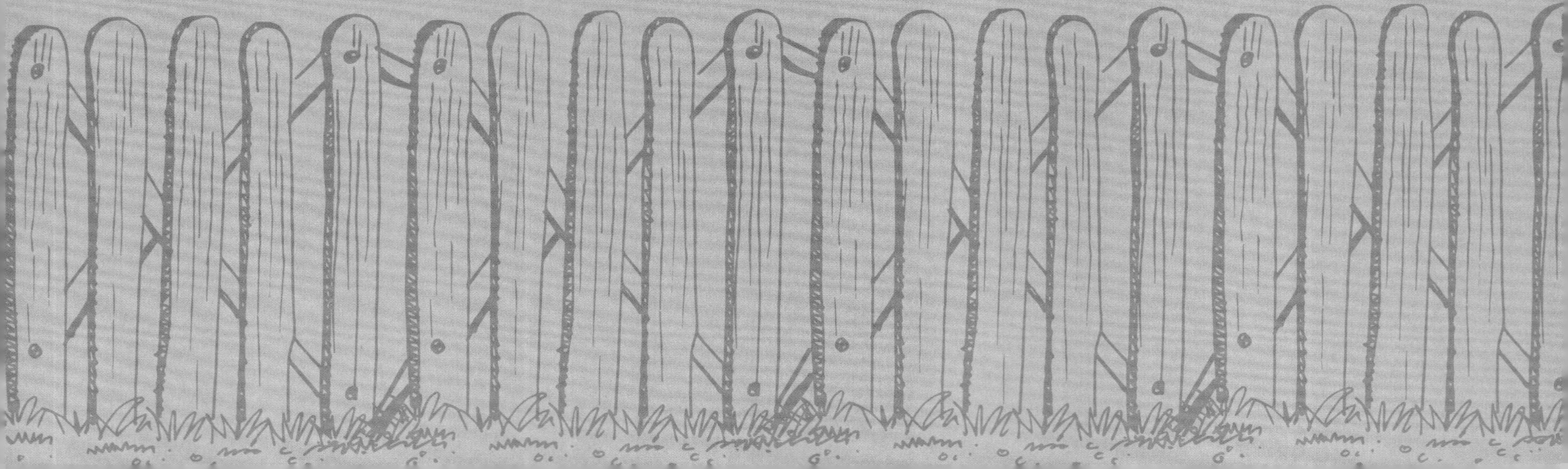

October 2017

Peter and Meredith,

It is a bittersweet pleasure to share this with you.

Much love,

[illegible]

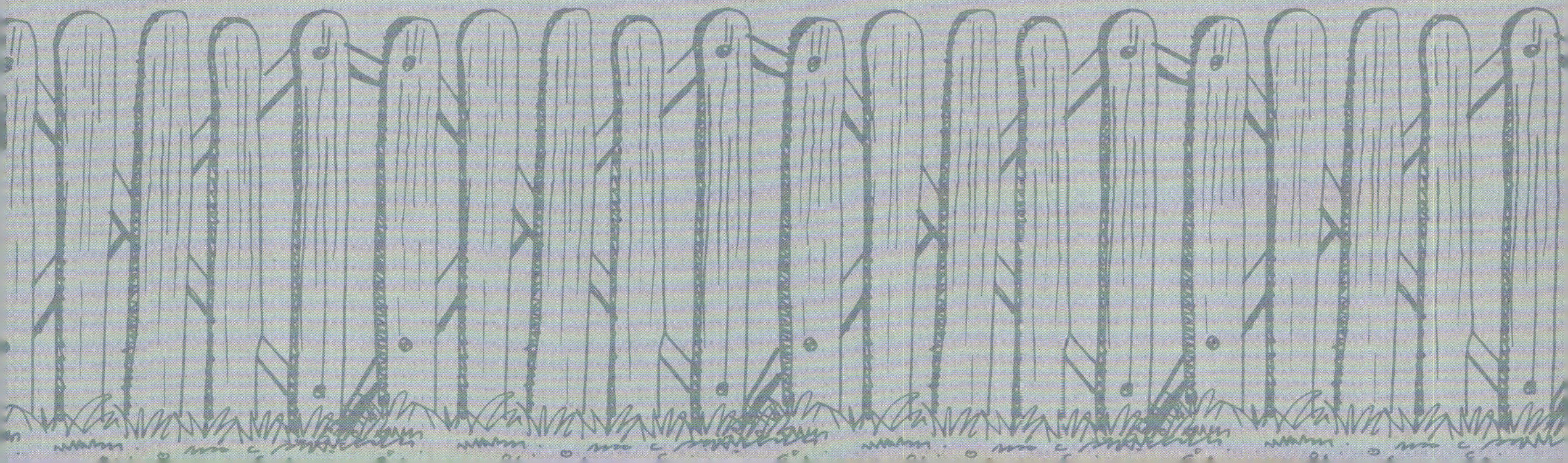

For almost 70 years Larry photographed hundreds of fences around the world because they caught his attention and he wondered about the stories behind them. He dreamed of creating a book of these stories which would encourage others to observe and think about the structures we humans impose on the natural landscape and the similar barriers we erect among ourselves. He carried this dream in his head for decades before starting to shape it into a book. Unfortunately, he had completed only the concept and a small start on the text when he became seriously ill and died in 2016.

To honor Larry and the value of his concept, I decided to take up his notes and complete the process of making his dream a reality. It was a bittersweet challenge. The photographic essay you hold now in your hands rings with Larry's voice and his enthusiasm for learning and understanding—an enthusiasm that those who knew him found infectious. I hope you will too.

Linda S. Hamilton

June 2017

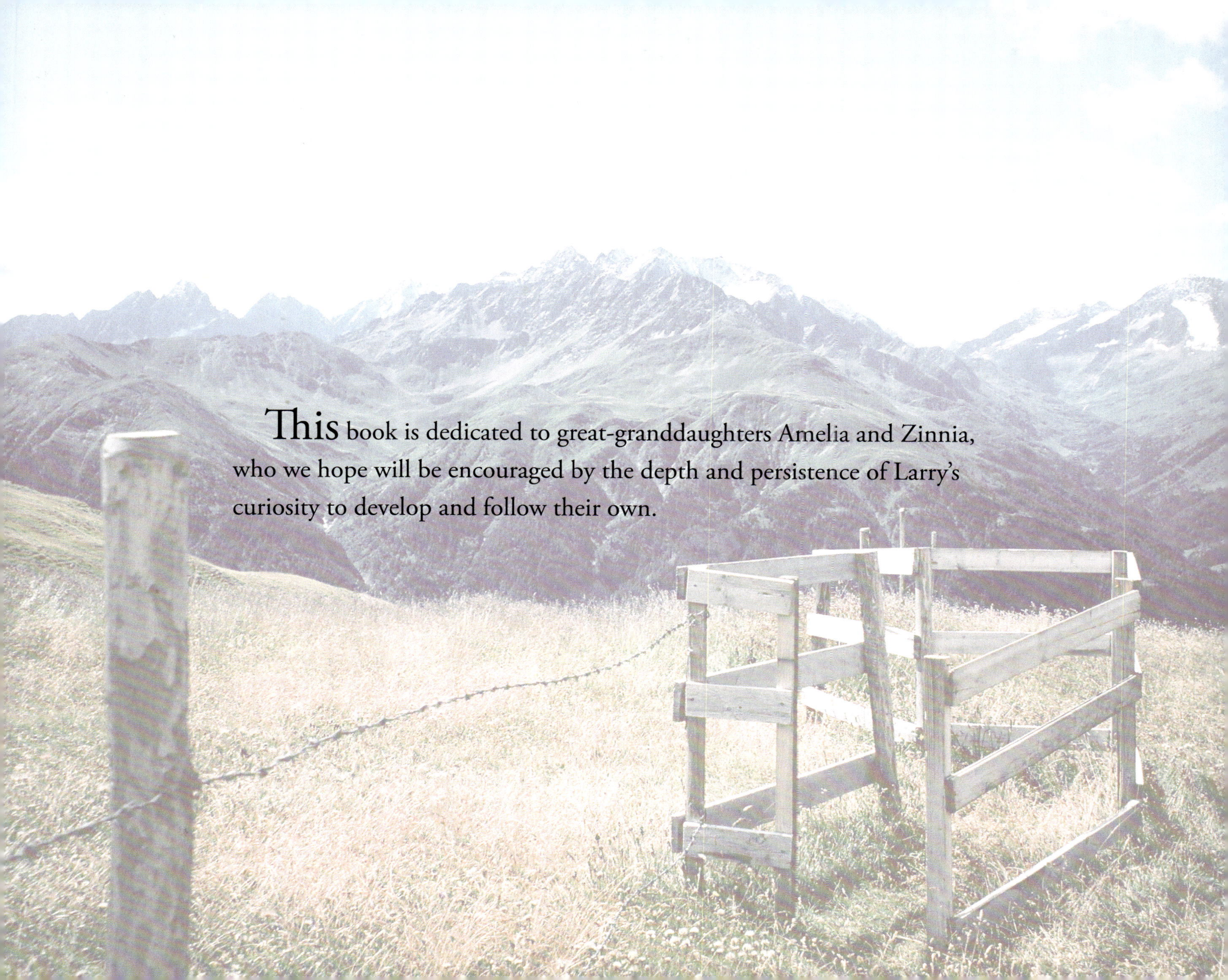

This book is dedicated to great-granddaughters Amelia and Zinnia, who we hope will be encouraged by the depth and persistence of Larry's curiosity to develop and follow their own.

MASCOT BOOKS

www.mascotbooks.com

Fences in the Landscape Talk—Are We Listening?
A Whimsical Photographic Essay

For more information, please contact:
Mascot Books
560 Herndon Parkway #120
Herndon, VA 20170
info@mascotbooks.com

Library of Congress Control Number: 2017907752

CPSIA Code: PBANG0717A
ISBN-13: 978-1-68401-087-5

Printed in the United States

FENCES IN THE LANDSCAPE TALK
ARE WE LISTENING?

A Whimsical Photographic Essay

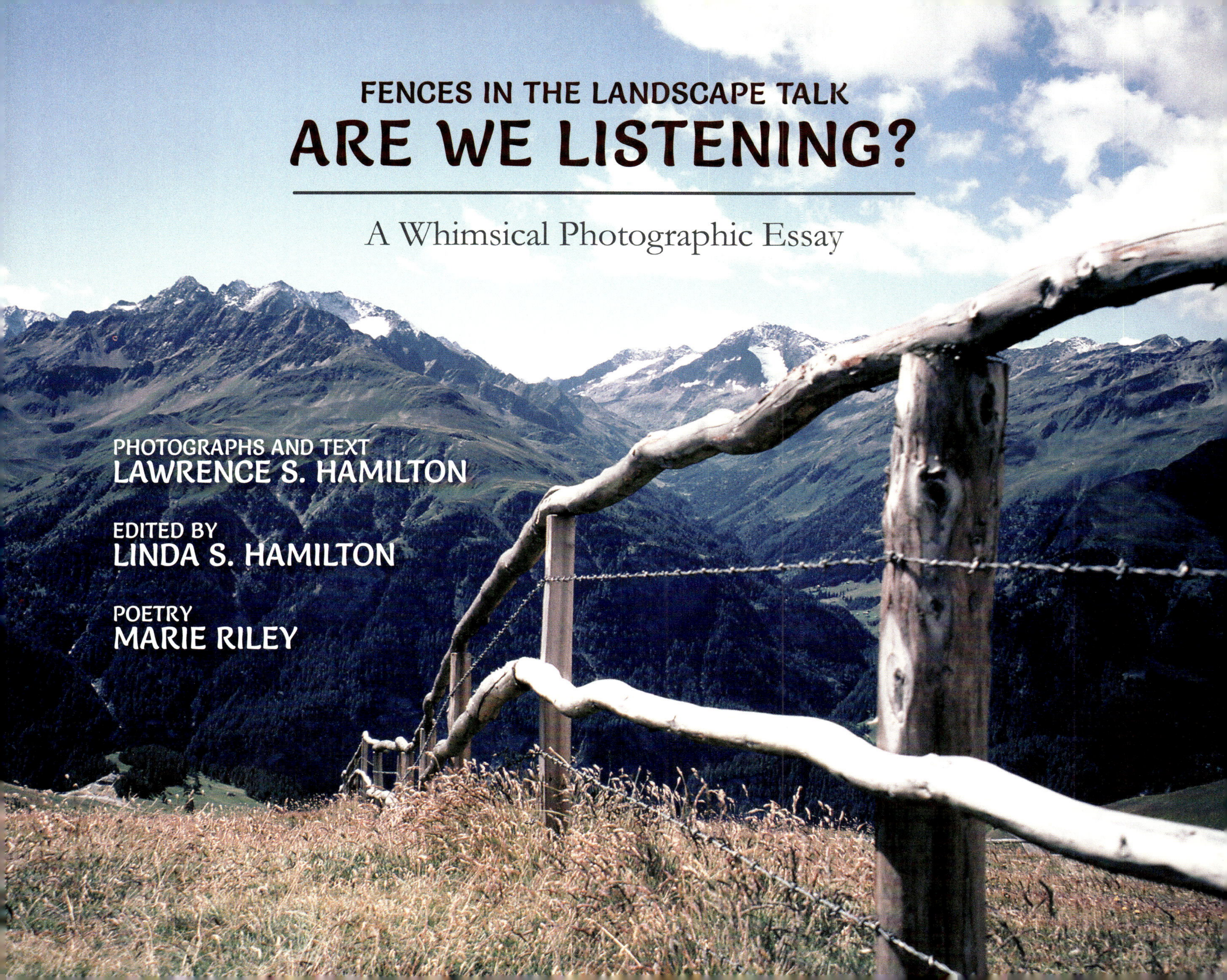

PHOTOGRAPHS AND TEXT
LAWRENCE S. HAMILTON

EDITED BY
LINDA S. HAMILTON

POETRY
MARIE RILEY

Welcome to the world of fences. The gate is open, so come on in. Be careful of the judder bars underfoot. These are in place to prevent cattle from getting out through the always-open gate on this farm in Yorkshire, England. Does this fencing and gate not speak to you of a friendly welcome? In this photographic essay, we are going to explore some of the various messages that a keen observer can read in these markers on the landscape.

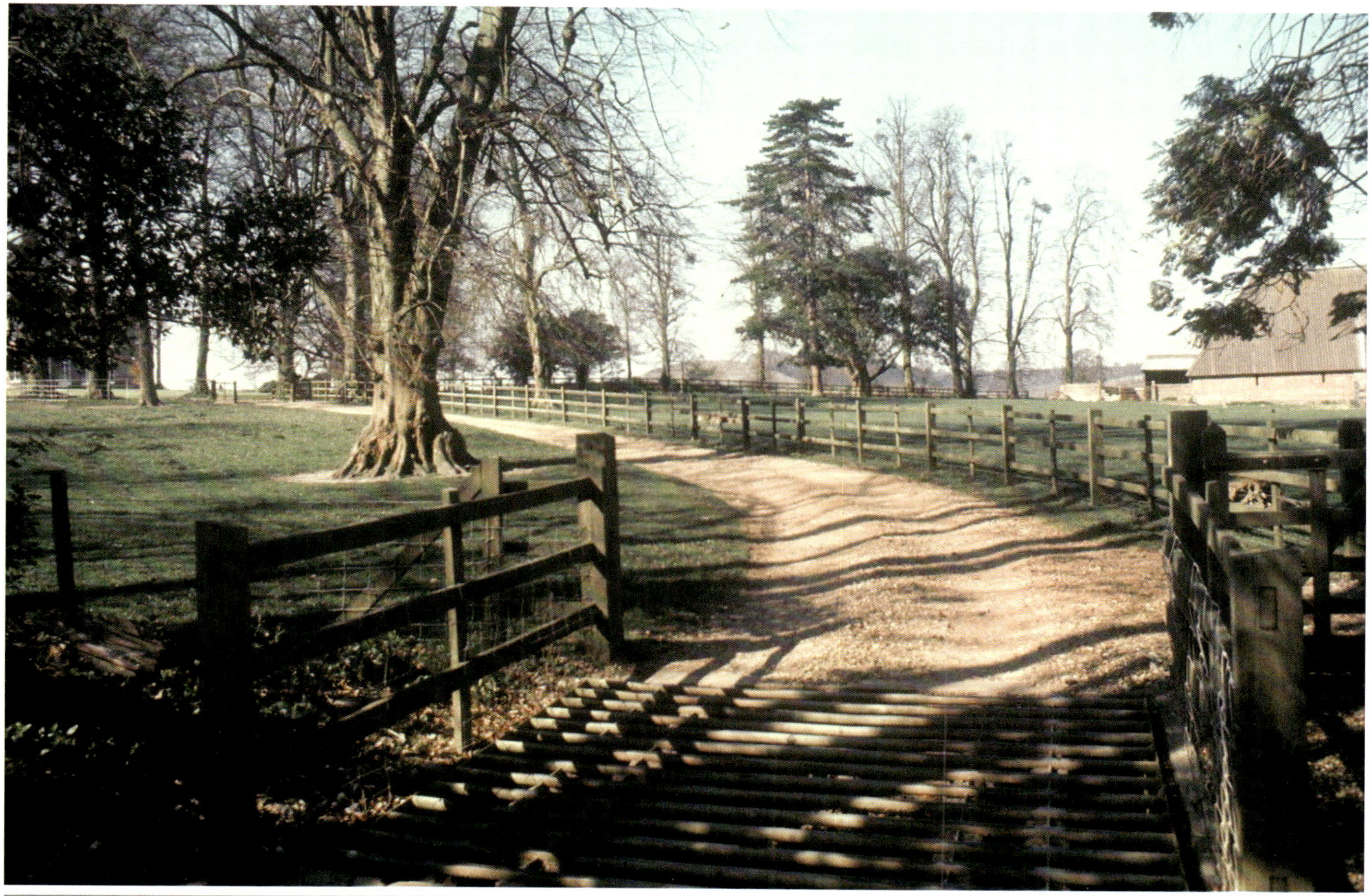

The gate is open and you are welcome to come in.

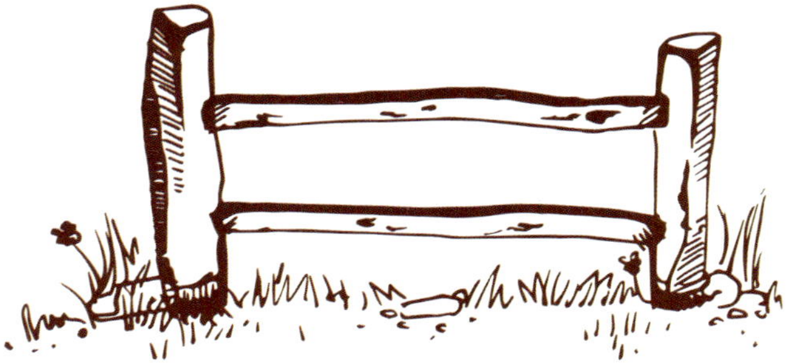

THE PURPOSE OF FENCES

The small African dik-dik antelope will insert a twig or grass blade into a scent cavity just under its eye to mark its territory. A meadowlark in Vermont sits stroppy on a post or rail and warbles its territorial claim. Wild canines scent boundaries with their urine, and bears mark signal trees with claw marks.

To stake out and announce one's territory is an inherent characteristic of many animals. Humans exhibit this trait, and very strongly, using various markers on the land, and sometimes on water. These may then be recorded in legal documents, on maps, or in the collective memory of a community.

The most common territorial markers worldwide are fences. They not only mark the limits of ownership, but may separate various uses and serve other purposes within one ownership. The materials from which they were constructed, the way they were constructed, their height, width, length, appearance, and fit in the landscape can tell us much—much about the land, the purpose, the builder, the present-day steward, and history. These human-made markers in the landscape can tell a story to those who choose to listen and learn from a landscape. This is the world of fences.

Historically, the major purposes of fences have been:

- Territorial boundary markers. *(This is mine!)*
- Keeping something in or out. *(Go no further!)*
- Privacy screen. *(No peeking!)*
- Protection from wind, sun or noise. *(Please give me a break.)*
- To segregate space within boundaries (to separate different uses, i.e. cultivated crop types or rotated pastures). *(Everything in its place.)*
- Aesthetic reasons, since many fences appear to be merely attractive, charming, or funky, without a utilitarian function. *(Beauty is in the eye of the beholder.)*

In erecting these markers, the builders reveal something of their own personality, the area's land uses and history, materials available, and the purpose. Let us look at a few of these from around the world and see if we can hear what stories they are telling. I'll draw from a collection of photographs I've taken over the last 68 years, a "hobby" born of my interest in Nature, the use of natural resources, human ecology, and the fact that I love a good story.

The first fence that really caught my attention was a pine stump fence near Guelph, Southwestern Ontario, Canada. It was this pine stump fence that enticed me to study the world of fences. It was an "Oh, wow!" moment for me in 1948, as a young man on my first job as Ontario Zone Forester. *(Yes, this is an old photo!)*

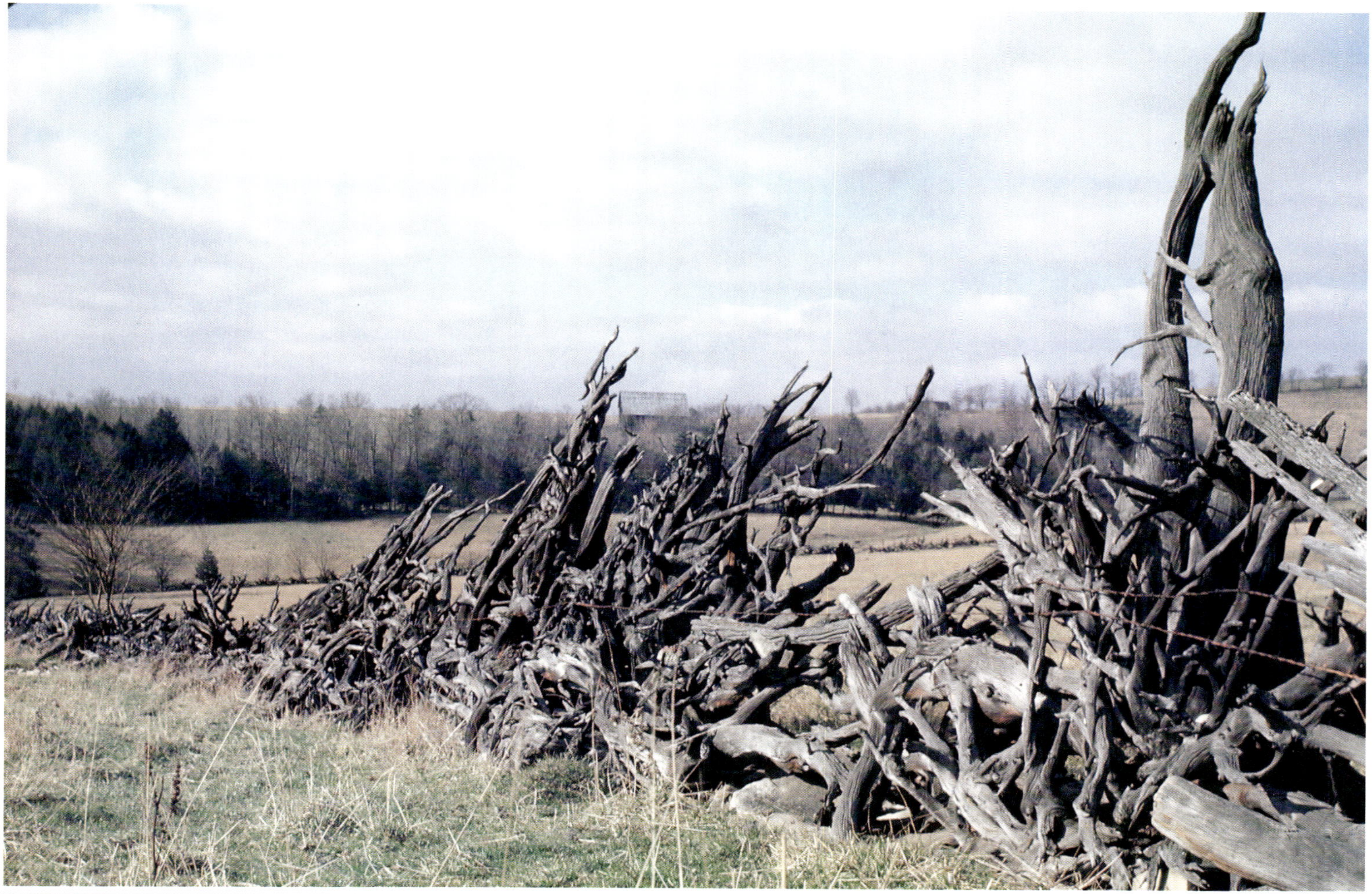

Pine stump fence, Southwestern Ontario, Canada

The gnarled roots, like bony fingers, pointed to a pioneer past when the land was cleared of giant white pines, the trunks were used to build shelter, and the stumps with roots pulled out were placed in this row as a barrier to something. The gun-metal gray, weathered roots were an interlaced web that grabbed my heart, head, and imagination. I realized that I was hearing a fence speak, and I was hooked.

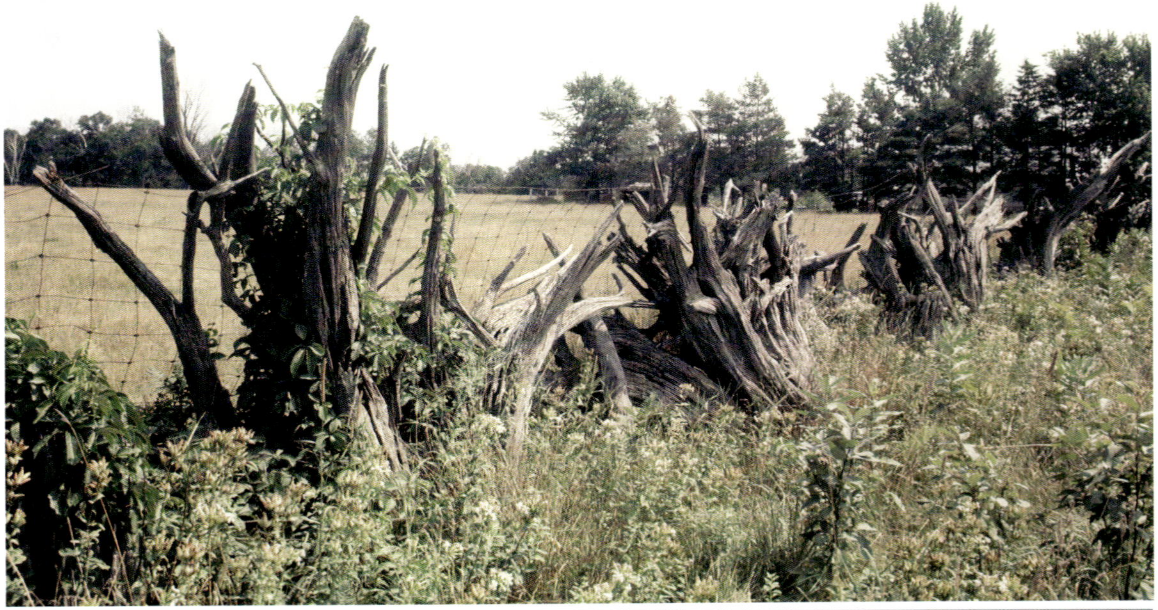

Aesthetically weathered pine stump roots,
Southwestern Ontario, Canada

Stacked in rows, the stumps proved to be a useful and long-lived fence because of the pine resin in the wood. Most of these have since been dismantled and taken away to be lucratively sold in the landscape trade in modern suburbs where individual stumps with their root networks may support rambling roses, ivy, bird baths, or other decorative material. There are even pine stump rustlers, operating at night. Perhaps pine stump fences remaining substantially intact should be registered as historic cultural artifacts.

By day,
The greyed and crackling joints
point wildly
into a thrifty pioneer past,
where everything had its use.
Branches burned for potash.
Rotting molars of pine yanked
to clear the land for plows,
strewn long and dense,
woven sometimes.
"Here," the deadwood says along its bristly stretch,
"here you cannot pass."

I hope this has peaked your curiosity, because I would like to show you some of the photos I have taken, give my interpretation of what these fences can tell us, and share the questions they raise in my mind. Make your own observations. You may see different things, and have different questions. But beware—once you start the practice of observing the landscape carefully, you may not be able to stop. Your senses and curiosity will be opened and the pleasure will be addictive.

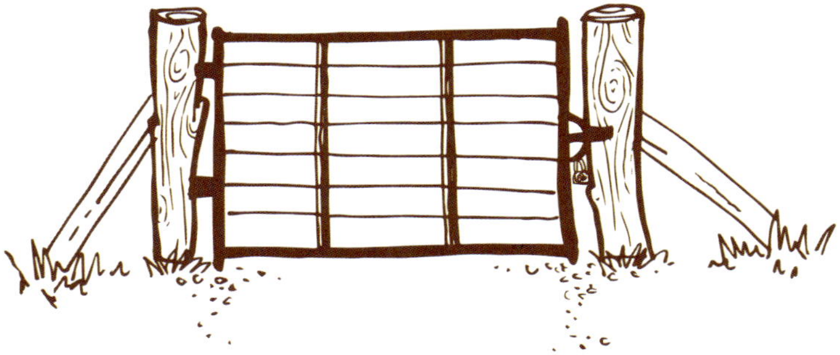

THIS IS MINE!

GO NO FURTHER!

The word fence derives from the Latin *defendere*, to defend, and then Middle English *fens*, also referring to defense. Defense was the earliest purpose of both walls and fences. Pictured on the next page is Dundrum Castle in Northern Ireland, which was built in the early 13th century in Norman style by a de Courcy. It has an outer "defensive" wall of stone, as well as the stone curtain wall, tower, and bastions of the castle itself. Note the capping with vertical flat stones to make getting over more difficult. This capping was also often used in domestic fencing to dissuade goats and sheep from climbing over. None of these defenses were effective, and many battles resulted in the castle changing owners many times. It was finally taken by Cromwell's troops and mostly demolished around 1652. It is now a National Historic Property.

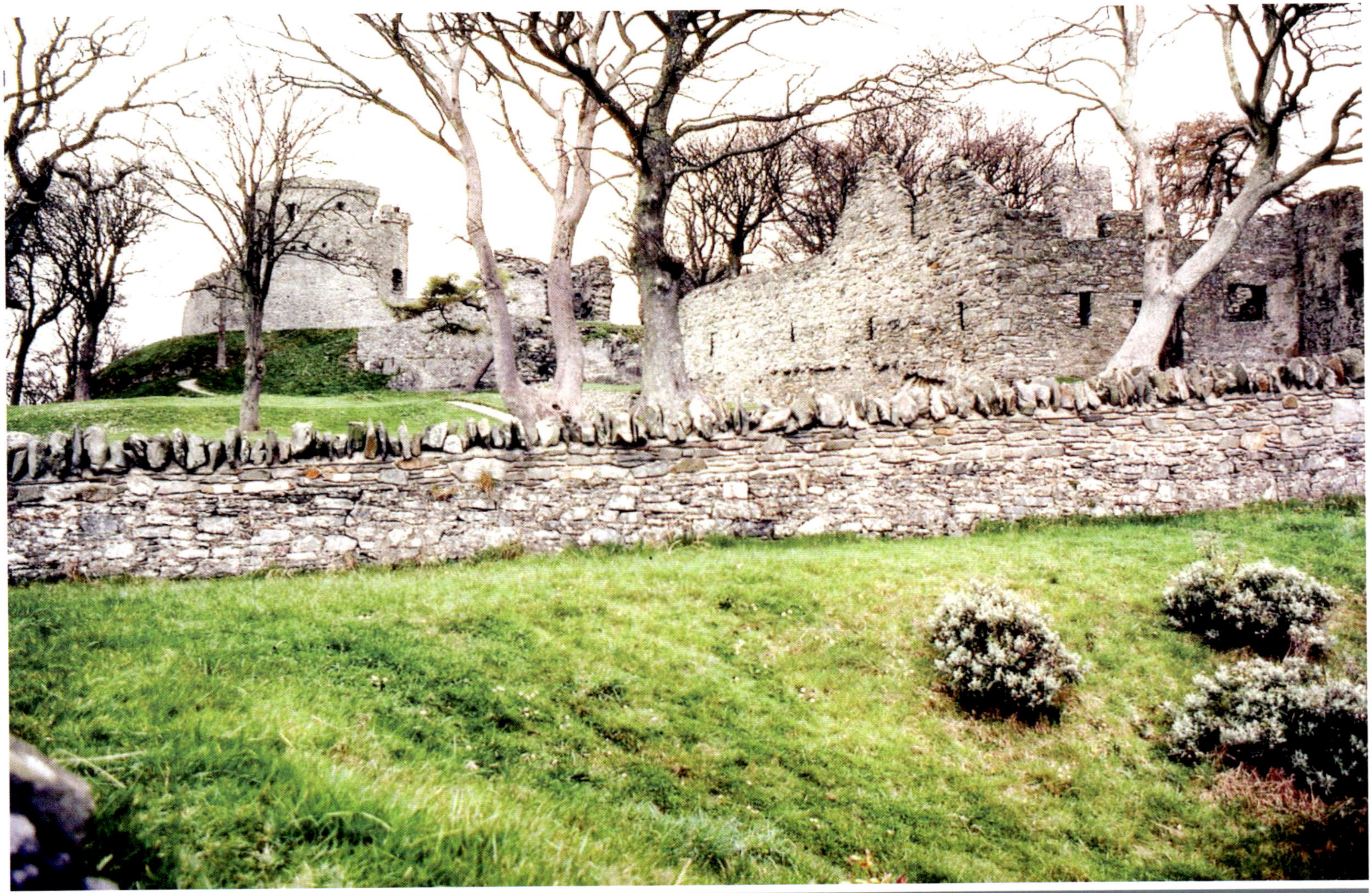

Dundrum Castle, County Down, Northern Ireland

The fairies whisper from crannies
old tales
of battles won and lost, kingdoms razed,
or lives forever muted in the grey misty rockland.
Gauze whispers, insubstantial
as all high goals
wind into shades, advancing and retreating
into the large landscape
until he who would reign must count the stones,
the bones
between ambition and glory.

Not only walls, but also fences, have been important barriers to military ground operations. Certainly in the days of foot soldiers, or even of cavalry, and prior to armored tanks, they were landscape features that provided impediments to battle advancements and a modicum of cover for those attempting to hold ground. They played a prominent role in many battles of Europe, where thick hedgerows and stone walls were also obstacles to military advances. In World War I, fences of barbed wire were deliberately set up to impede the enemy. In the northeast of what is now the USA, during the Indian Wars, War of Independence, and War of 1812, even wood rail fences were defensive positions at times. The early settlers had adopted the zigzag snake rail fence where trees were abundant, since they were relatively easy to construct, and durable wood such as cedar, juniper and chestnut were available.

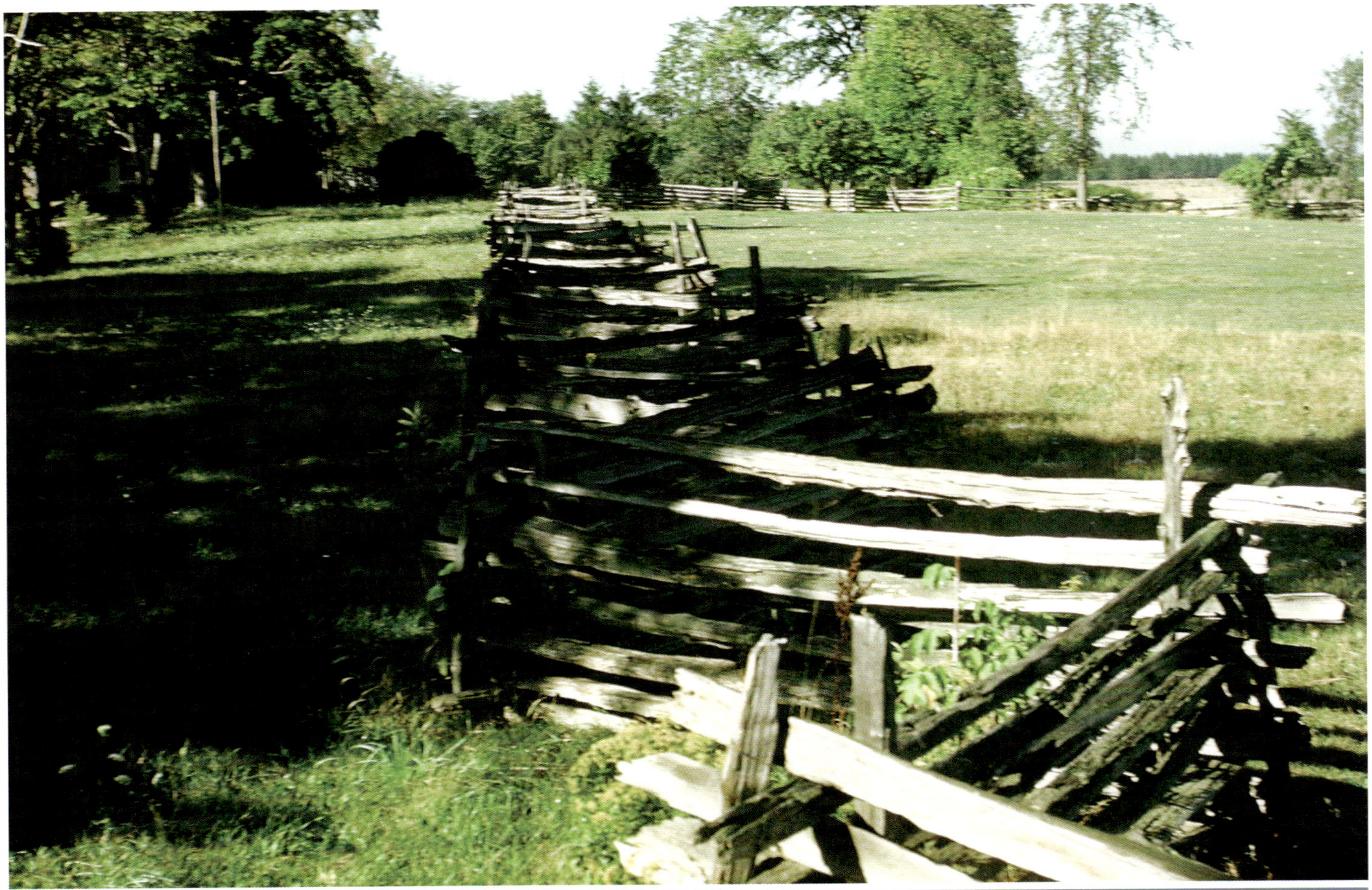

Snake rail fences, like this one in Vermont, USA, provided some cover and a battle station in farmland during military conflicts.

The barrier function is undoubtedly the primary reason for most fences. They have been erected in both rural and urban areas, not only as property markers, but also to prevent easy access of neighbors' animals, and sometimes of the neighbors themselves, or to prevent the fence builder's animals from straying. Walls may be constructed with stone or other easily-available material, but fences are commonly made of wood, especially when forest or woodlands are near at hand; stump fences or snake rail fences are good examples. Often, they are composed of living plant material, for example gorse, blackthorn, or hawthorn on European farms, or of cactus in dry country. Following the invention of woven wire and barbed wire, metal entered the scene, though sometimes with wooden posts or to reinforce a less-than-sturdy fence. On some rural properties several of these may co-exist, and so may tell an interesting time-lapse history.

Several types of fences together denote different materials being available over time, from early land clearing to recently-purchased woven wire and metal posts.

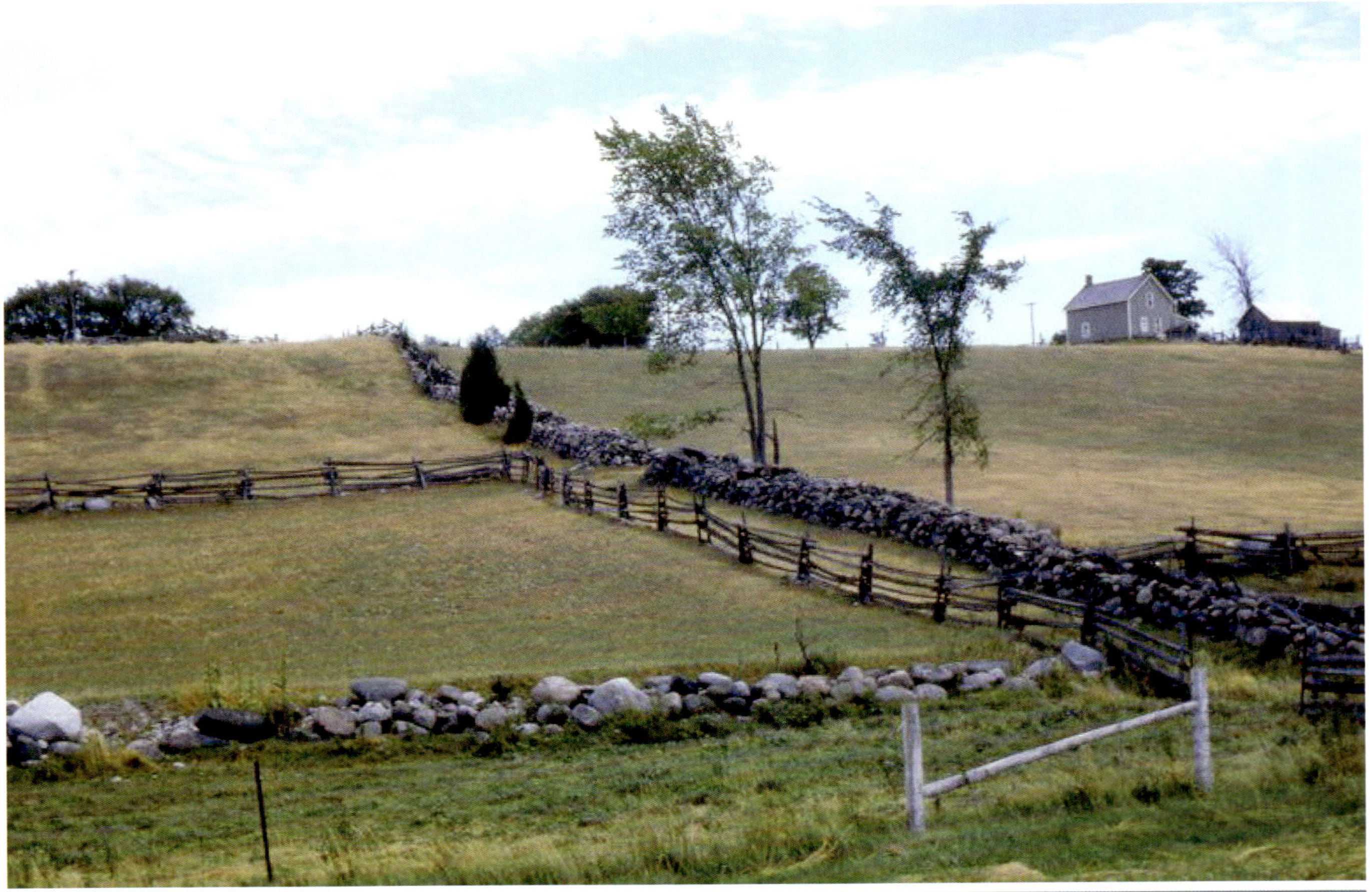

Materials of stone, cedar posts and rails, barbed wire, and woven wire are all seen here in Southeastern Ontario, Canada.

Fences vary greatly in length, and can be as small as an enclosure around an individual tree.

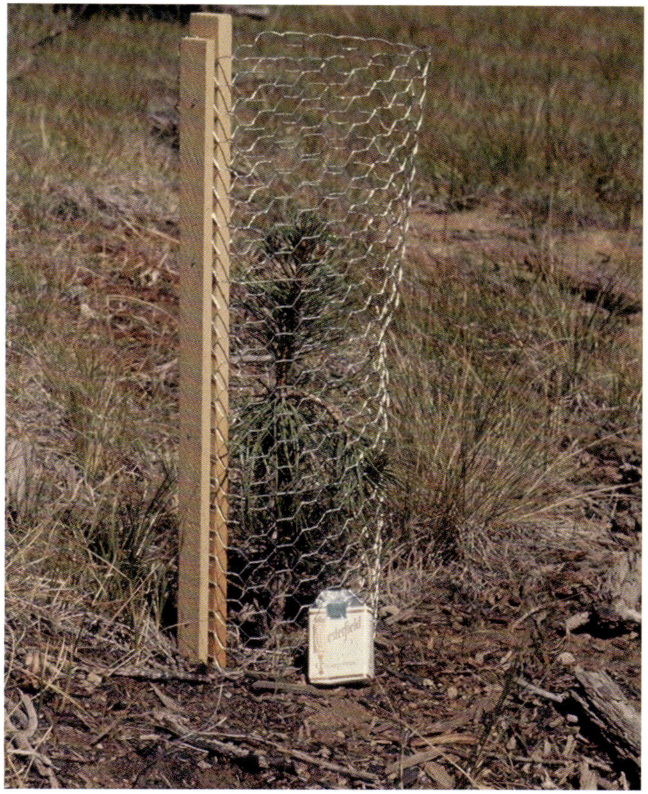

A chicken wire fence guards a planted pine seedling, probably from deer, in Deschutes National Forest central Oregon, USA.

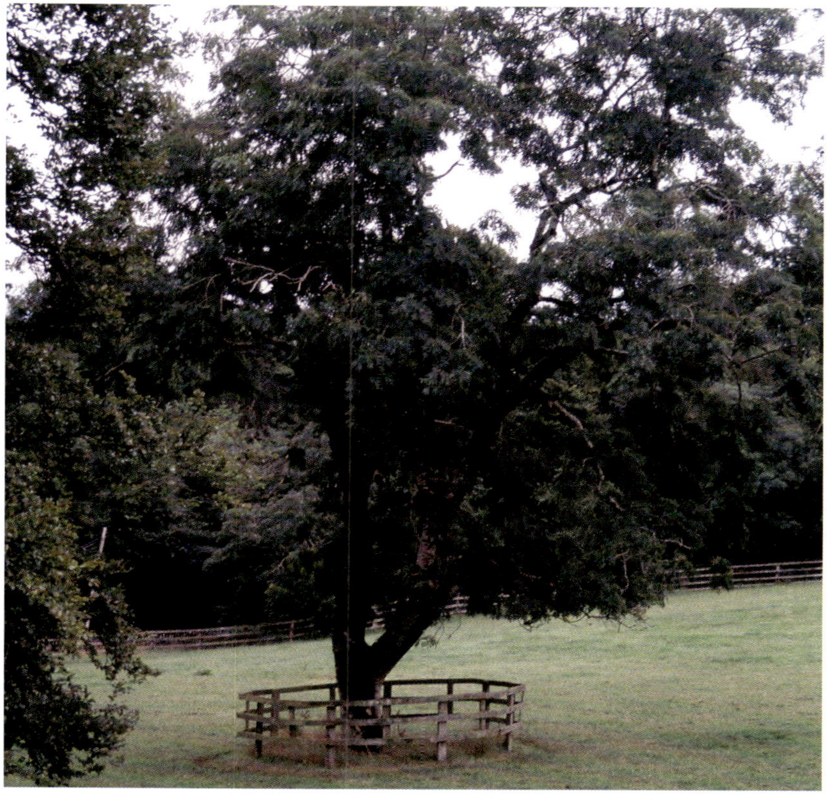

This one in Tipperary, Ireland encircles a valued mature shade tree, protecting its trunk from rubbing by the enclosed animals and keeping them from resting and compacting the soil immediately around the trunk.

This fence provides important protection from browsing goats for a young tree in Venezuela.

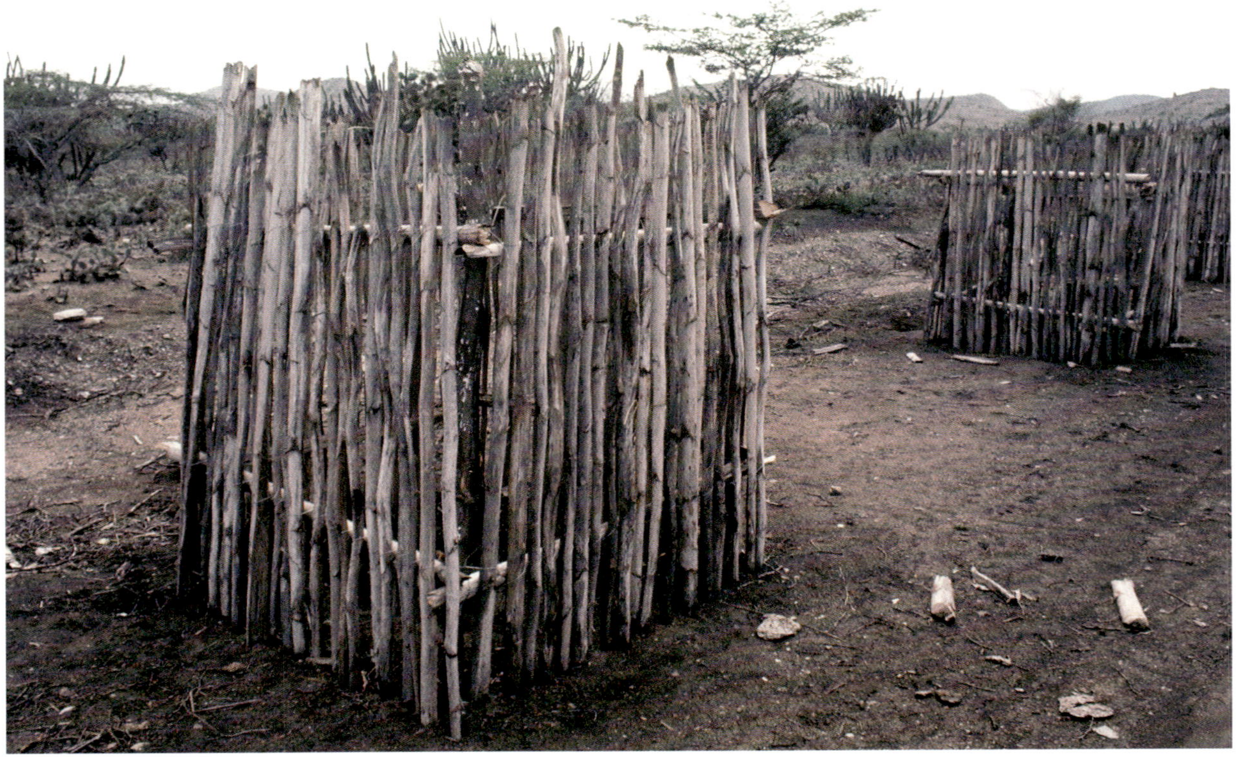

Fences can also be impressively long. This one traverses more than a thousand miles continuously in Eastern Australia. It is the famous Dingo Fence, meant to limit their territory and protect livestock. Dingoes, being the clever animals that they are, frequently outsmarted the makers of this barrier.

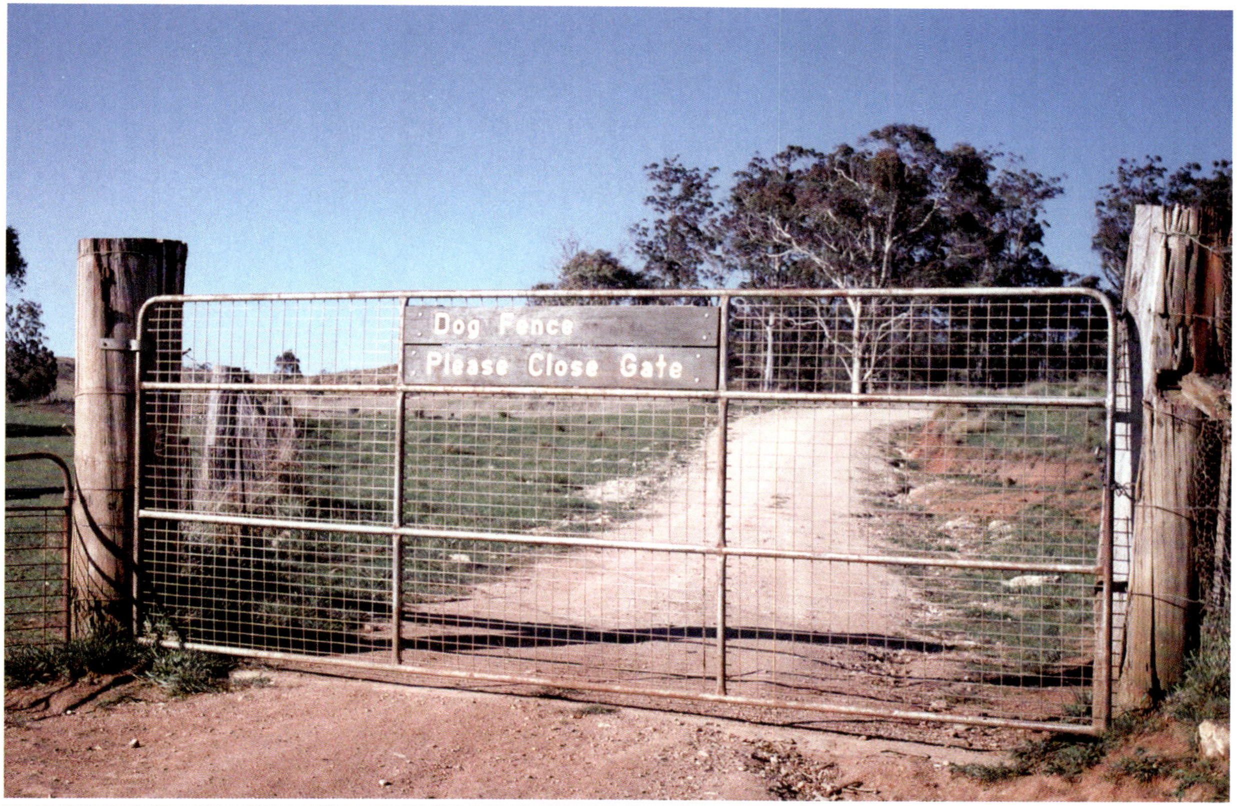

A farm gate in the great Dingo Fence on the Tableland, New South Wales, Australia.

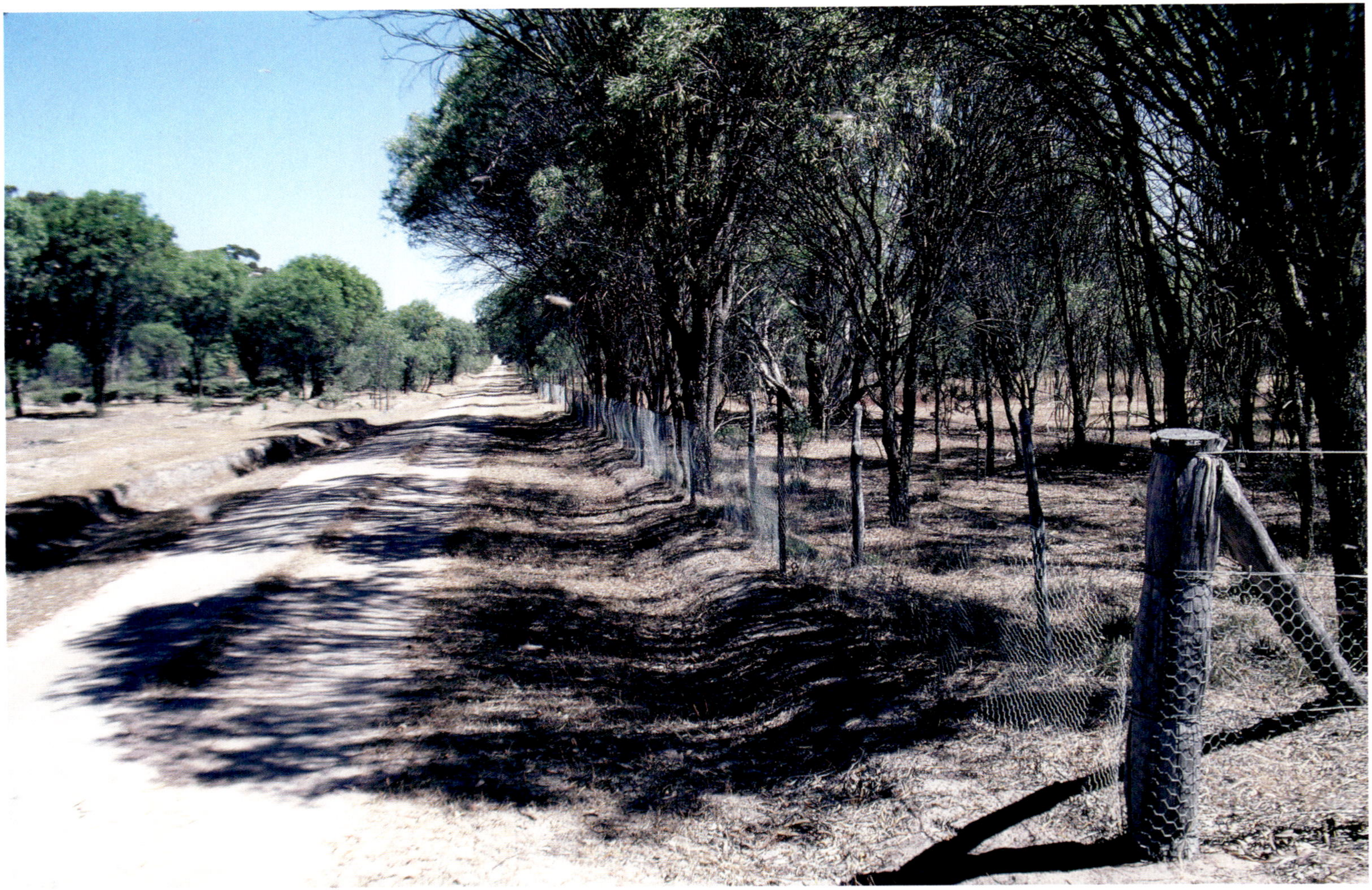

Maintained section of the famous Rabbit-Proof Fence in Western Australia.

In Western Australia, there is another champion for length: the so-called Rabbit-Proof Fence. Rabbits had been introduced in 1859 for hunting purposes, but without predators to control their numbers, the population exploded to plague proportions. In an ambitious effort to reduce the destructive and competitive use of livestock herbage by this introduced species, a State Barrier Fence was erected in 1907. It ran a distance of 1,139 miles north to south. Two additional supplemental fences were erected, making the total length of the Rabbit-Proof Fence some 2,023 miles! Not surprisingly, it was only partially successful. The later approach of targeted introductions of the disease myxomatosis knocked down the rabbit populations, and the fence is no longer fully maintained. The fence did, however, still help to limit the number of emu moving into agricultural lands in search of browse during heavy drought years in the 1930s, 1970s, and early 1990s. A remnant portion of the fence is still maintained and has small enough wire weave to still be effective in excluding even small mammals.

These fences were almost as ambitious as two of the world's most famous walls which also tried to establish *This is mine! Go no further!* In the end, the walls were not successful either. And they took vastly more effort to construct and maintain than any fence. The Great Wall of China linked a series of fortifications in an east-west direction to protect the northern border of China at various stages and through several dynasties. It was begun in the 7th century BC, with the longest and best areas constructed using bricks and stones instead of rammed earth, being built in the Ming Dynasty. It ran for roughly 5,500 miles, had up to 1,200 watchtowers, and was 15-30 feet high plus ramparts and 16 feet across the top. It failed ultimately in its purpose, and much of it has fallen into decay. Some sections are currently maintained and restored, however, as one of the world's great tourist attractions.

Also built to protect a northern border from "barbarian" invaders was a wall built by the Romans across England from sea to sea at the time of Emperor Hadrian; construction began in AD 122 and was finished in about 6 years. It ran 73 miles and was fortified at regular intervals. Part of it used turf that was 20 feet wide and 11 feet high. Another long section consisted of squared limestone blocks, 10 feet wide and 16-20 feet in height. The entire wall was made more effective with a ditch or dry moat on the northern face. Hadrian's Wall is now a tourist attraction, the site of a National Trail, and was declared a World Heritage Site in 1978.

Constructing a wall is generally a much greater investment of material, time and effort than a fence. So it is no wonder that fences are used extensively to not only make clear statements about boundaries and ownership, but also to address practical problems and to show off the creativity of the builder.

Join me now to listen to more stories told by fences, like not only "This is mine!" and "Go no further!" but also "No peeking!" "Please give me a break," "Separate but equal," and "Beauty is in the eye of the beholder." I offer my interpretations, which have occasionally been confirmed by the fence builder or owner. You may see additional story lines. Let's look and listen.

The photos are grouped generally by the type of material the fence builders chose—WOOD, LIVING VEGETATION, DRY VEGETATION, MOSTLY WIRE, and then there is STRANGE STUFF.

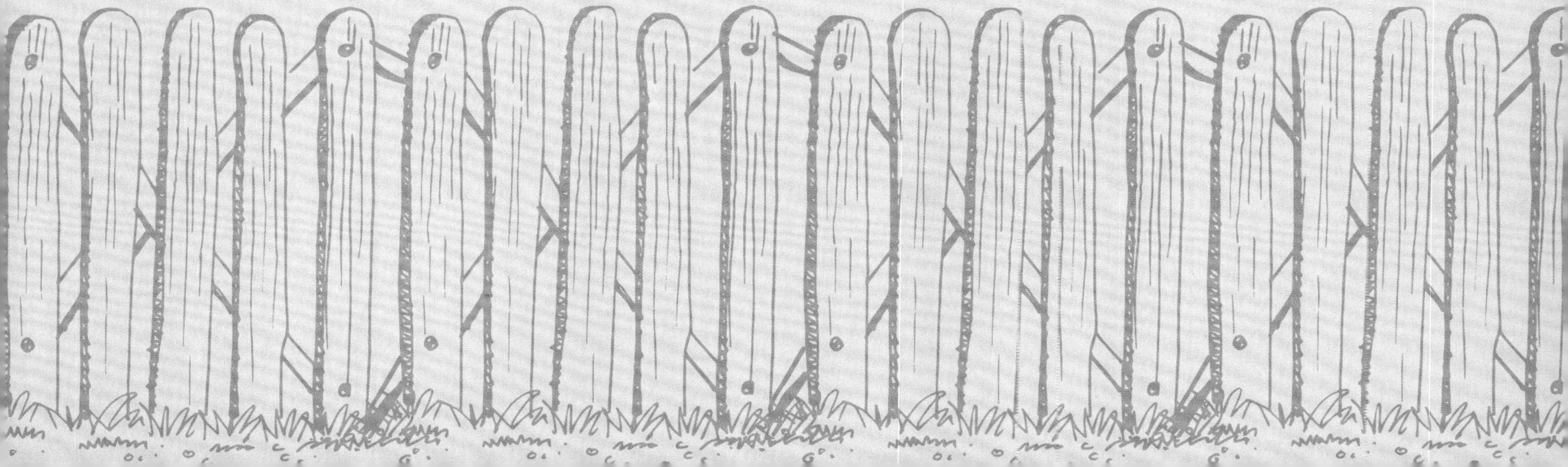

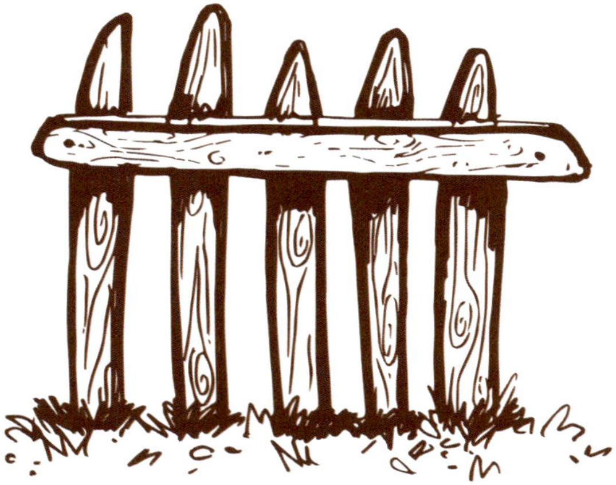

In the World of Fences,

WOOD IS GOOD

When forest land is cleared for farming, a source of wood for posts and rails or poles becomes readily available. Land clearing took place so long ago in the Old World that almost all wooden fencing has disappeared there, either through decay or use as fuel. It is therefore in the New World, particularly North America, that the wooden fence remains an important characteristic of the landscape. Land-clearing fence builders soon learned which species would decay to uselessness very quickly, and which were good for the long haul. Eastern North American colonists soon learned that species such as the cedars (white, red, and Atlantic) and the abundant chestnut were the very best, though as shown at the beginning of this book, pine stump-roots, which are naturally impregnated with resins and terpenes, were not only satisfactory for longevity, but attractive to boot.

In regions of the eastern USA where the American chestnut once thrived, rails and posts were usually fashioned from that long-lasting species. In the Northeast, white cedar, common in swampy areas, was long-lasting and easily split. Where shallow soils made digging post-holes difficult, rails were simply placed on the ground in a zigzag pattern three, four, or even five rails high. This was the iconic snake rail fence.

A square 40-acre field, for example, would typically require 8,000 fence rails for many kinds of rail fencing. By 1850, there were an estimated 3.2 million miles of wood fence in the United States![1] Since then, various types of wooden fences have been constructed, many of them giving clues to geographic location or to some characteristics of the builder/owner. What do you read in the ones that follow?

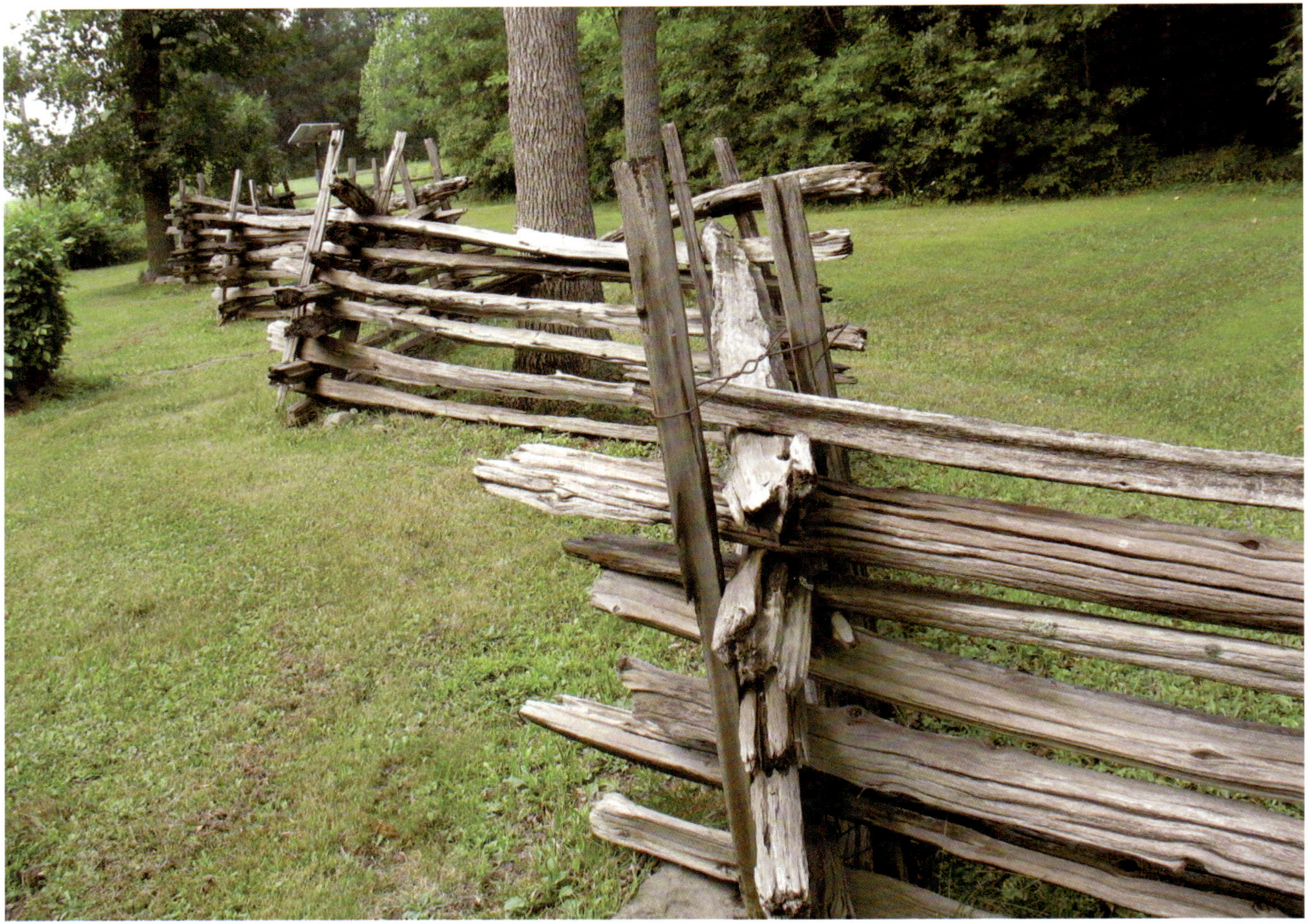

This is a modified 6-rail snake rail fence. Upright posts are not deep in the ground, but are used for bracing, and braced again with wire. This wood has seen more than 150 years in service, with this fence being constructed in Vermont, USA from cedar salvaged from an original fence dating to the 1800s.

Snake, they called it, or worm,
wooden trail of serpent, 60 degrees for security.
Creating havens for critters
and every weed you can imagine;
A wide swath of unplanted land:
farmers' grievance.
Invention of New World plenty and New World waste-
The long-lived snake and the shrinking forest.

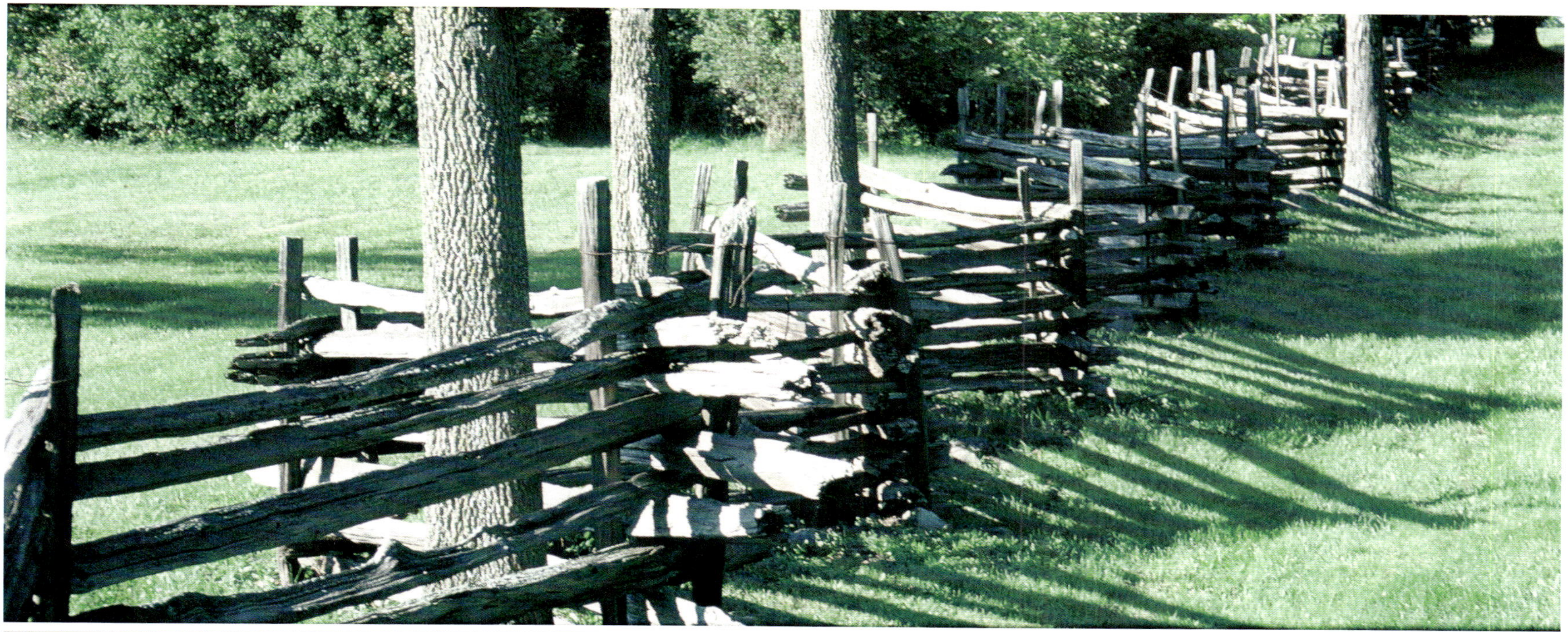

This Vermont, USA split cedar rail fence demonstrates how flexible the building style is, as it easily snakes around trees.

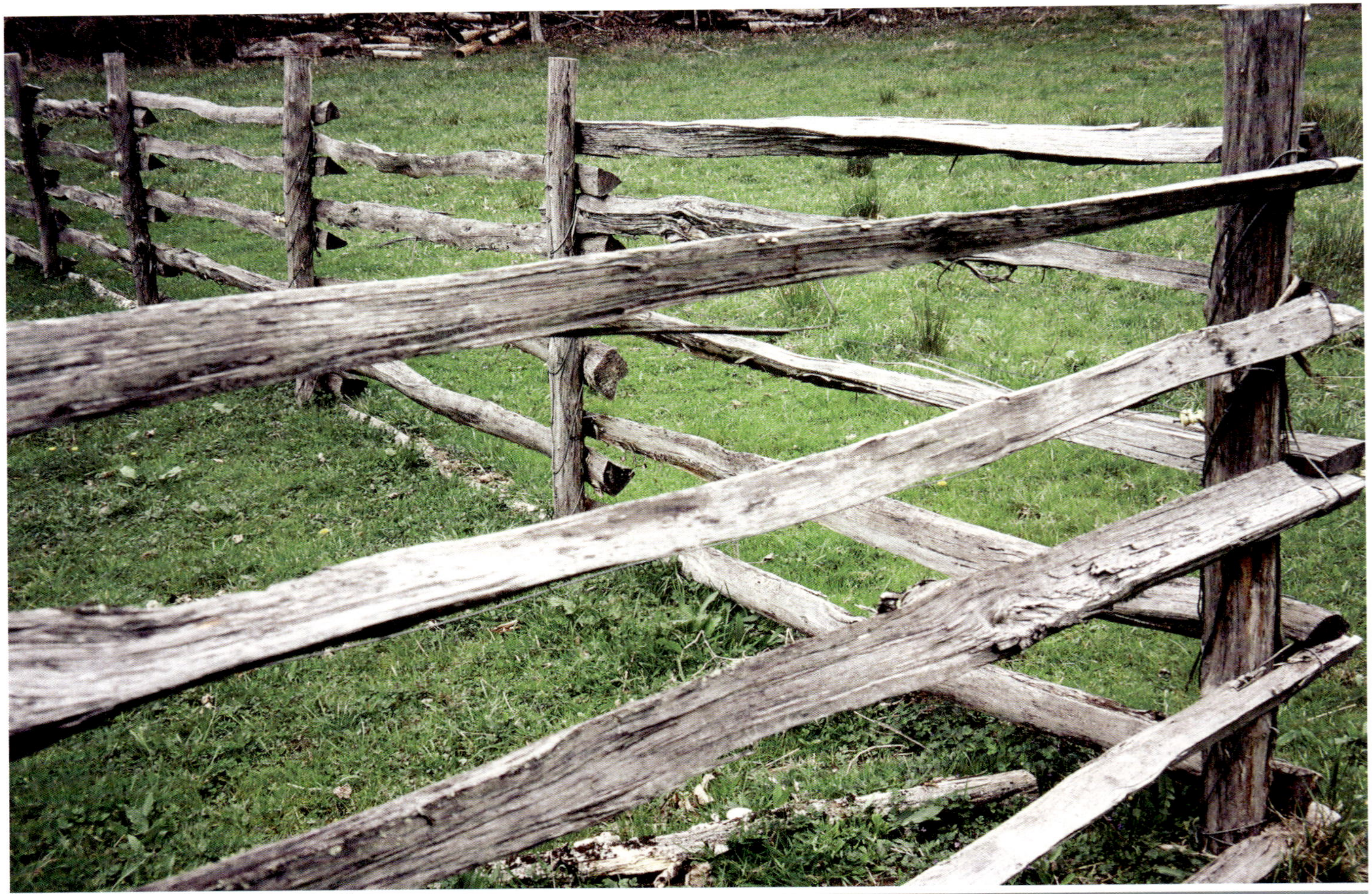

Chestnut also makes excellent rails, as used here in the Southern Appalachian Mountains of the USA. These rails are attached to the uprights with wire.

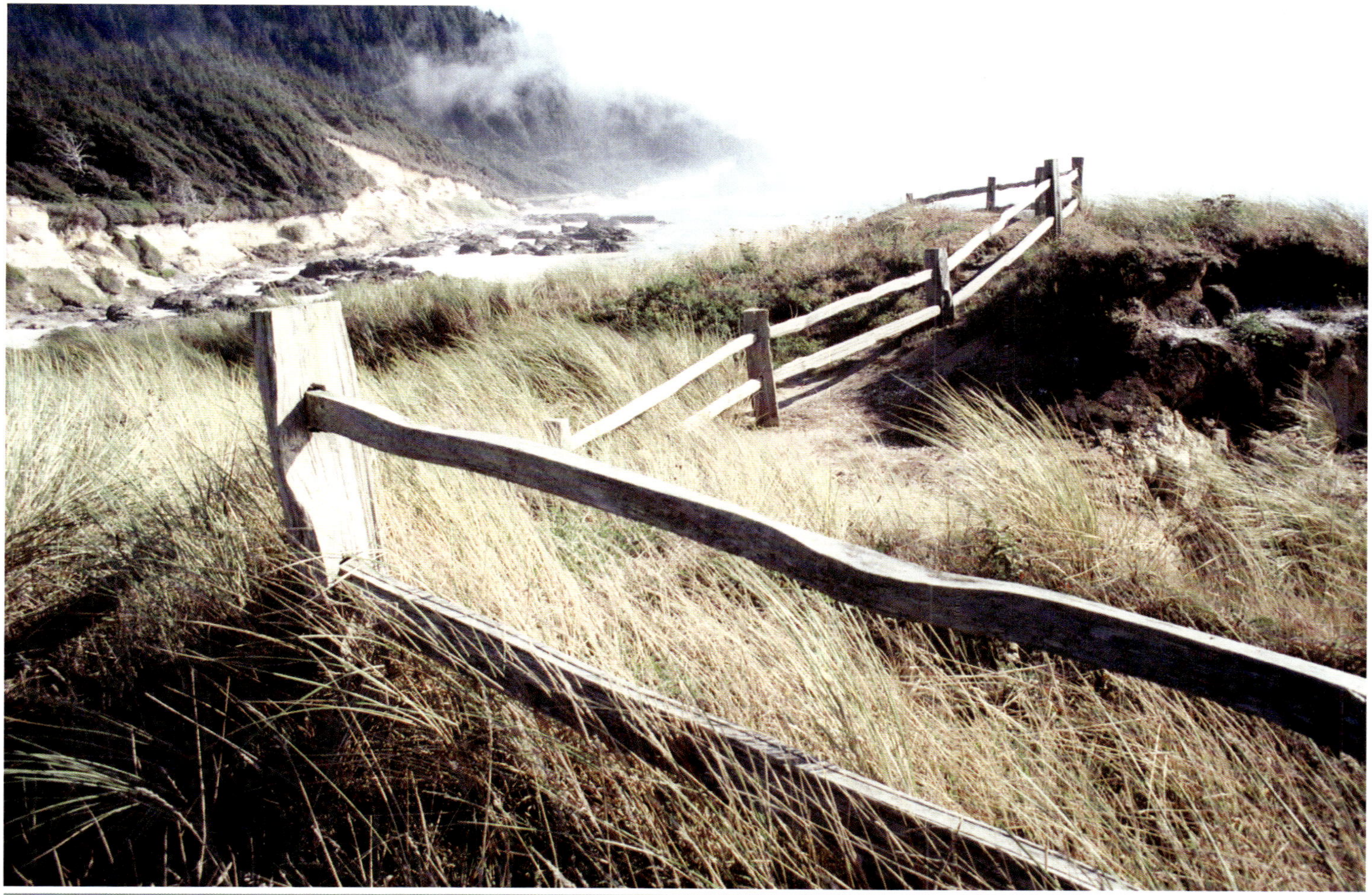

The rails of this coastal Oregon, USA fence (near Yachats) are inserted into slots in the uprights.

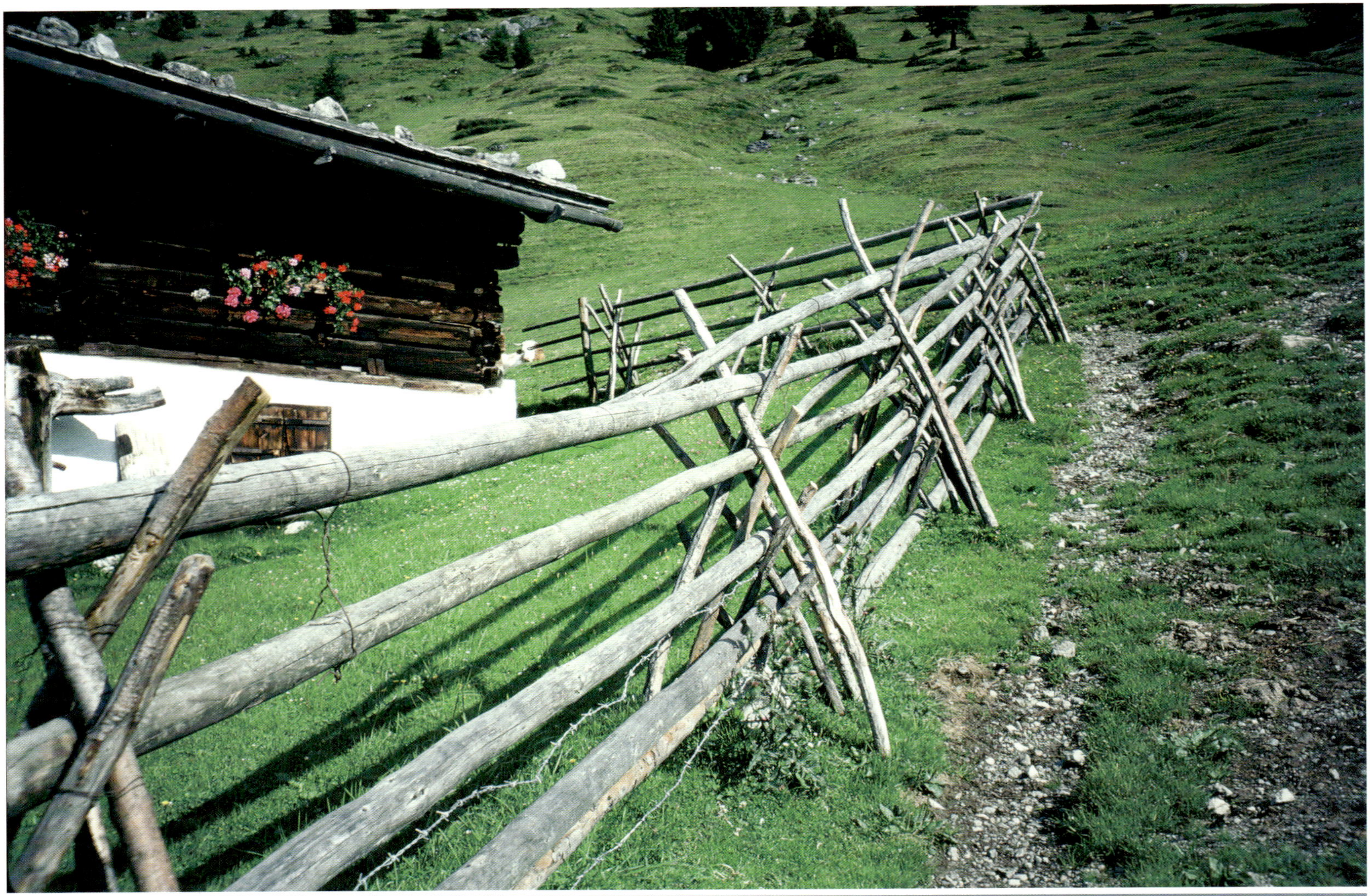

These rails are cleverly supported with a crisscross of light-weight uprights (plus a little wire), in Kalkalpen National Park, Austria.

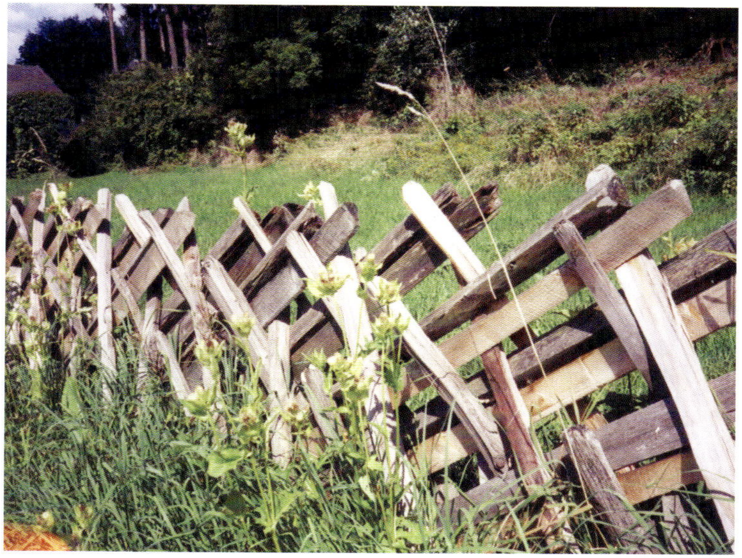

This fence near Beschtesgaden, Germany perhaps carries crisscross rails to the extreme.

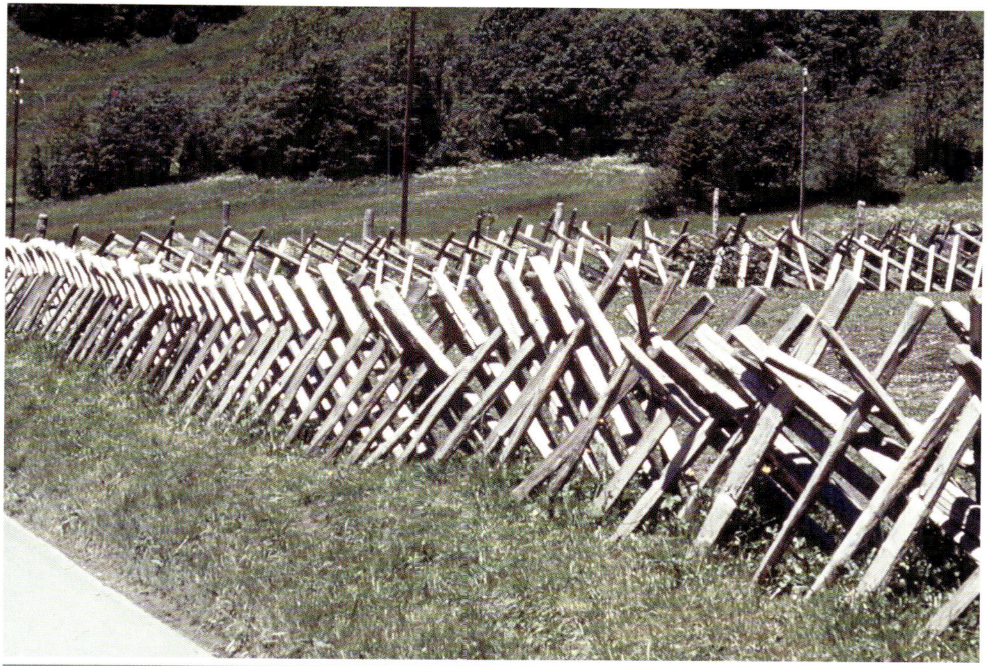

In this enigmatic crisscross lumber fence near Villars, Switzerland, no nails or wire employed. But what a profligate use of wood! I was unable to ascertain the motive behind this fence. What do you think?

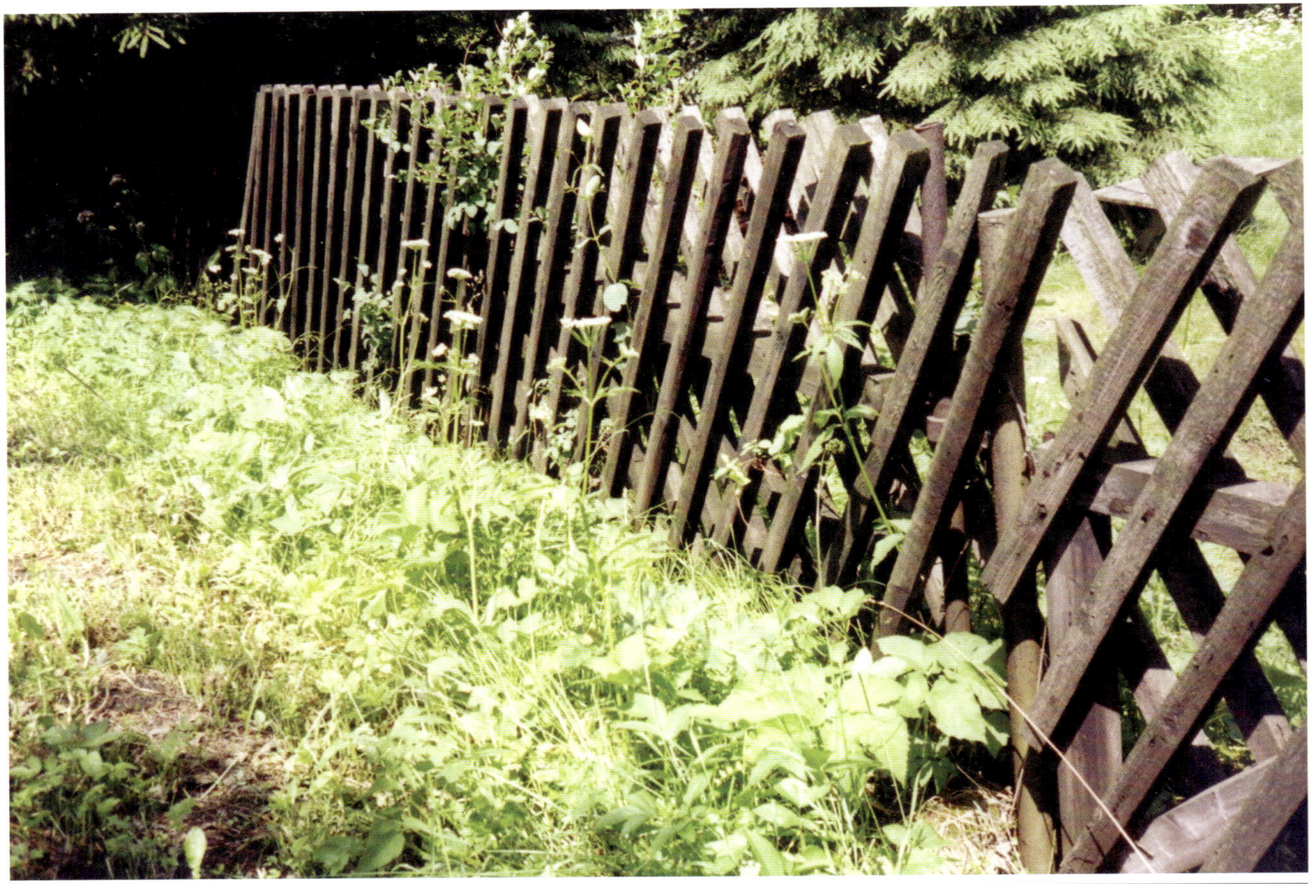

Here is another unusual wooden fence whose story is unclear. I wonder what is going on here in Chribska, Czech Republic.

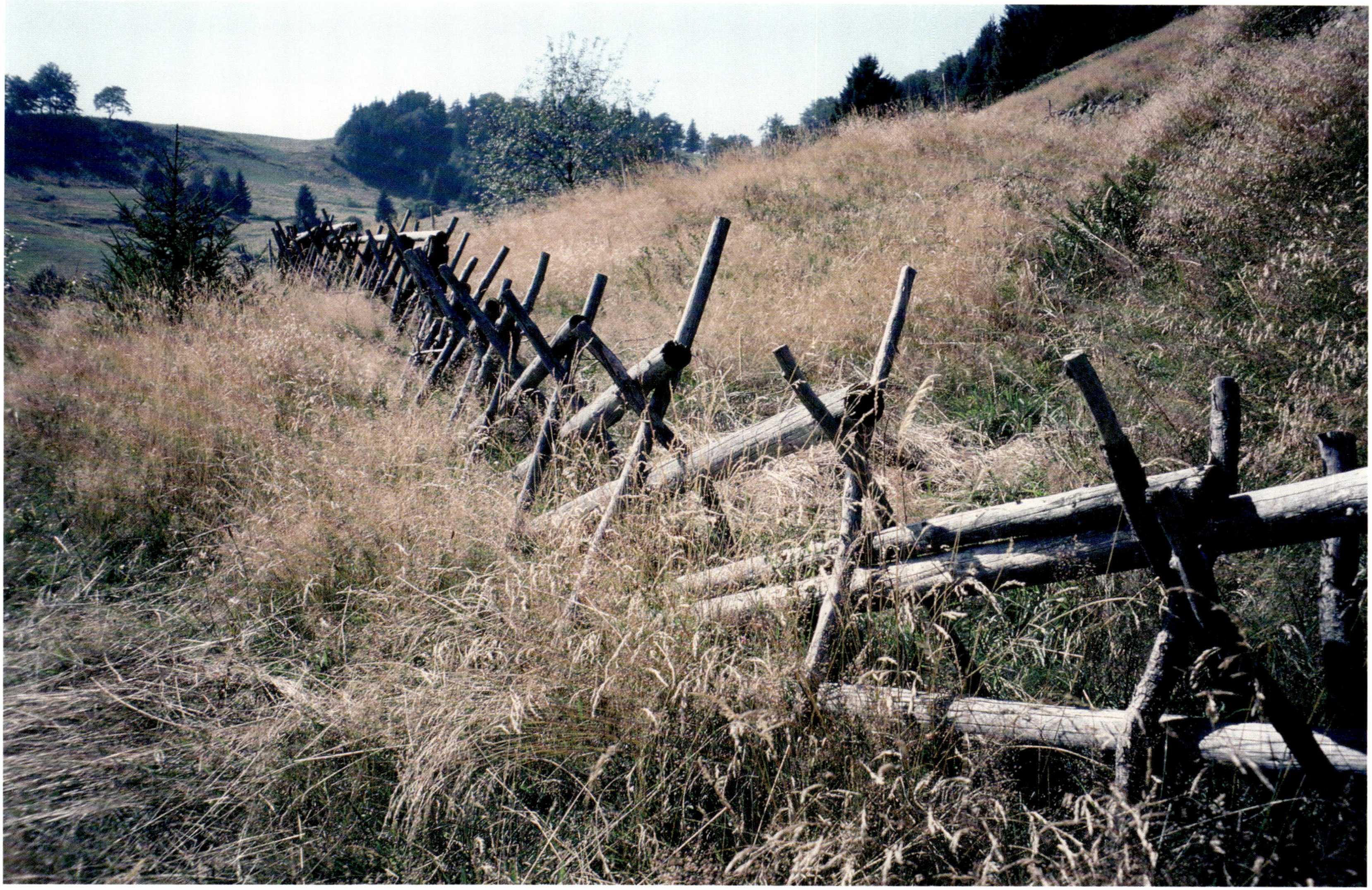

Here is a traditional German Black Forest fence near Freiburg which is light but sturdy, with little need for wire or other ties.

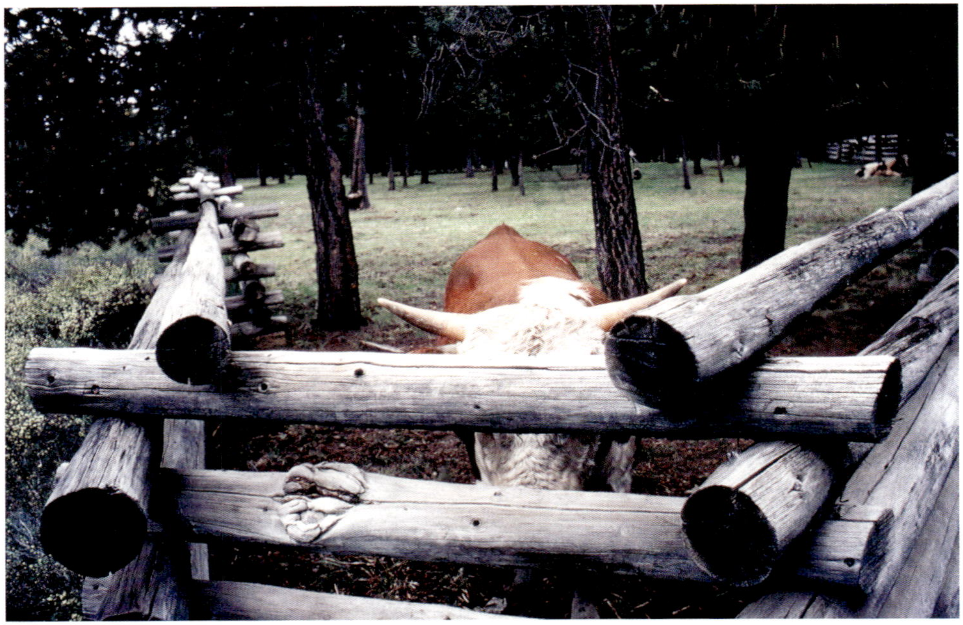

If you need to, you can make a fence sturdier.

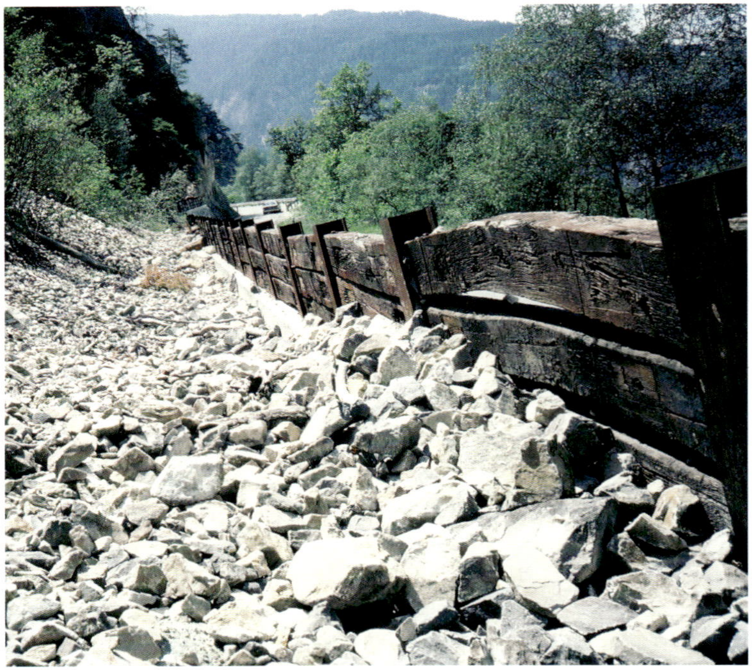

Or really sturdy, as here near Grimnetz, Germany.

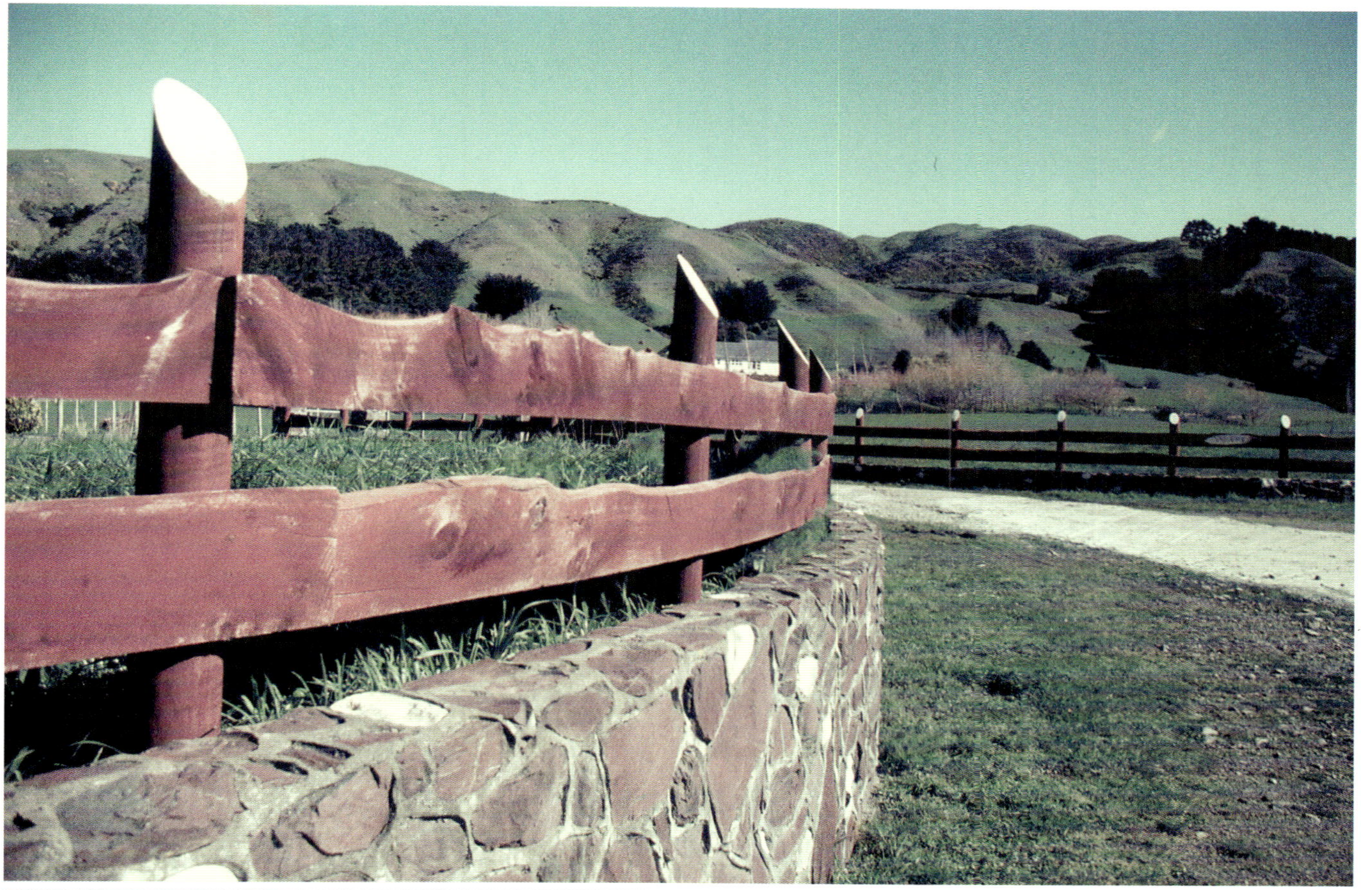

Farms with animals really do need strong fences, but like this one in New Zealand, sometimes the builder seems to go beyond utilitarian.

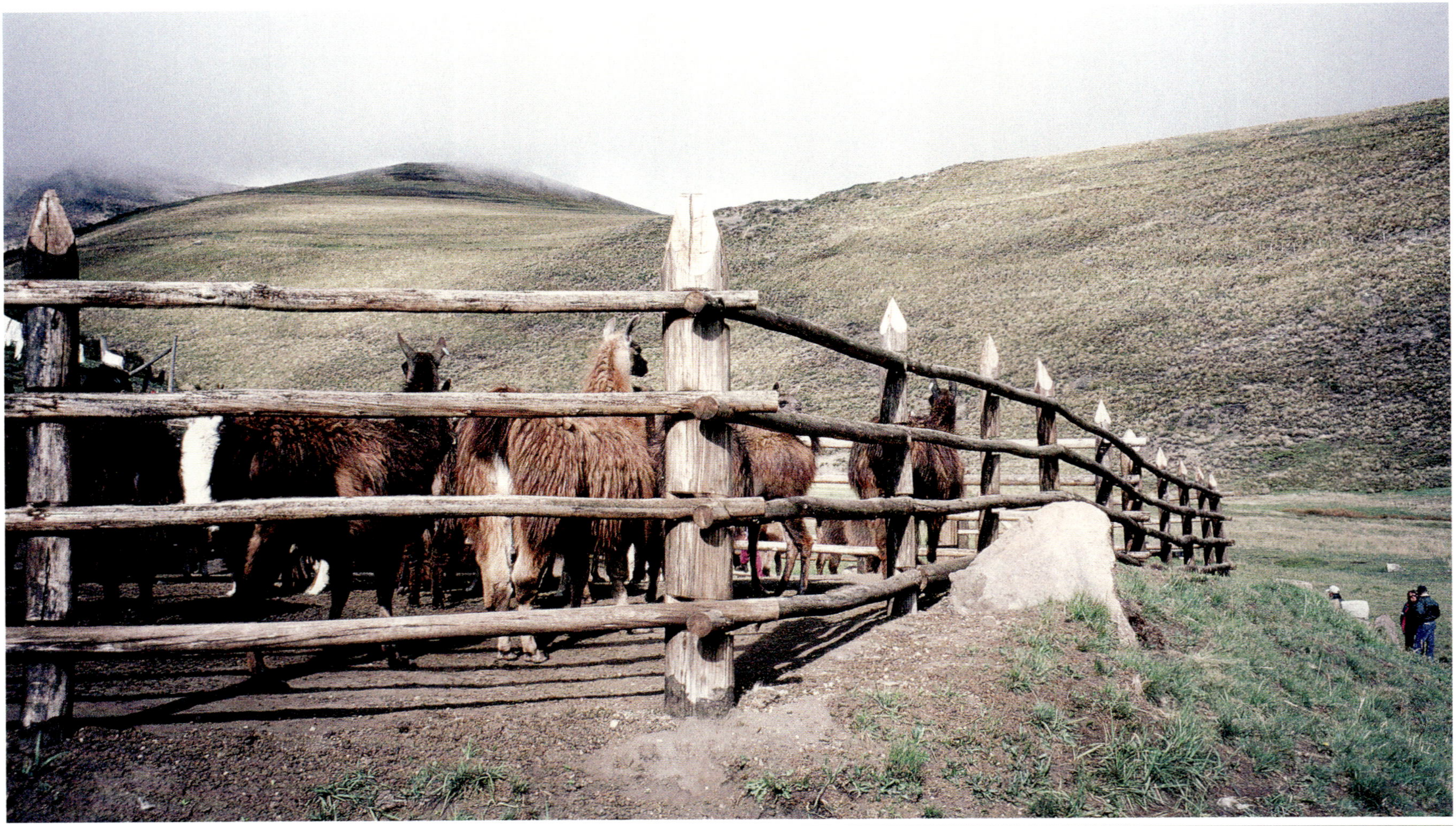

This would be a more typical wooden fence approach to large animal confinement. This one is in Ecuador near the base of Chimborazo (the highest mountain in the world, as measured from the center of the earth; height above sea level 20,564 ft). Note how pointed the builder made the top of the posts. Did he think this would discourage mischievous spirits from sitting there and bothering the llamas?

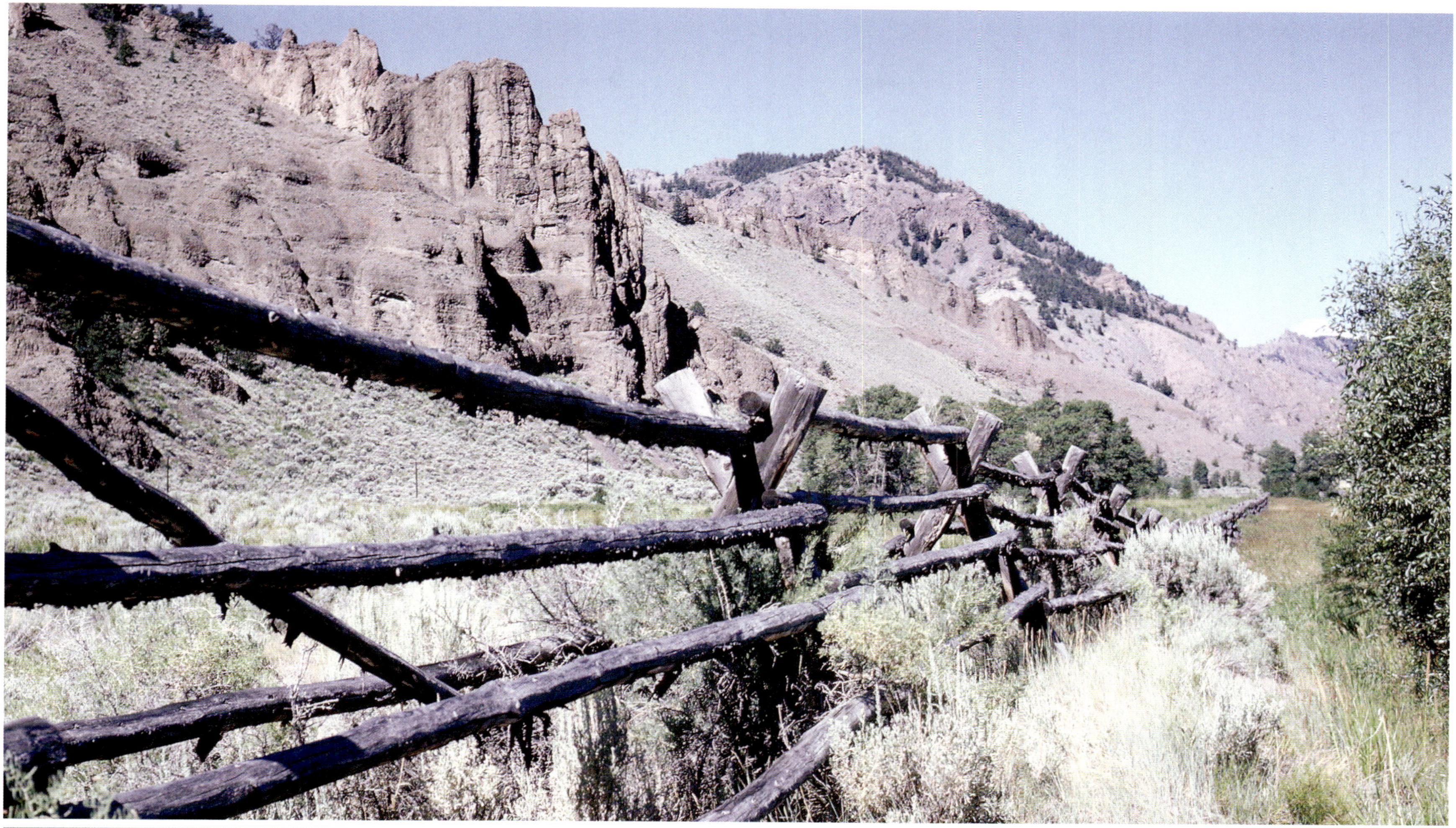

This rail fence from the Shoshone Valley of Wyoming, USA has been a typical style of animal fencing in the American West.

If digging is not easy, and enough wood is available, today's fences on horse and cattle ranches in the American West often utilize an X-bracing style.

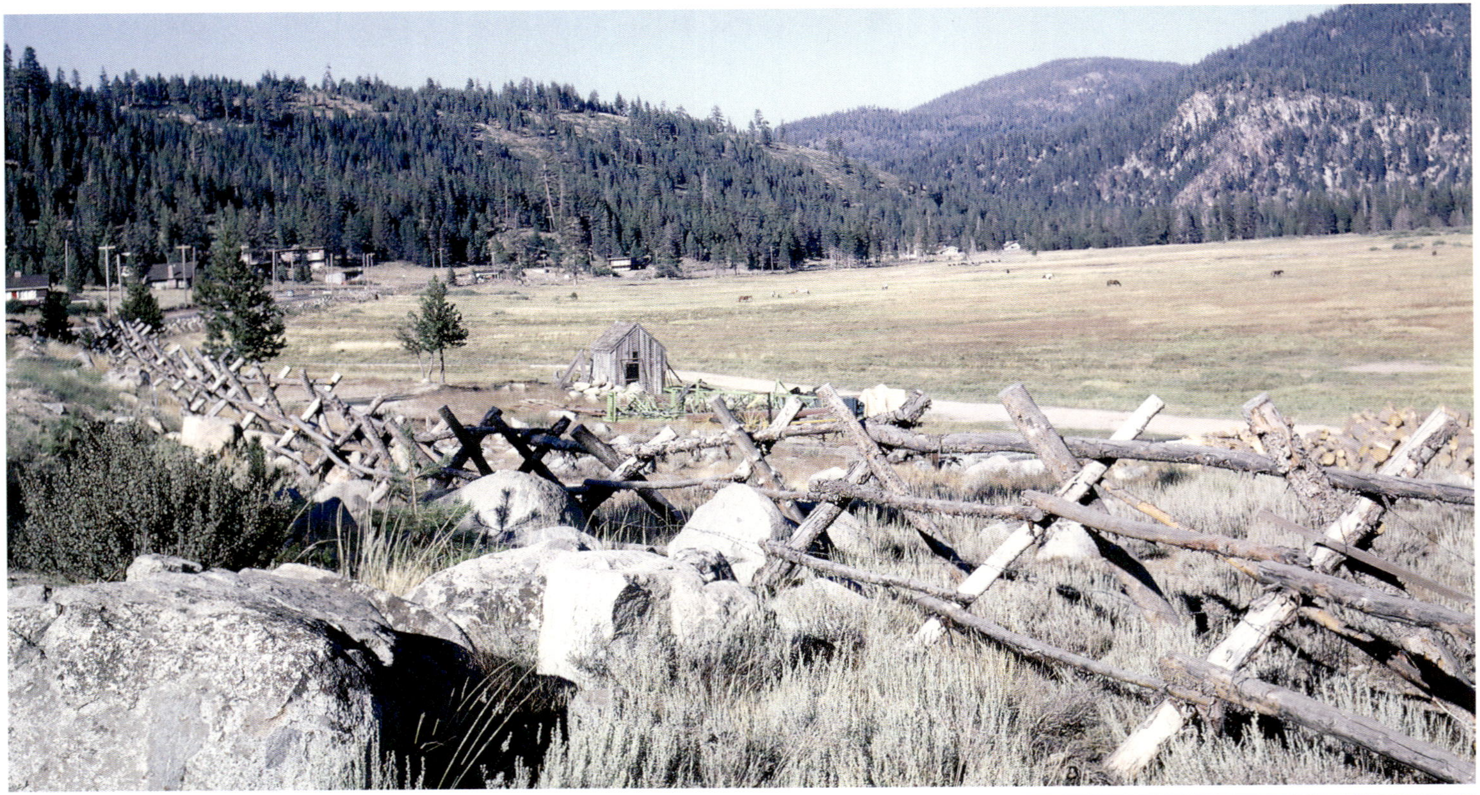

X-braced small poles and rails are nailed in place. The style is known as buck and rail. This one in Wyoming, USA is probably of lodgepole pine which, in the dry climate and with posts not sunk into ground where they rot quickly, will probably serve for at least 10 years.

X's file across the Wyoming field.
Cousin of the snake, the buck and rail braces, balances,
muted by sun and rain
to the suggestion of line,
in the rounded landscape

For situations in the American West where wood is scarce, ranchers often turned to the stake and rider fence. Modern barbed wire, which was developed in Illinois in 1874, made such a fence feasible. Indeed, barbed wire made possible the fencing of much western USA rangeland since prairies offered neither rocks for walls nor trees for fences. When fencing came to the open range, it was contentious, as settlers under government-sponsored agricultural Homestead Acts became "sod-busters," plowing the land and fencing out their neighbor cattlemen's steers. Barbed wire was part of the "wild west," where these conflicts were often settled directly and violently. Meanwhile, barbed wire soon spread throughout the world.

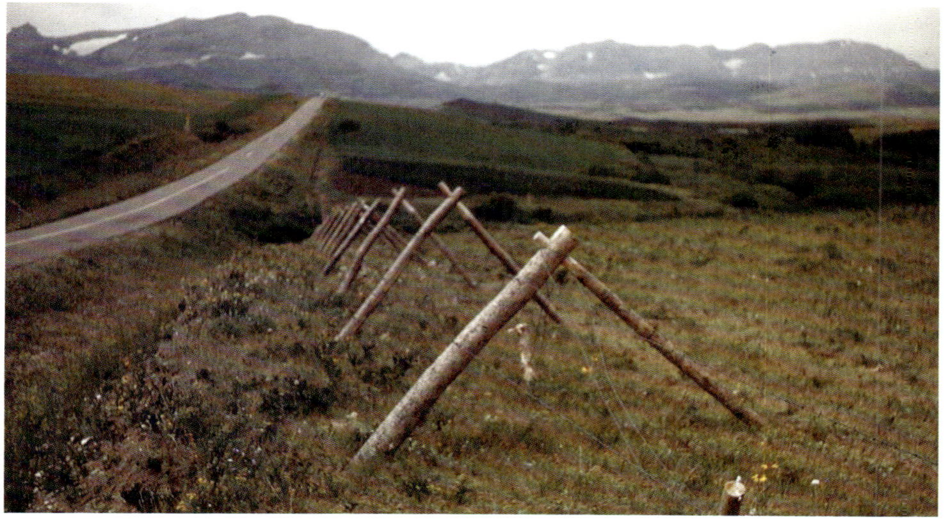

Stake and rider fence in Montana, USA in an open area approaching the foothills.

Smartly
the posts salute.
No palace guards more ramrod proud.
"Hang the expense, man,
this here's no ordinary farm!"
Staunch sunflowers bloom white paint, --
between them
lines strain in a mathematician's dream
of right angles.
Tactical grid.

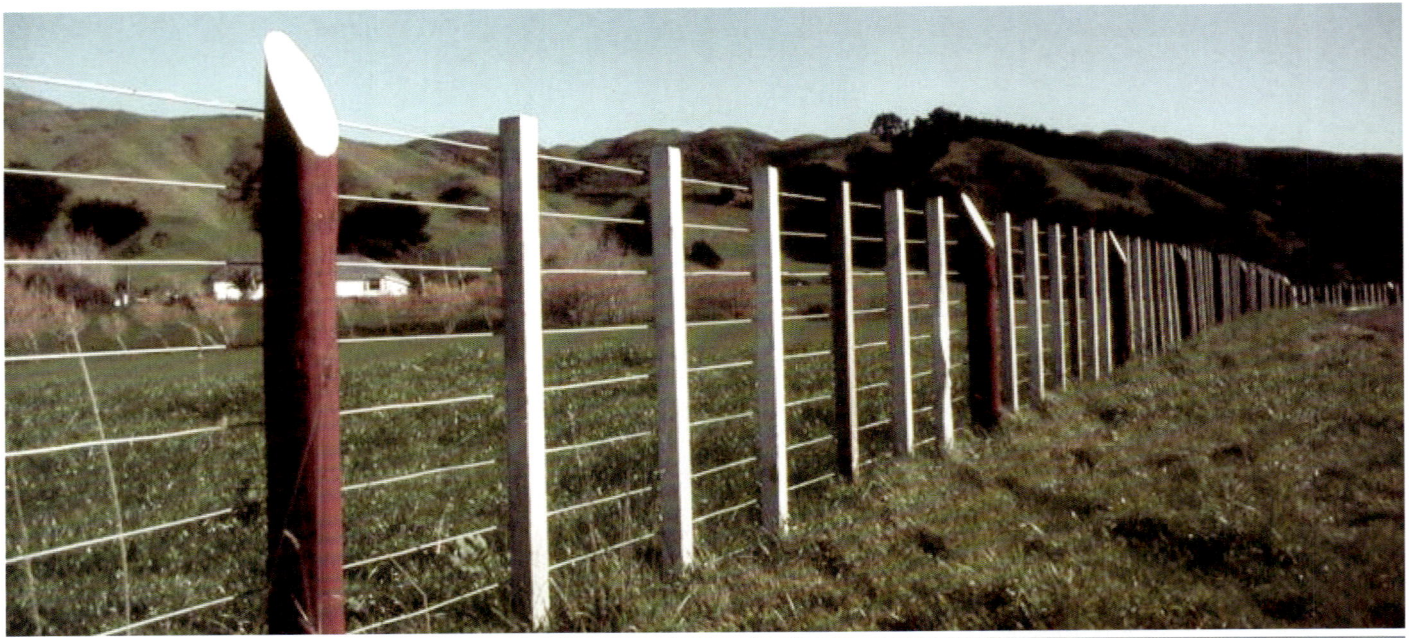

Where farms are smaller and conditions less harsh, as here in New Zealand, ranchers can take a different approach to fencing. This one is obviously proud of his/her enterprise and has made a significant investment in painted posts and mesh wire—functional certainly, and also quite a public statement.

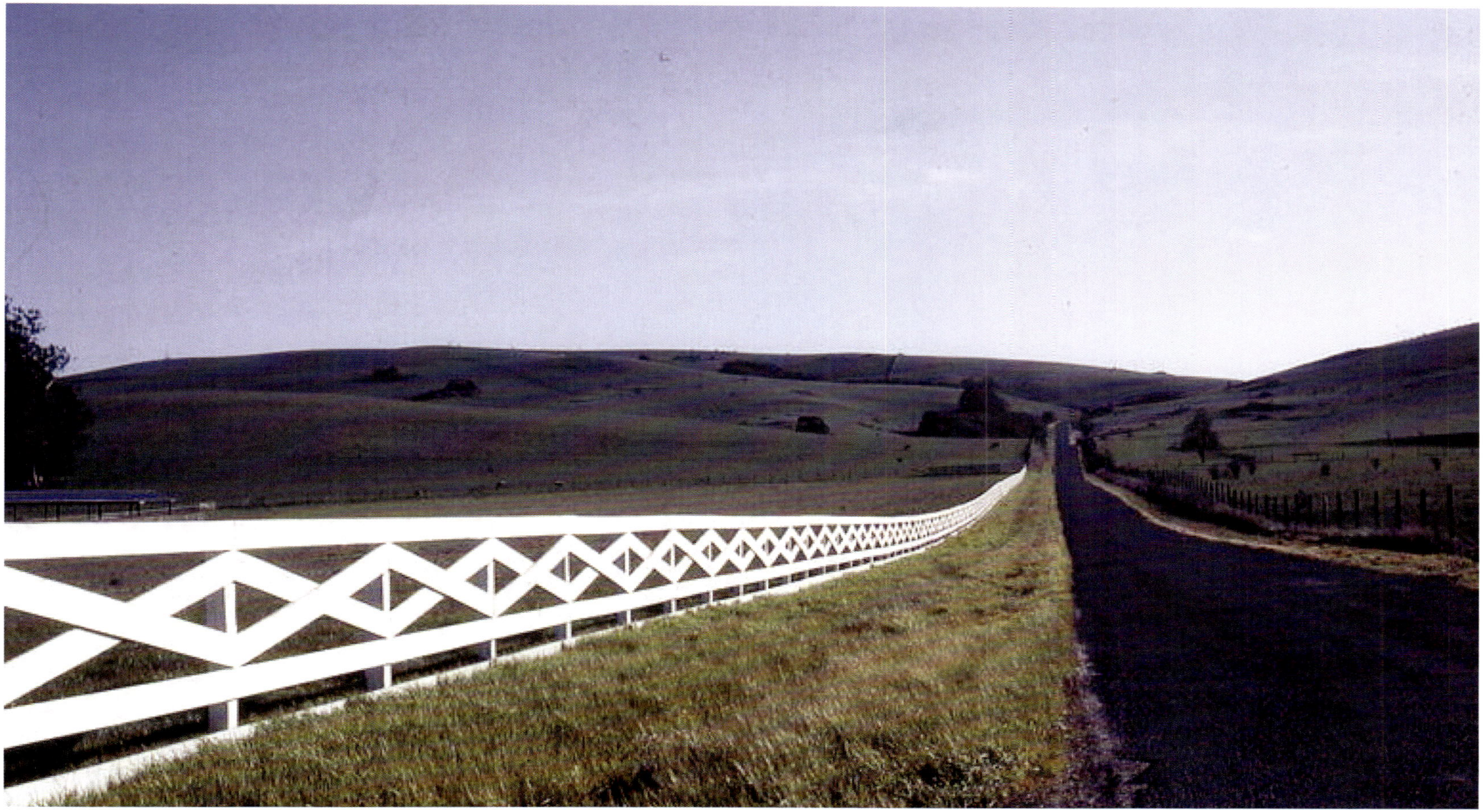

To me, this cattle ranch north of San Francisco in California's Coastal Range is another case of where appearance seems to be just as important to the owner as containment of animals. If it were a horse ranch, the posts would have been on the outside to prevent rubbing injury to the valuable animals inside. It certainly is a showy fence, indicating that the owner thinks the animals (and perhaps the owners themselves) are valuable and important.

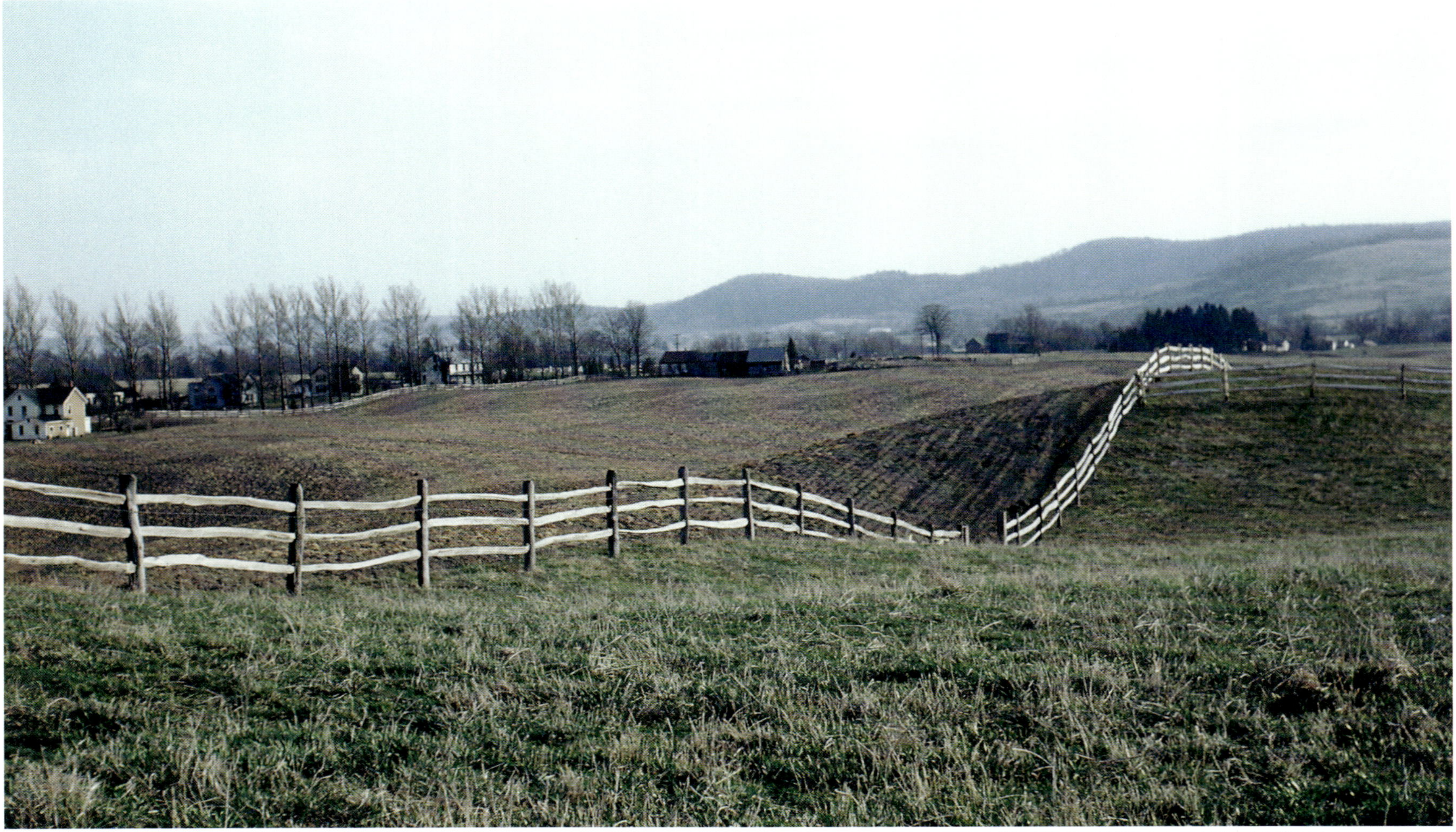

Here is a more modest, but very graceful and long-lasting chestnut split rail fence dividing pasture and cropland near Cooperstown, New York, USA. Three split rails inserted into holes drilled into posts make a scenic fence, as well as an effective one, in dairy country.

Coarser in style, but probably just as effective for dividing off pastures, is this fence on the Big Island of Hawai`i, USA made of wood salvaged from clearing former Eucalyptus plantations. This is ranching country. Cattle were introduced into Hawai'i by Captain Vancouver around 1793. A few Mexican cowboys were recruited in the middle 1800s and soon Hawaiian cowboys, called paniolos, developed great skill in stock handling and were employed by large family ownerships, such as here on the Parker Ranch, one of the largest in the USA. The interesting shapes of the wood makes for a scenic structure at the base of the well-known volcano, Mauna Kea.

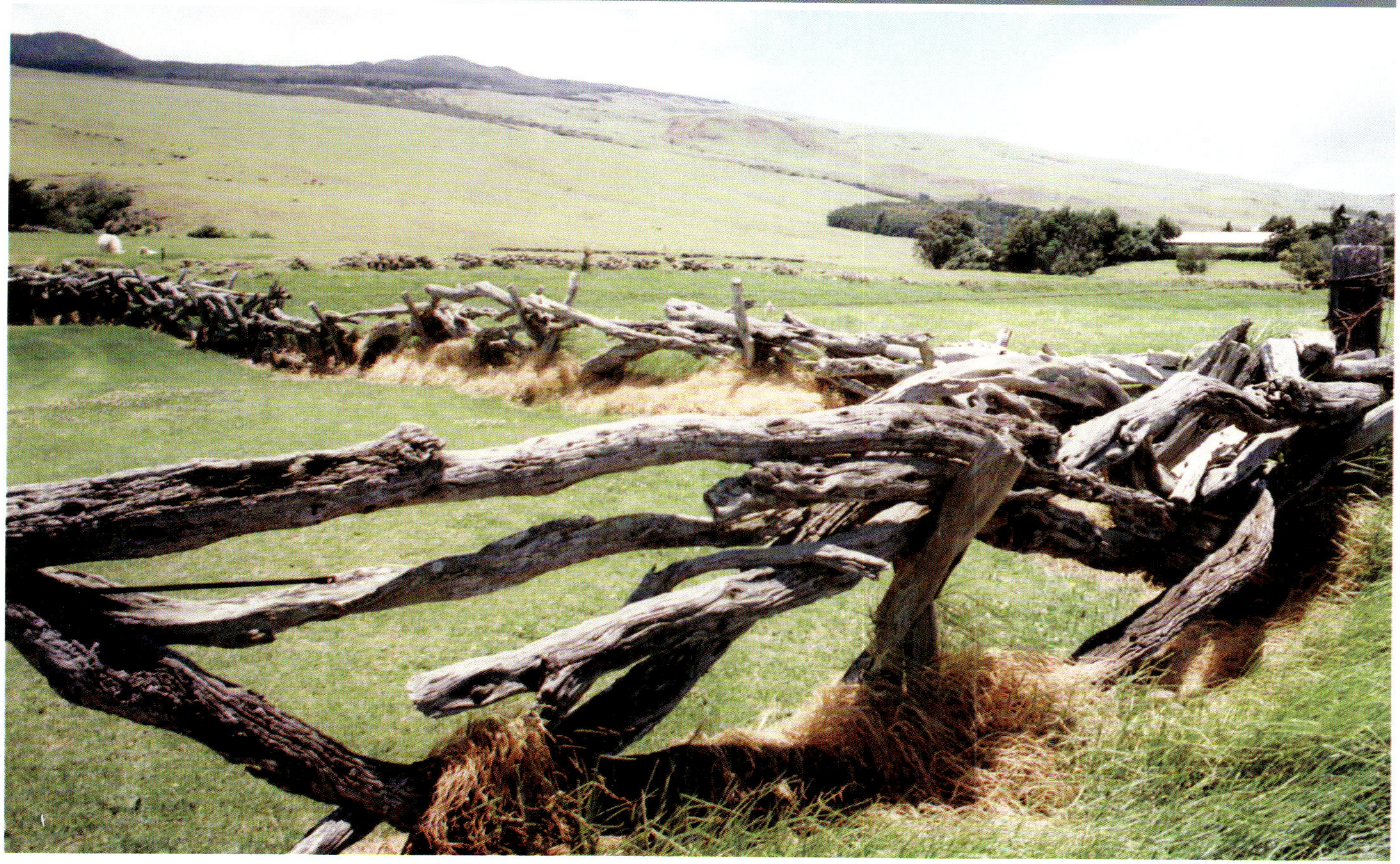

Another by-product of land clearing can be the iconic pine stump fence. This one in Ontario, Canada near Stoufville has been reinforced with woven wire fence.

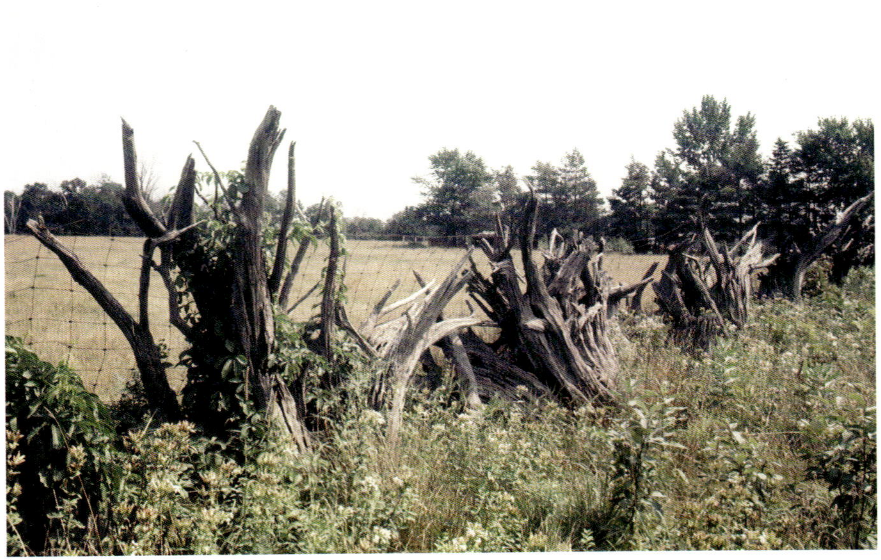

The combination of wood and wire can make for a very effective and reliable fence, as seen here in the Midlands of England.

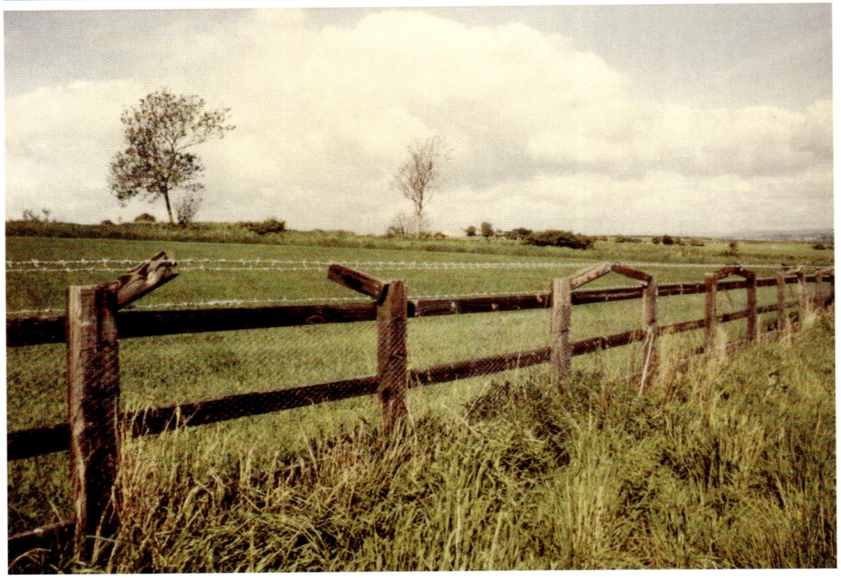

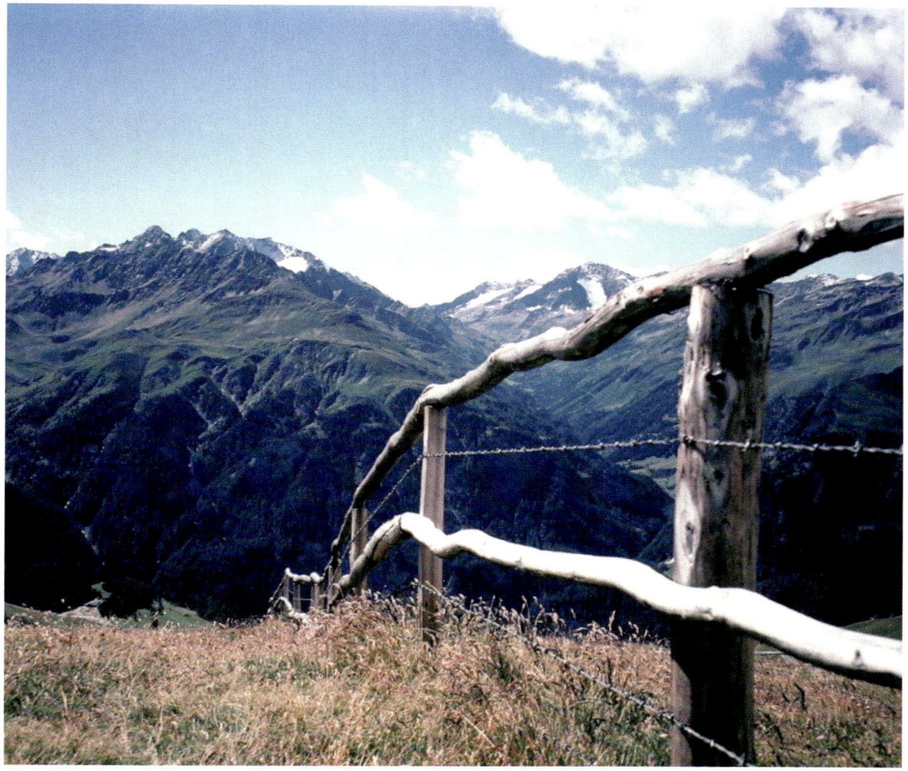

Or an effective and elegantly simple one such as this combination of rails plus barbed wire in Hohe Tauern National Park, Grossglochner, Austria.

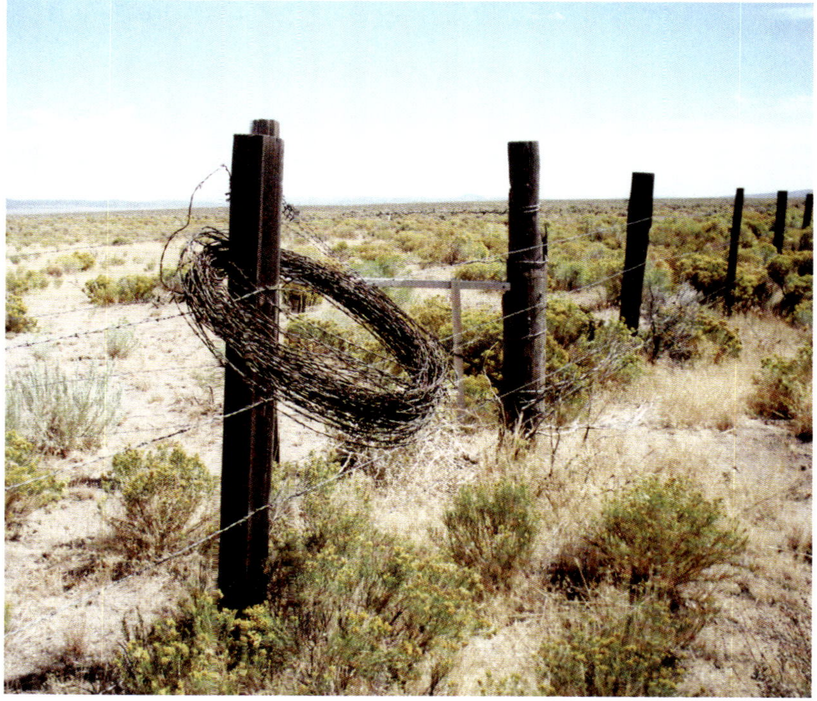

Using more wire than wood in fencing became very common in the American West after modern barbed wire became available in the mid-1870s. This 3-strand barbed wire rangeland fence is near Steens Mountain in Oregon, USA.

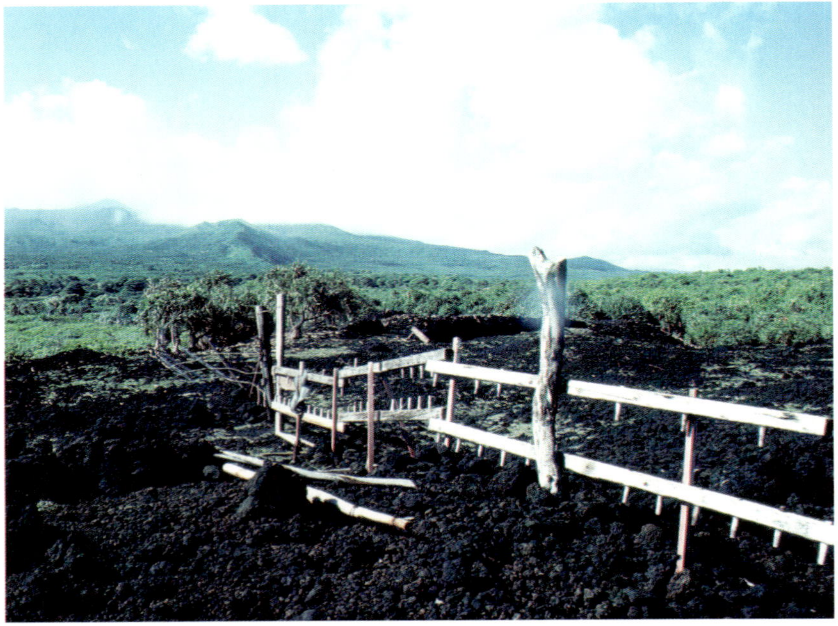

Using discarded crossarms from utility poles for this fence near Hana, Maui, Hawai`i USA was probably not so much about sturdiness as about making use of available materials.

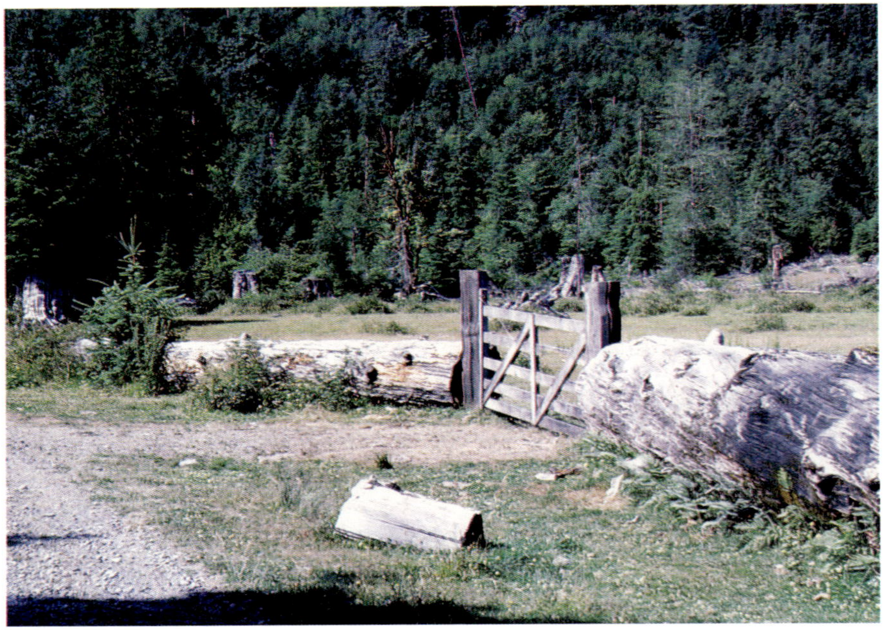

Also in the spirit of "working with what you have," here is a creative, if not extravagant, use of trees. This Douglas fir log fence on the Olympic Peninsula of Washington, USA does not exclude or confine the Roosevelt elk of the area, but works well as a barrier to cattle (and motorized vehicles!).

Sometimes, what are most easily available are cut wooden boards rather than rough-hewn rails. Here near Killybegs, Ireland, the builder has also taken the trouble to cap the tops of the posts—perhaps to ward off mischievous spirits, or just in hopes of slowing down the rotting of the wooden posts?

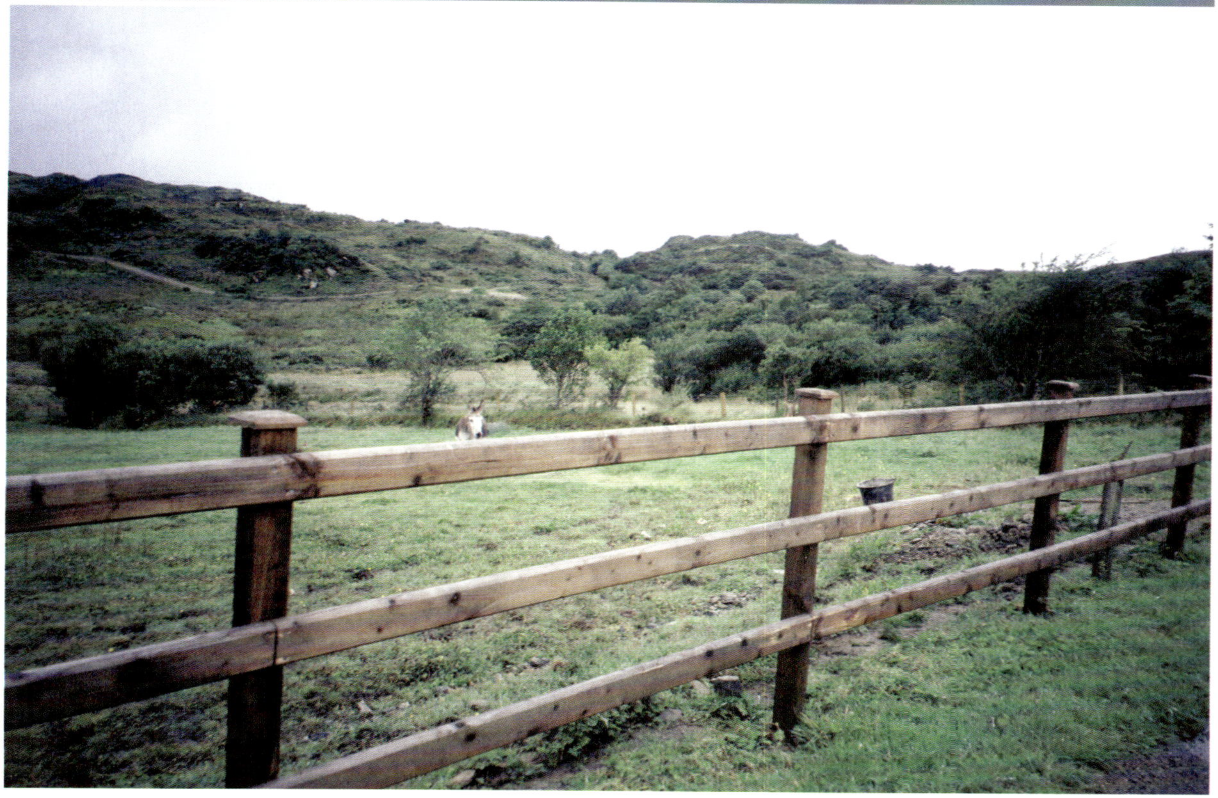

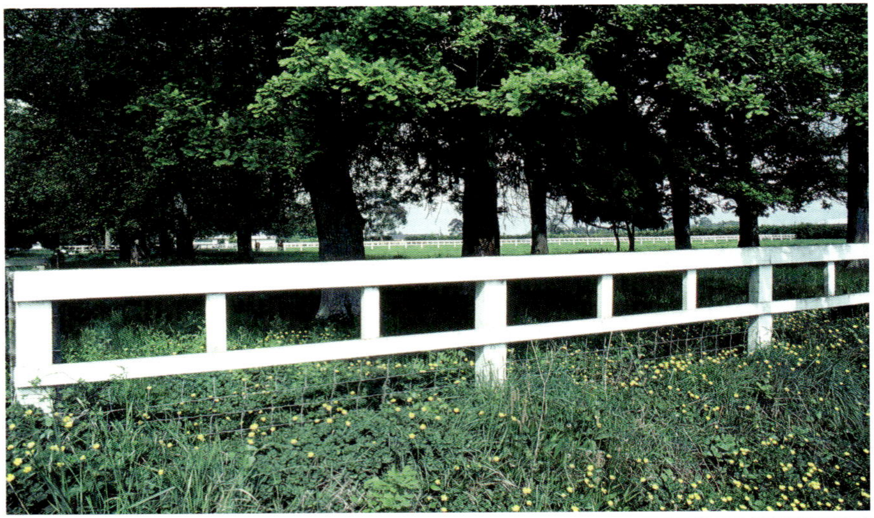

But for a trim and tidy working fence, nothing beats a horse pasture fence. As is common, this one near Cambridge, England is painted bright white and is purposefully smooth on the pasture side to avoid the horses being scratched or scraped. It does seem rather short for a horse fence, however. I wonder if perhaps this is a pony farm.

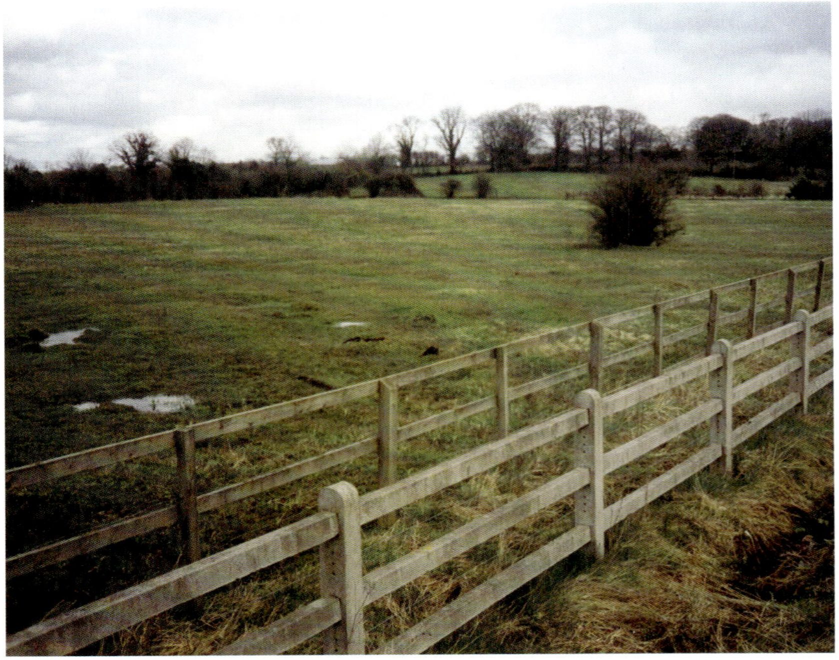

Is this a horse fence? Was the cast concrete fence on the right the original and the wooden board fence added later as better injury-protection for horses? Does the swath between them serve a purpose? The wooden fence is in such good condition, it seems unlikely the government would have put in the concrete one as a public works project, as can happen in the United Kingdom. Only the folks in Mullingar, Ireland can say.

Some wooden fences are testaments to considerable skill on the part of the builder and much care is taken with the process. Here is a farm fence north of Leningrad, Russia whose effectiveness and elegance is achieved through ingenuity and craftsmanship. Note how the uprights are "ladders" made using pliable saplings to create rungs, which support long rails threaded through them at a graceful angle.

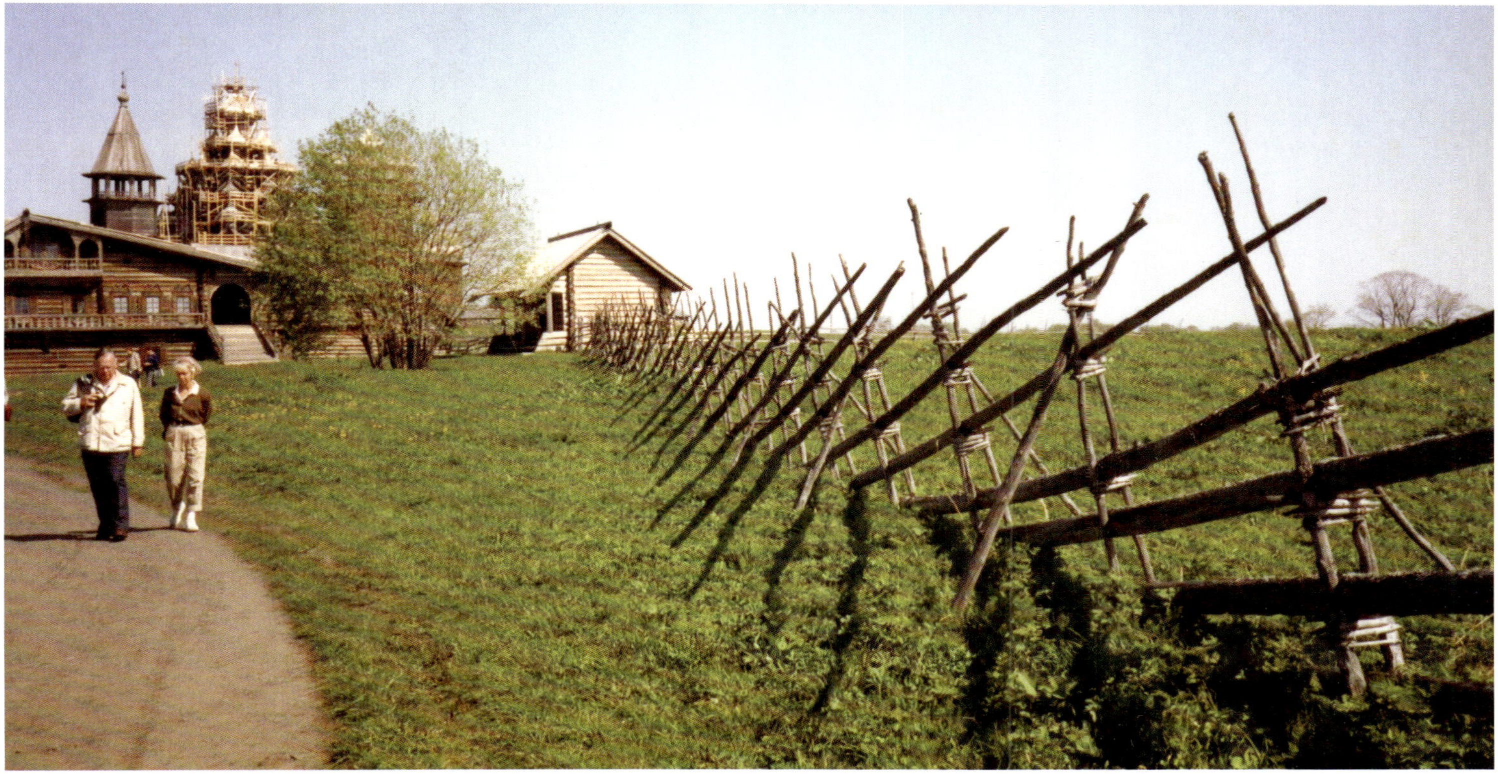

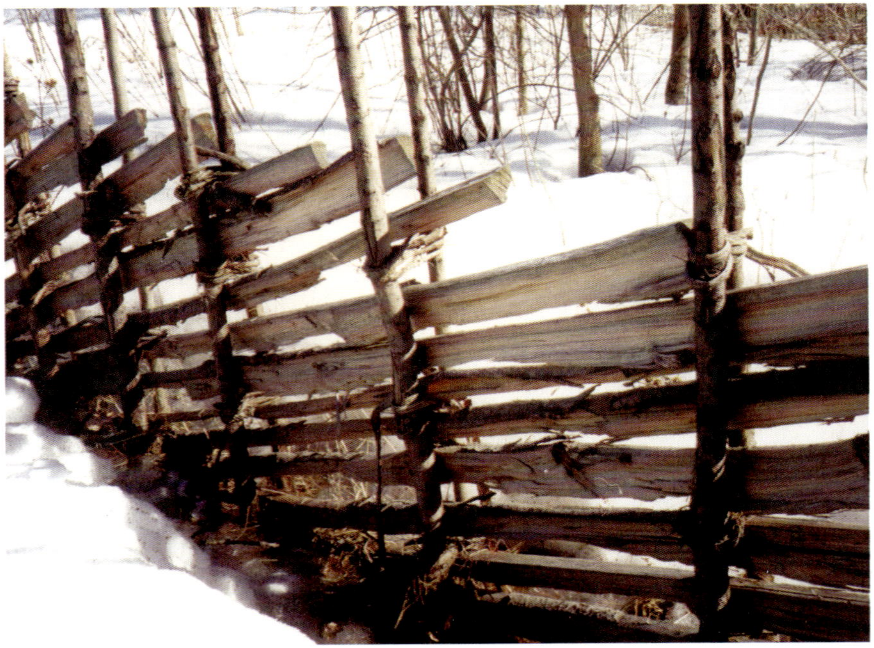

Here is a sturdier Norwegian version of that approach.

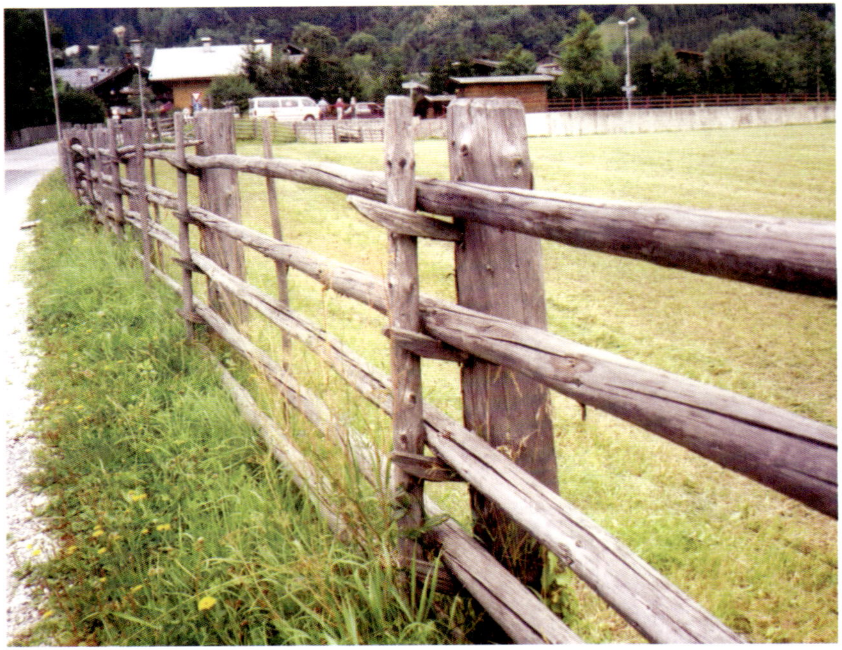

This carefully-made fence in Austria uses straight spruce rails and peg supports driven into the posts to make straight, almost uniform lines.

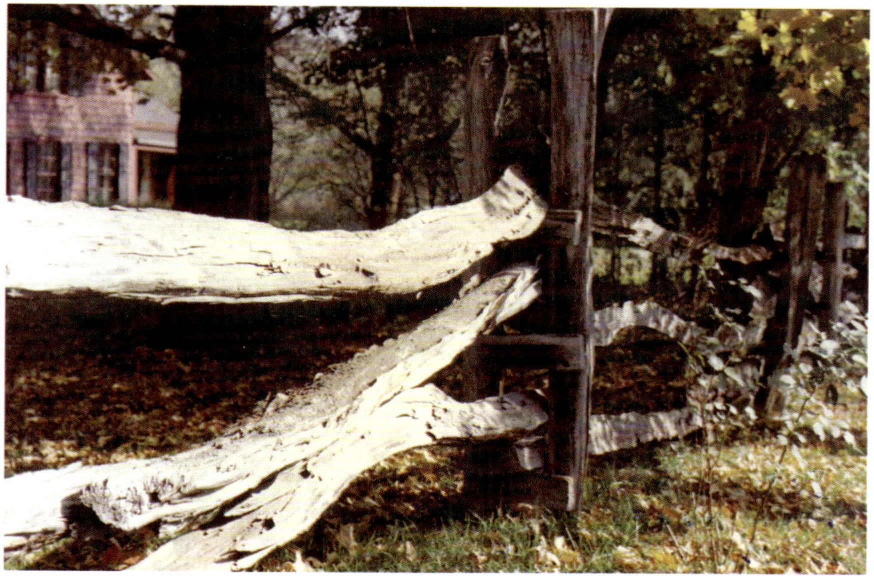

If what you want is a bolder statement, this hand-split heavy elm rail fence near Ludlowville in Upstate New York, USA will do it. It takes a double upright with nailed spreaders to hold it up.

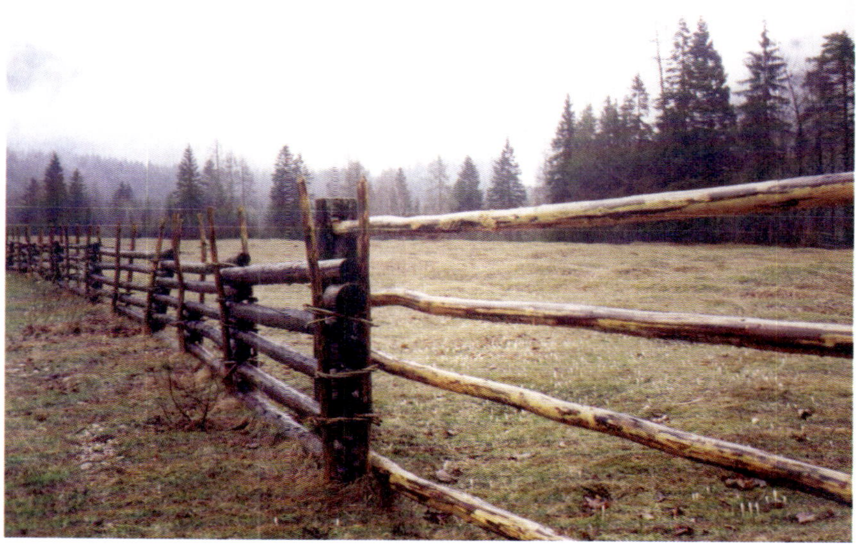

There are many ingenious ways to support a fence. This one in Triglav National Park in Slovenia uses lashings made of linden to squeeze together larch uprights and rails.

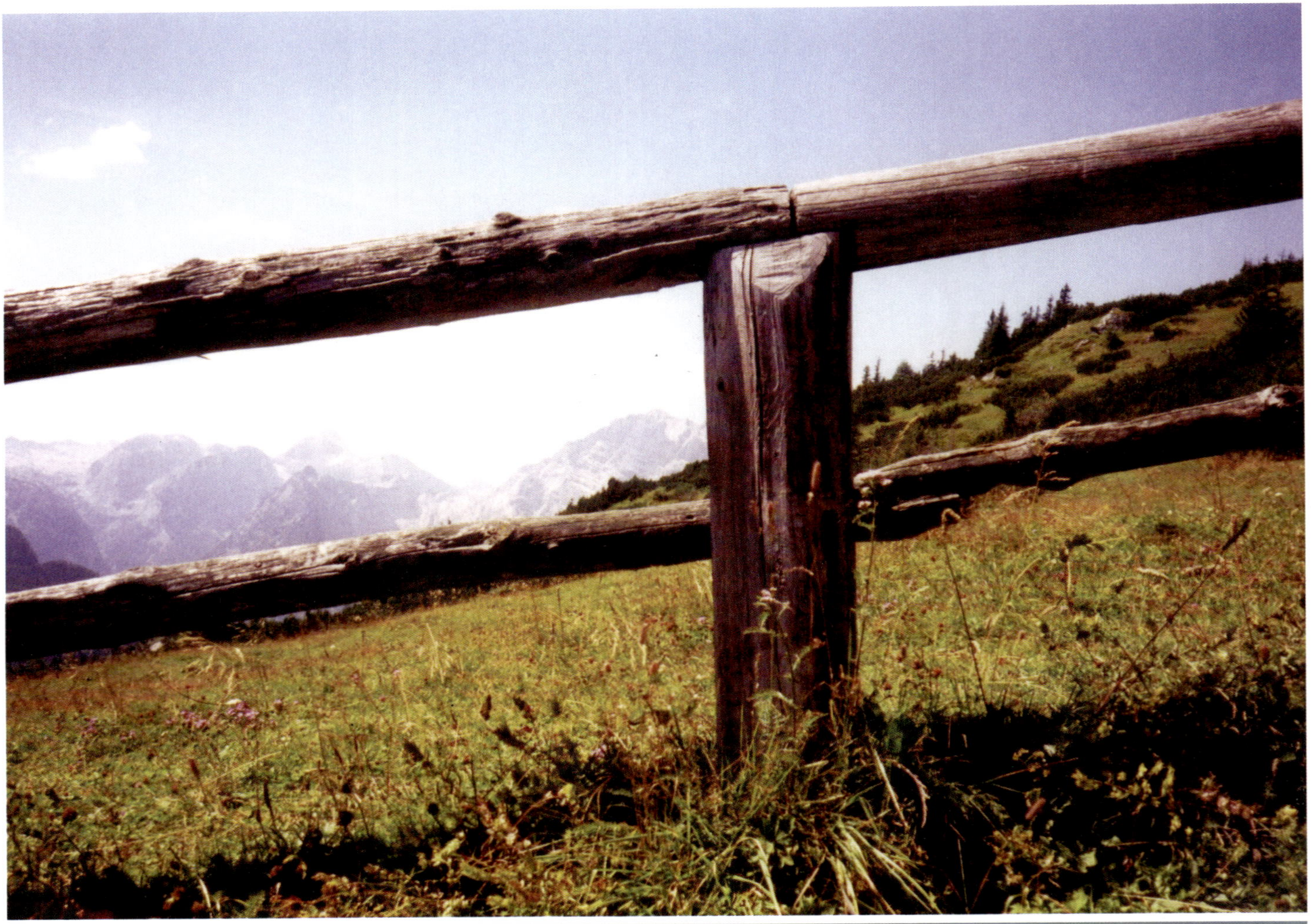

Sometimes it is more about precision notches and balance, as in this Austria-Germany border fence.......

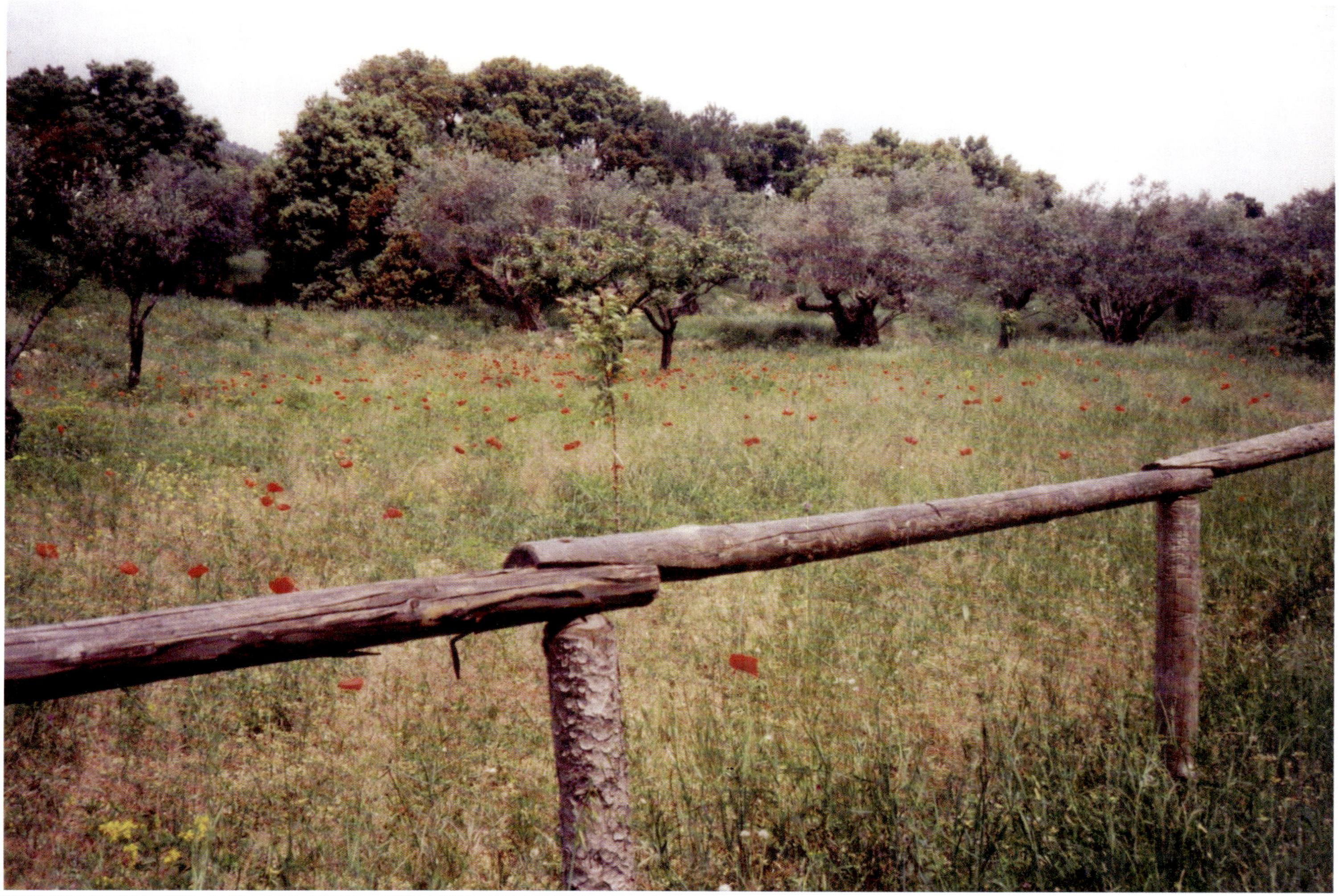

Or this airy demarcation of an olive grove property in Provence, France.

Sometimes significant resources and effort are put into attempting a solid barrier, such as with this solid board fence on the rough moors south of Blanchland in County Durham, England. What is going on here? See how far it stretches across the landscape? It reminds me of another attempt at a solid barrier—"the wall" under construction by the USA along the border with Mexico. In the end, both of these fences will be ineffective means for dealing with whatever the problems are between the two sides. Fences, after all, are temporary; time and Nature break them down. And in the long run, I believe that is a good thing.

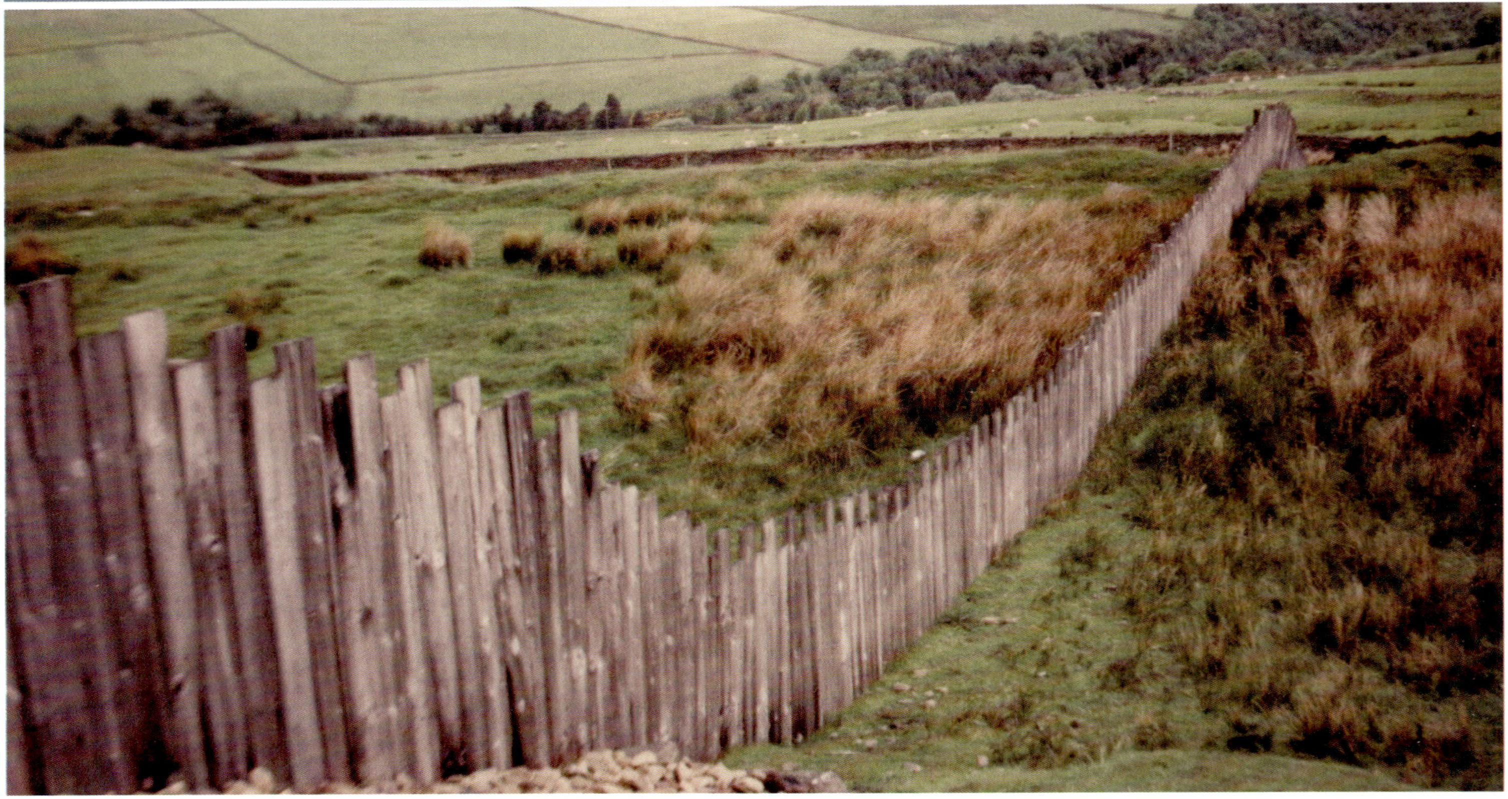

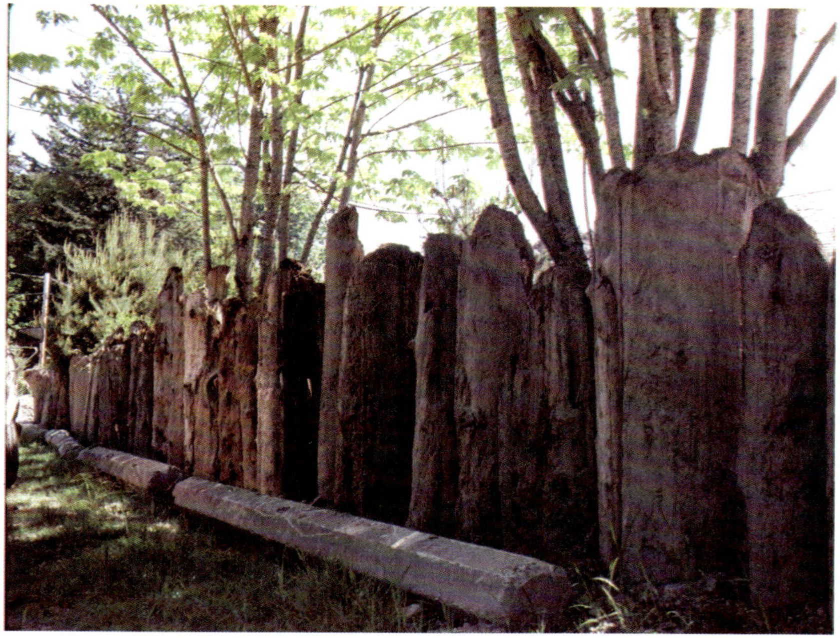

Is this a fence? It certainly is an attempt to create a solid barrier, using driftwood logs from Whatcome County, Washington, USA.

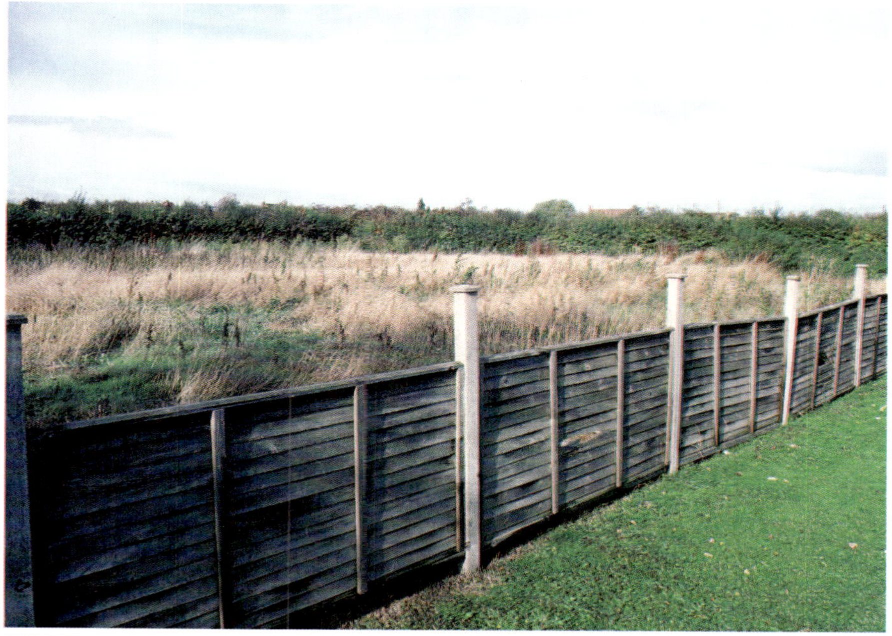

Why the need for such a solid barrier around this English lawn?

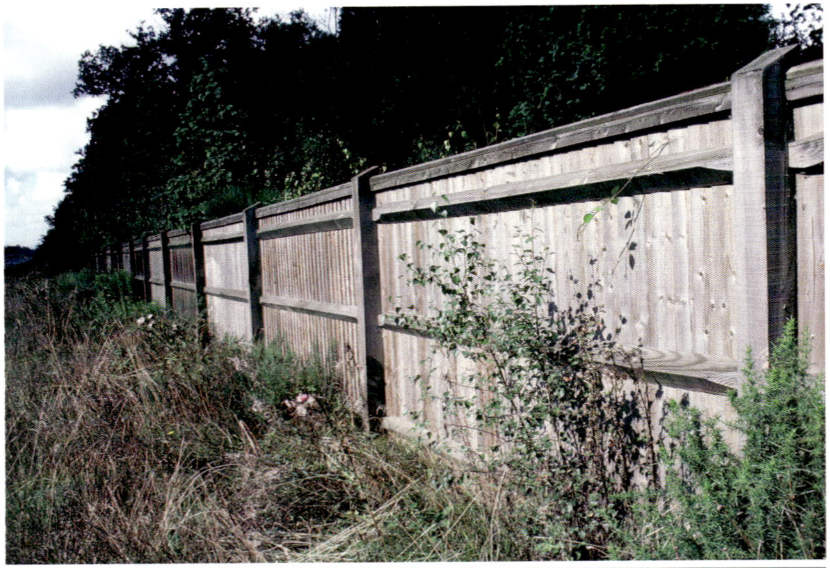

This one I know is a sound barrier fence, between a housing development and a busy road outside London, England.

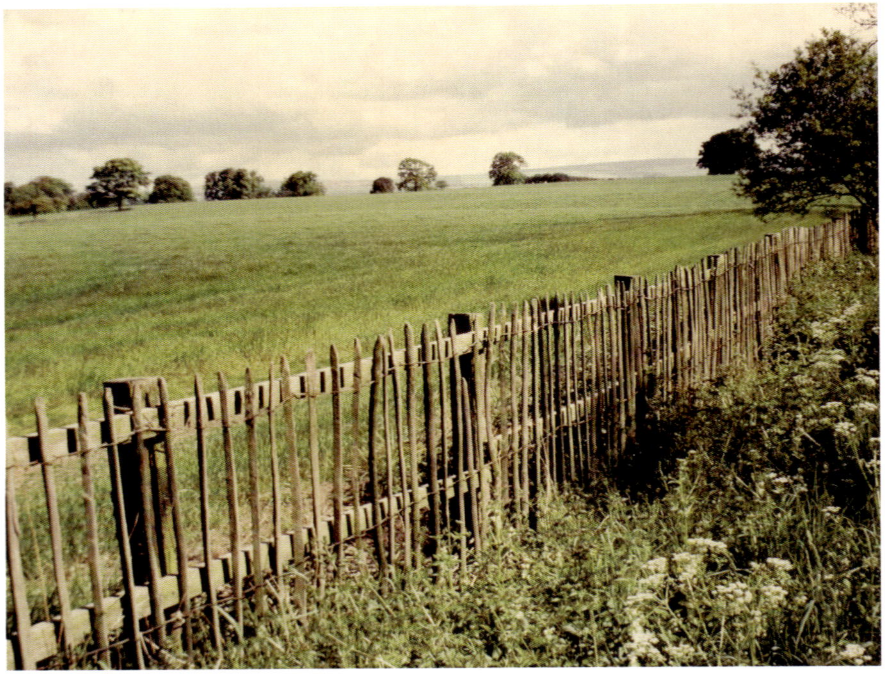

The lighter version of a solid fence is a picket fence such as this one near Berwick, Scotland, which makes a strong statement that the land is being used differently on each side, but which also allows for communication between the two.

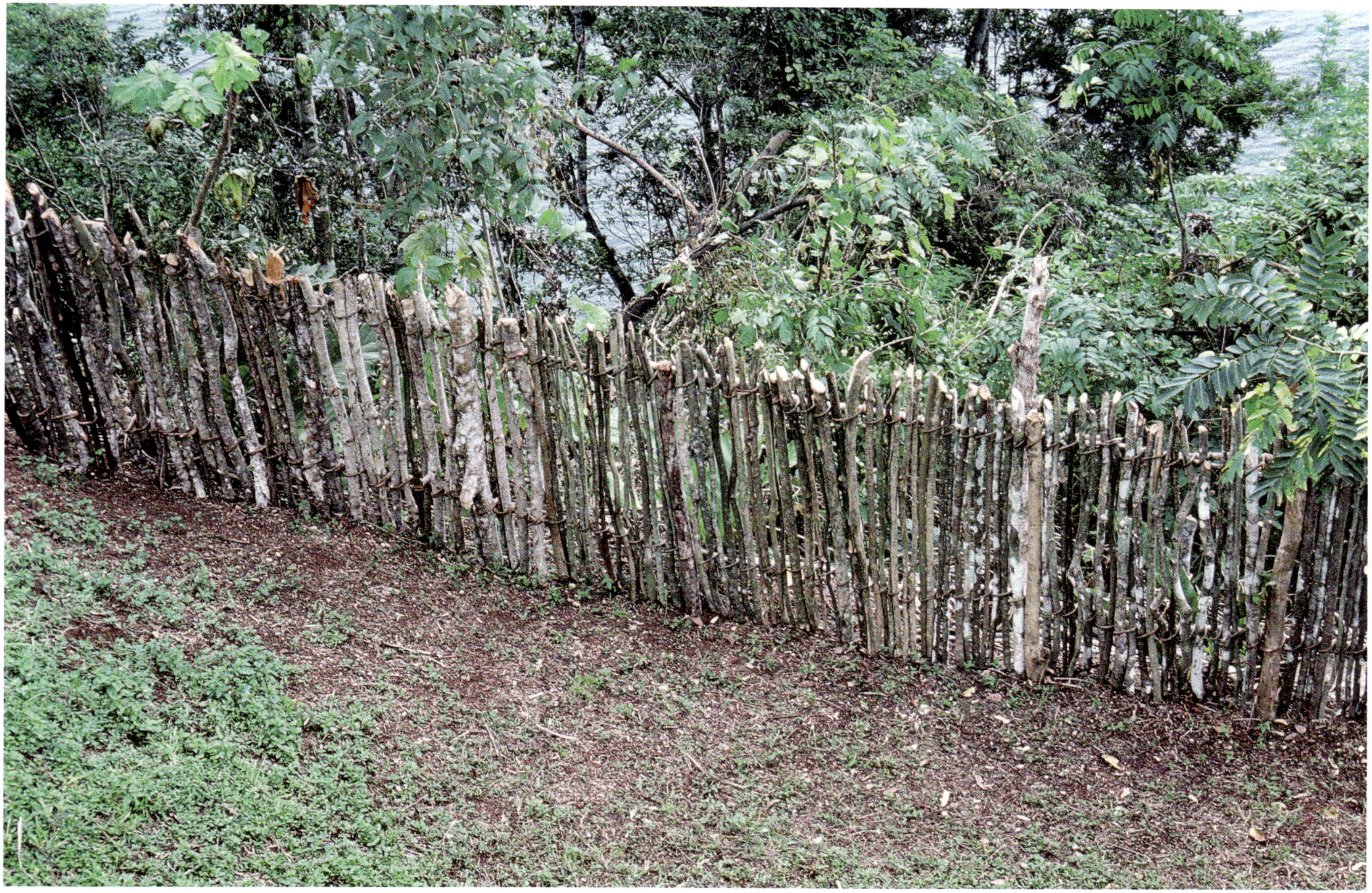

This Guatemalan picket fence message could be that the forest and forest critters are pushed back to this point. Or maybe because the slope drops off sharply on the other side of the fence it is there to keep animals and small children from falling out of the yard?

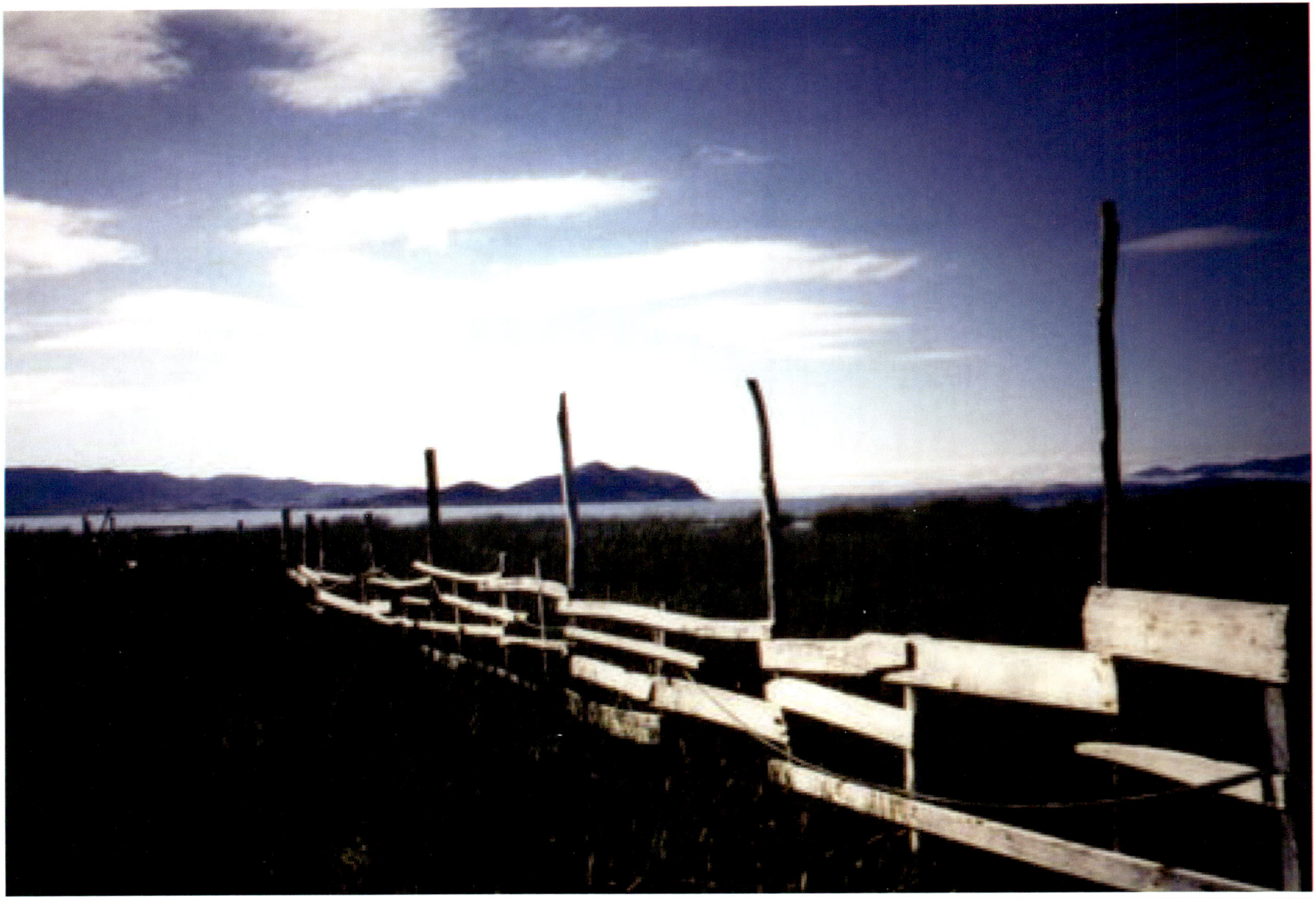

What is going on here with such an easily-penetrated fence on the shore of Lake Titicaca in Bolivia? Perhaps it is not so much a barrier as it is a rural version of the unambiguous ownership statement made by a suburban picket fence.

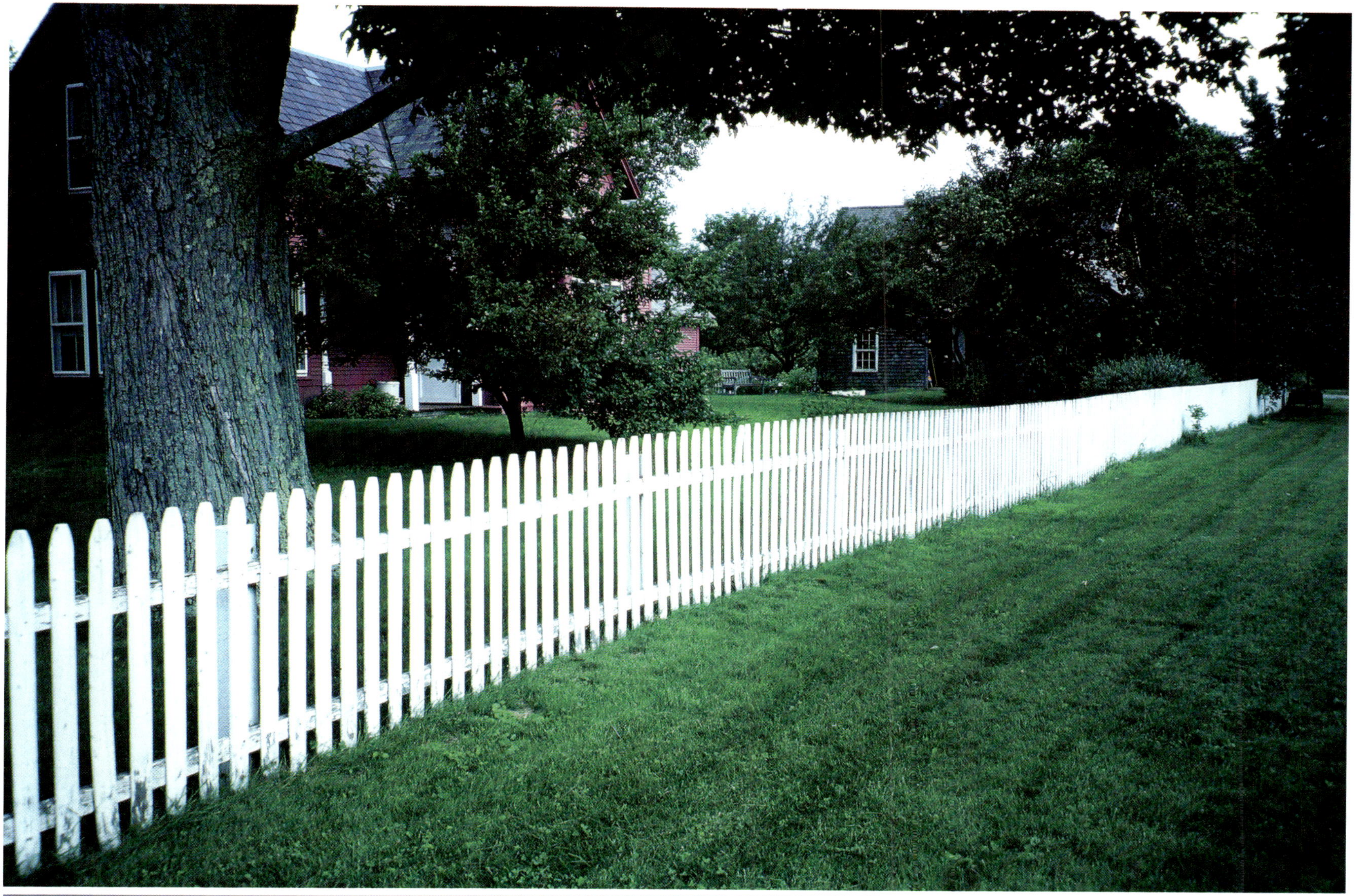

This classic white picket fence in the small town of Shelburne, Vermont, USA is being kept very white indeed, as is customary.

Not needing to be so fastidiously clean to serve its function and make its unique statement, this almost-solid picket of moss- and lichen-coated redwood stakes is built to keep smaller animals (probably sheep) in a California, USA paddock north of San Francisco. It looks like a little repair is needed. But even so, the wooden fence is certainly more scenic than the more modern wire fence in the foreground.

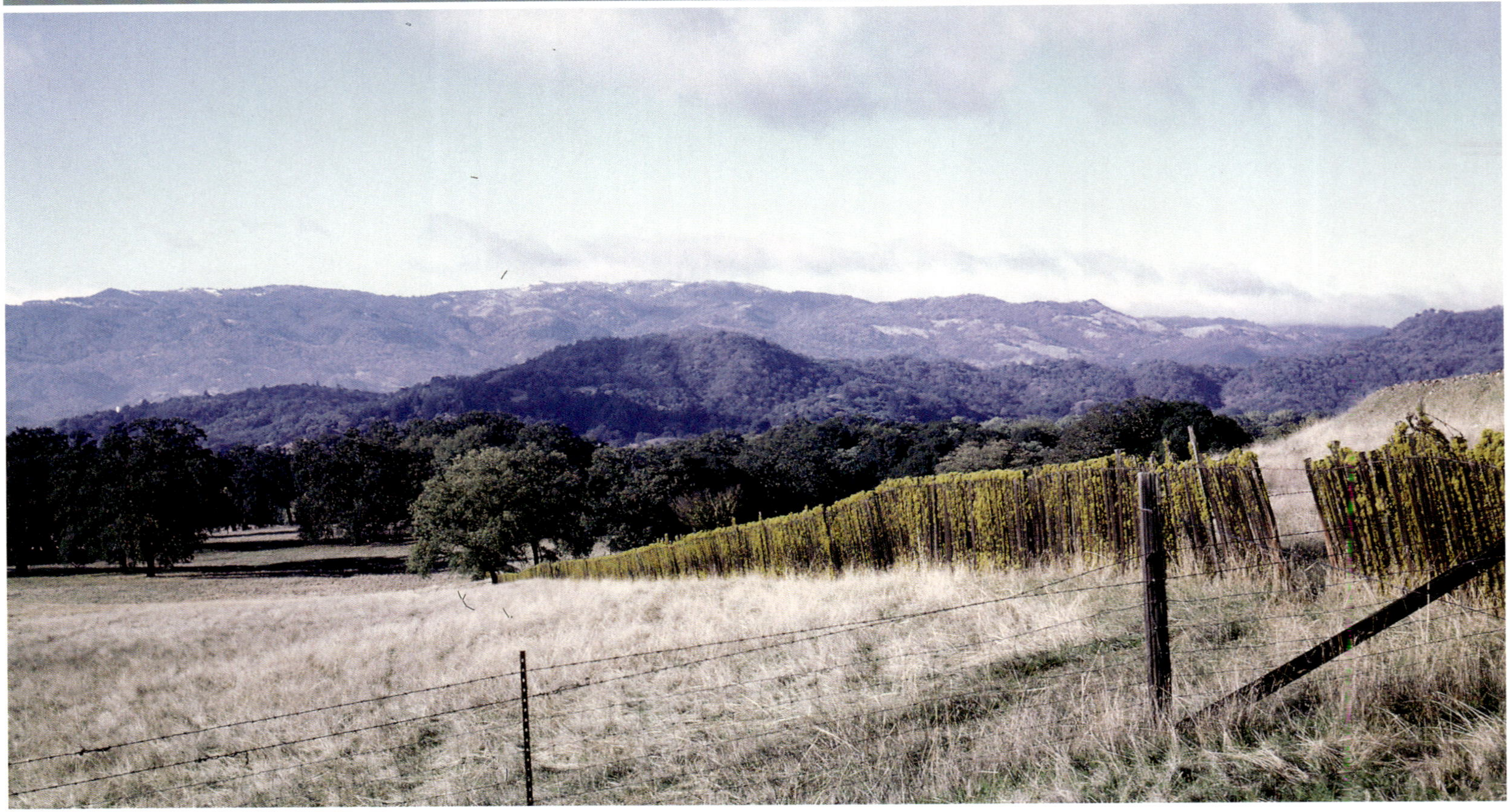

Under purple majesty
the deer and antelope
may play,
but not sheep.
"This is your turf, and this mine."
And redwood sticks, toothed with wire
insure wooly compliance.

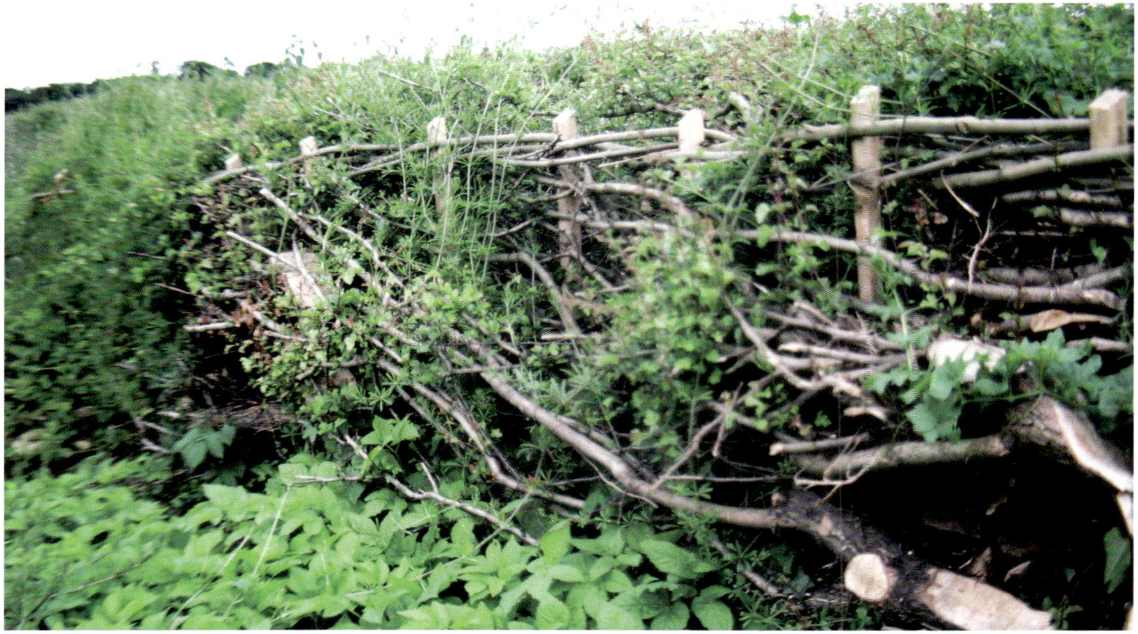

Here is another less-than-tidy but effective sheep fence, this one made by intertwining flexible limbs lopped from tree saplings in Wales. Some of the limbs seem to have sprouted, making for an even thicker barrier.

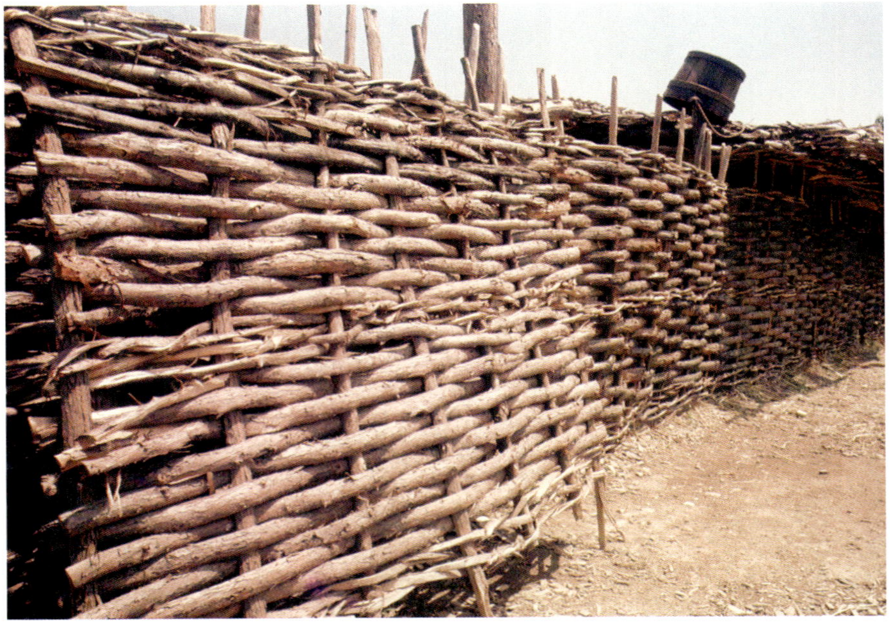

This impressive woven/wattle fence in the reconstructed historic Plymouth Colony, Massachusetts, USA deserves respect, both for how and why it was created. How great must have been the Colonists' fear of things on the other side of their (de)fence.

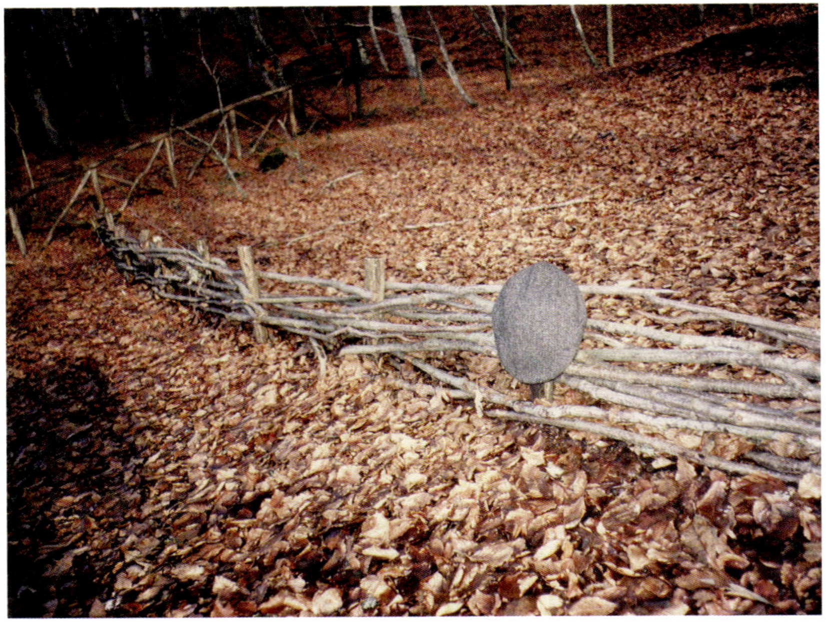

A much more modest woven fence is in the famous Fagetta del Monte Cimino, the beautiful and much-revered chestnut forest in central Italy. I'm not sure now what that is hanging from the fence, or even what the purpose of the fence is, but I bet there is a good story behind it!

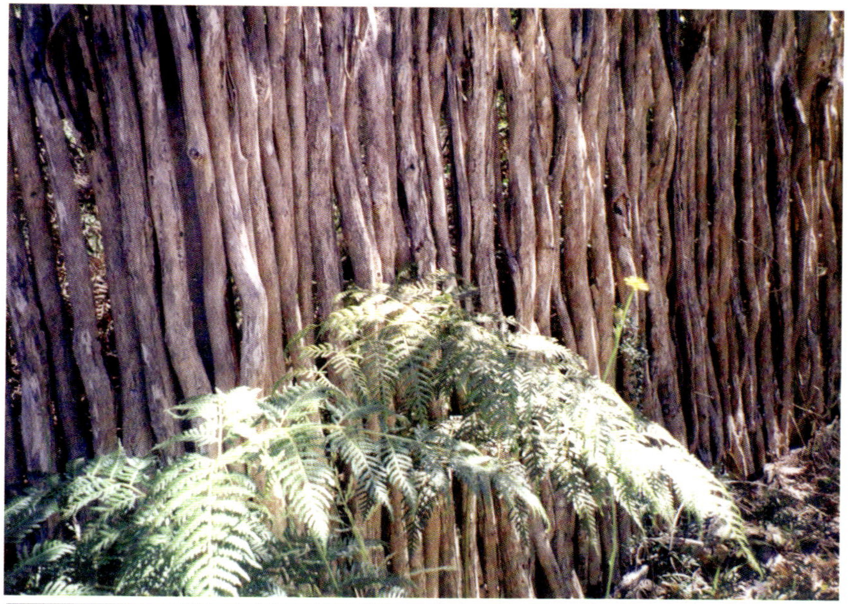

This barrier fence on Wilson's Promentory, Australia is made of tea tree saplings, apparently needing no wire or other support to keep it securely in place.

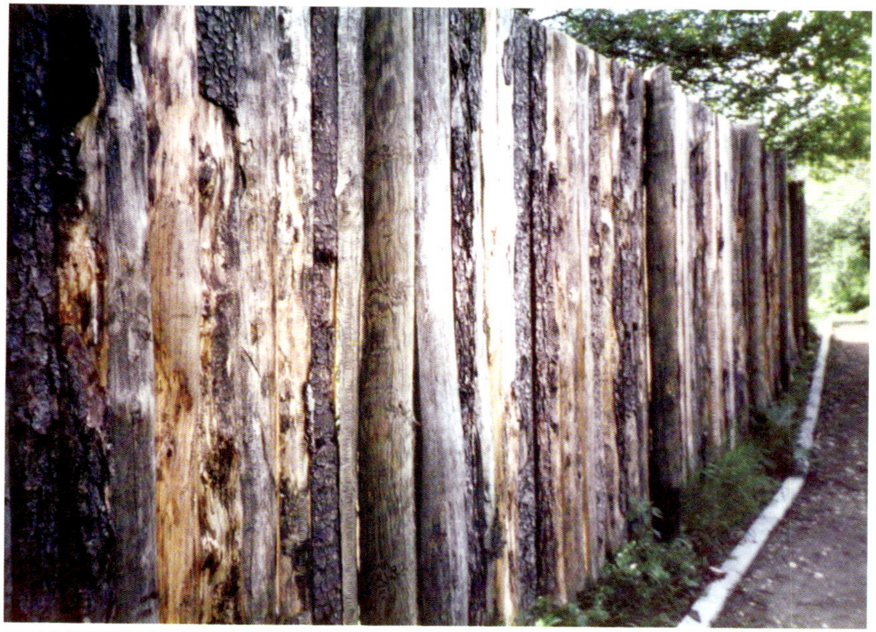

And this one is even sturdier and more visually solid. In this case, I know the reason for the fence is to insulate birds from the sight and sound of human visitors in this section of a bird sanctuary in Cuneo, Italy.

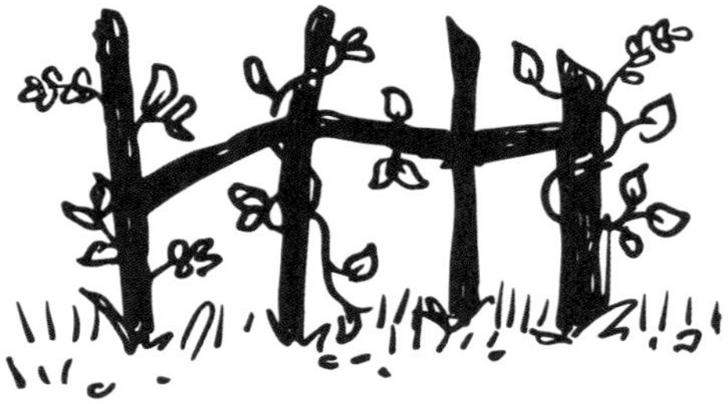

LIVING FENCES

Living fences are often ingenious, multi-purpose, and relatively long-lasting.

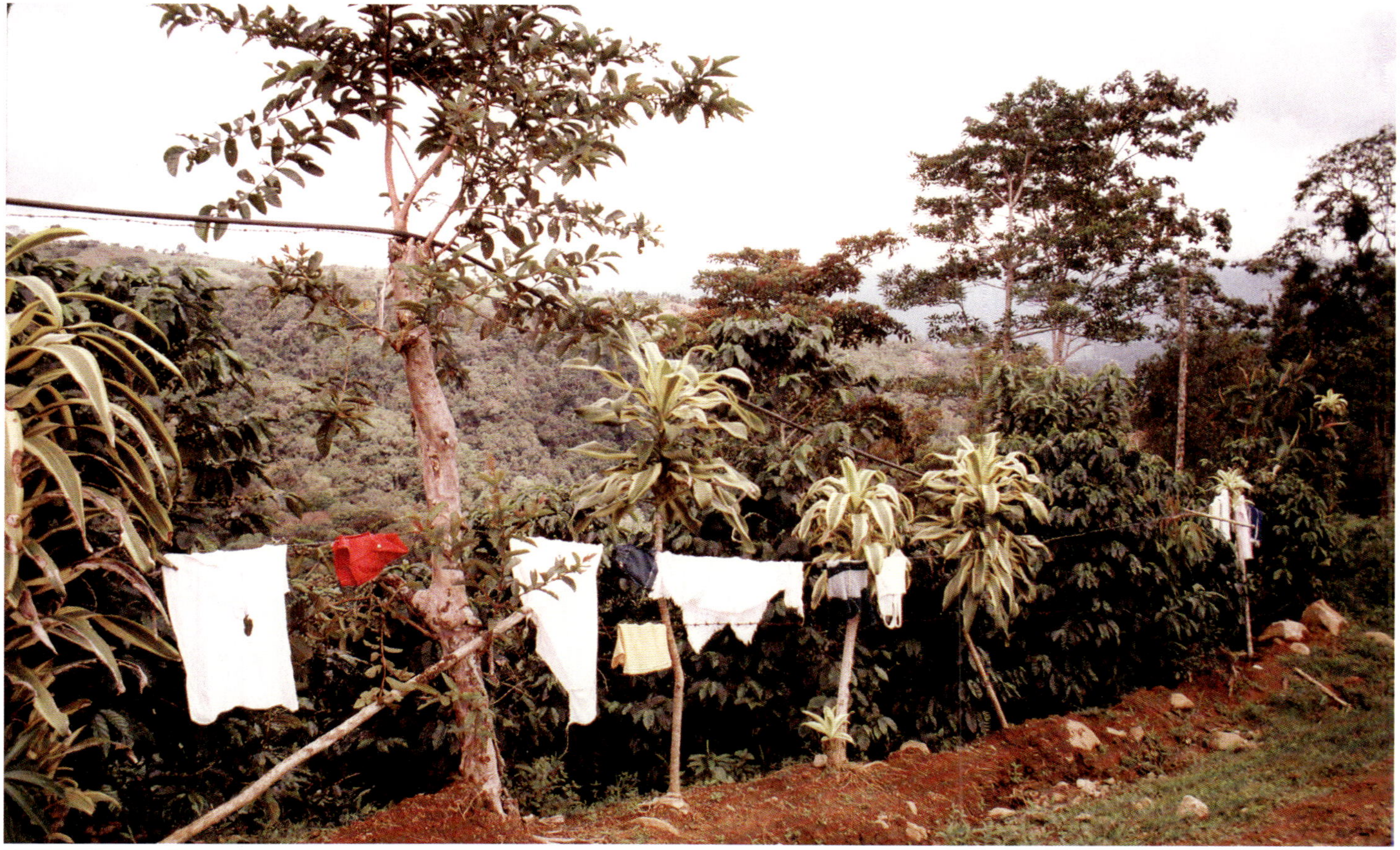

This living fence in Costa Rica was established by placing fresh cuttings of Erithryna trees at intervals and connecting them with wire (which provides a handy place to dry laundry). Farmers here will often plant small trees as living posts for such fences near their homes. These can be lopped periodically to feed the leaves to livestock and use limbs for firewood. This multiple use can be repeated sustainably, since the tree re-sprouts after cutting.

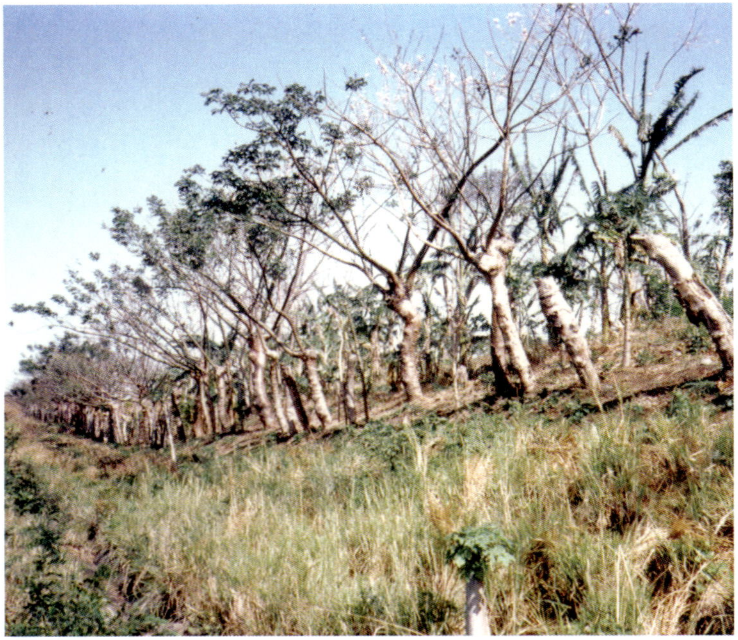

This living fence, also in Costa Rica, is made from Gumbo Limbo (*Bursera simaruba*), an introduced tree species which, like Erithryna, also re-sprouts readily. It is jokingly known as the tourist tree because of its thin, reddish peeling bark.

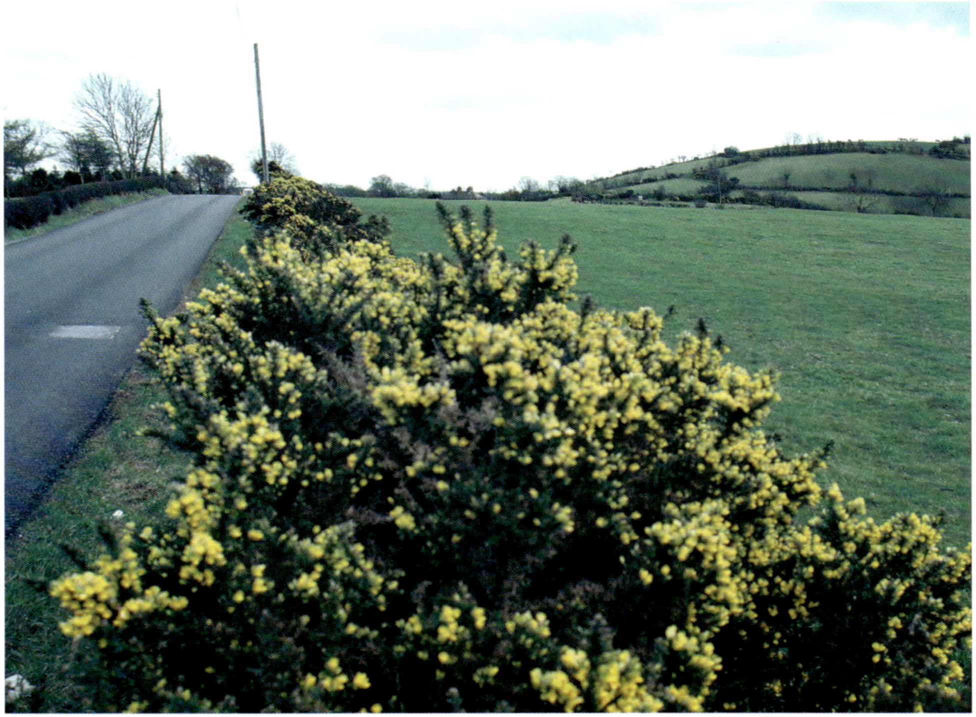

This kind of living fence of gorse (*Ulex europaeus*) is common in the United Kingdom. Gorse is native to Europe, but has been introduced into many other parts of the world. It makes a thick, prickly, evergreen barrier with attractive flowers; unfortunately, gorse also spreads aggressively and, without management, will invade open ground.

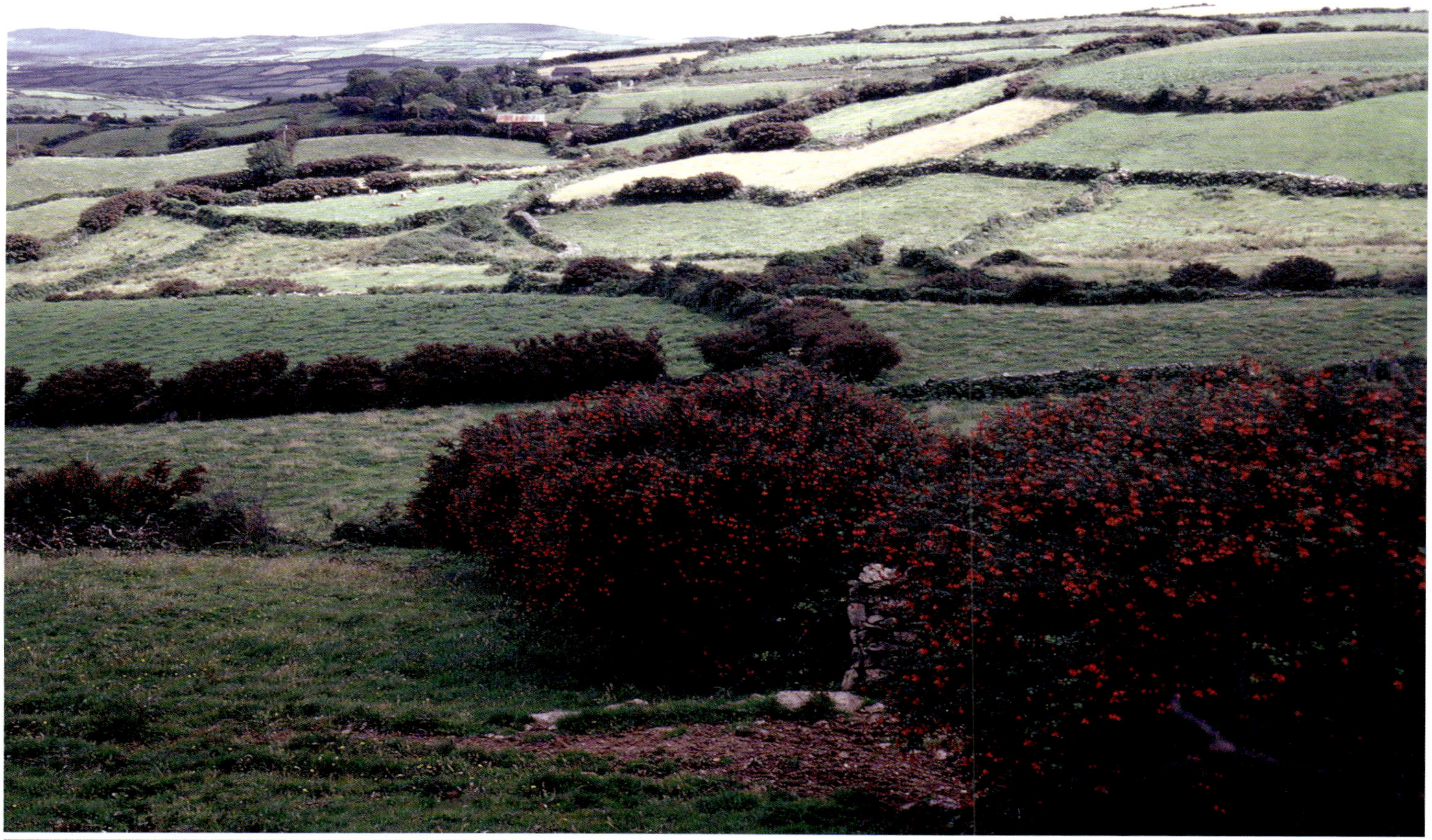

Equally attractive, effective, and somewhat invasive is this living fuchsia fence in West Cork, Ireland.

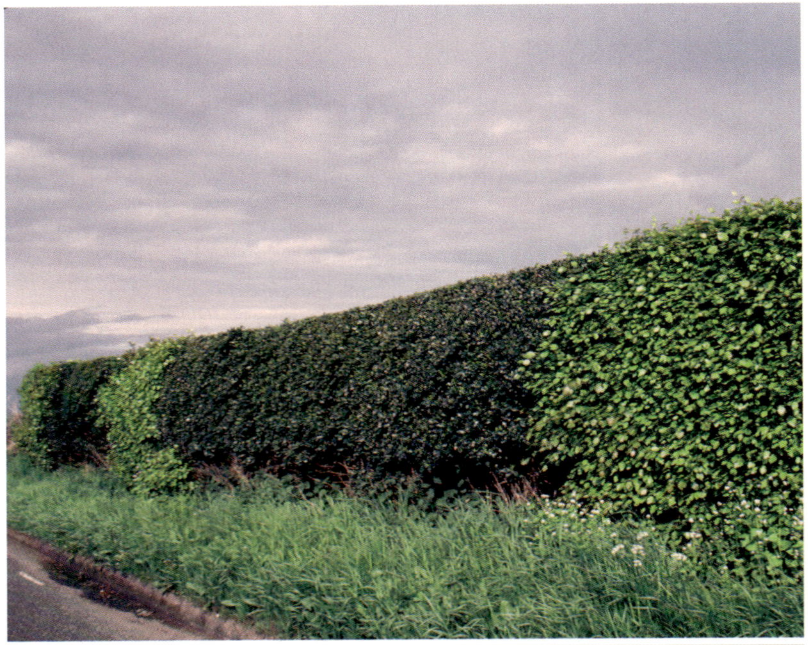

The iconic trimmed living beech tree fence is a special favorite in the United Kingdom. This one is near Comrie, Scotland. In the autumn, the leaves will turn beautiful shades of copper and reddish chestnut brown.

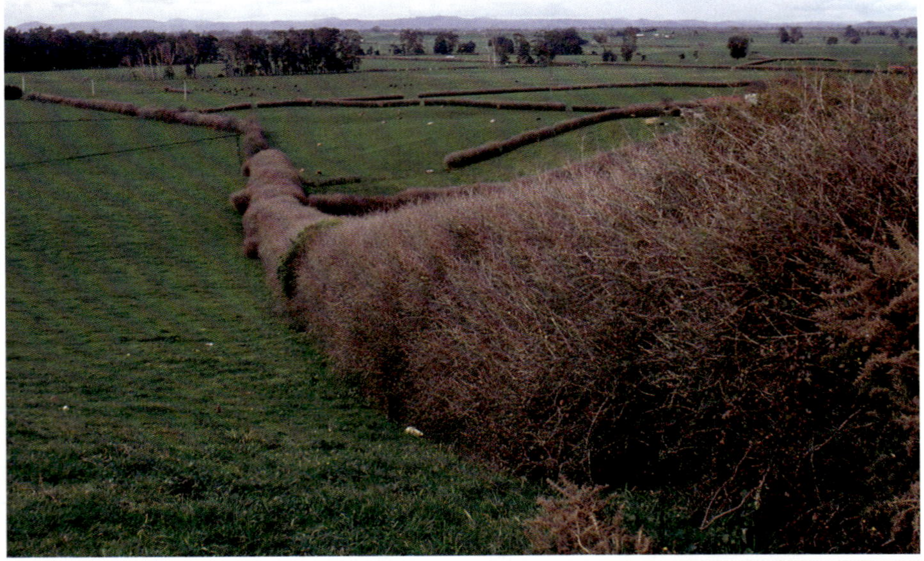

This thick thornapple fence near Waikato, New Zealand will be not only effective, but also very attractive when its small, dark green leaves and delicate white flowers come out.

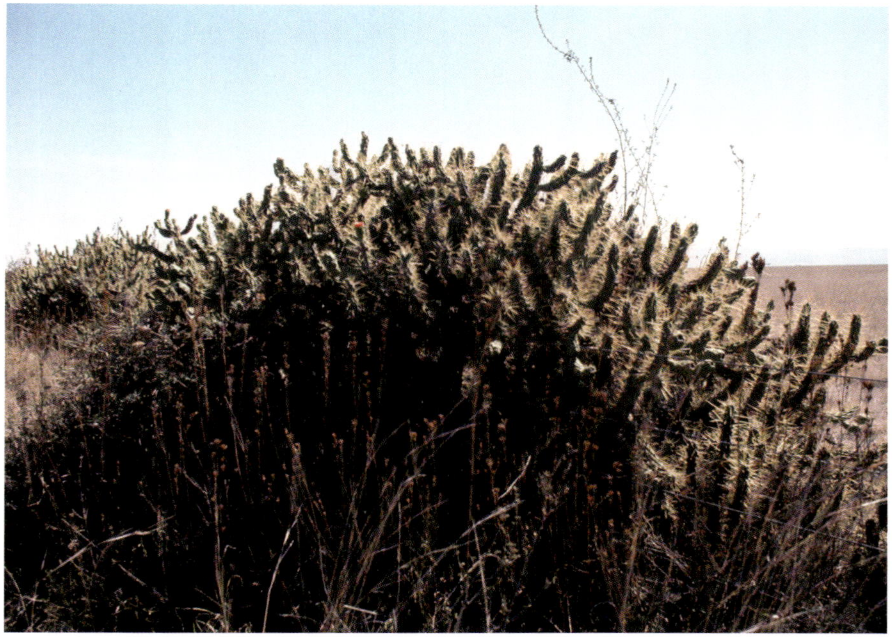

Sometimes the living cactus fence is so thick and thorny that reinforcement with wire is hardly necessary. But this one near Nairobi, Kenya has added wire to make sure there are no gaps.

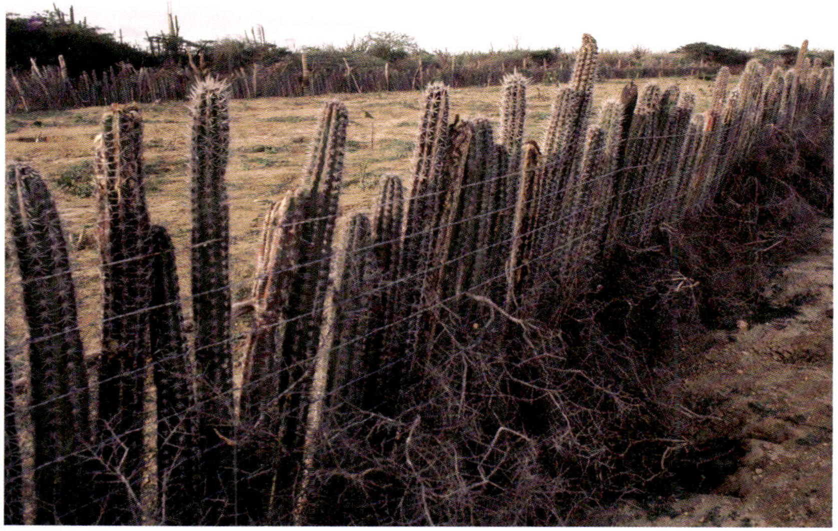

Here on the Península de Paraguaná, Venezuela, apparently something very sturdy was needed and so the living cactus is reinforced with both multiple strands of wire and cut woody shrubs. I wonder what they were trying to keep in?

More of a psychological or social fence, this living agave fence surrounds a highly-valued community forest plantation sponsored by an Australian Aid project near Chautara in Central Nepal. It effectively deters cattle from entering and damaging the plantation as the villagers walk them by each day on their way to water. Neither the agave nor the pines in the plantation are native to Nepal.

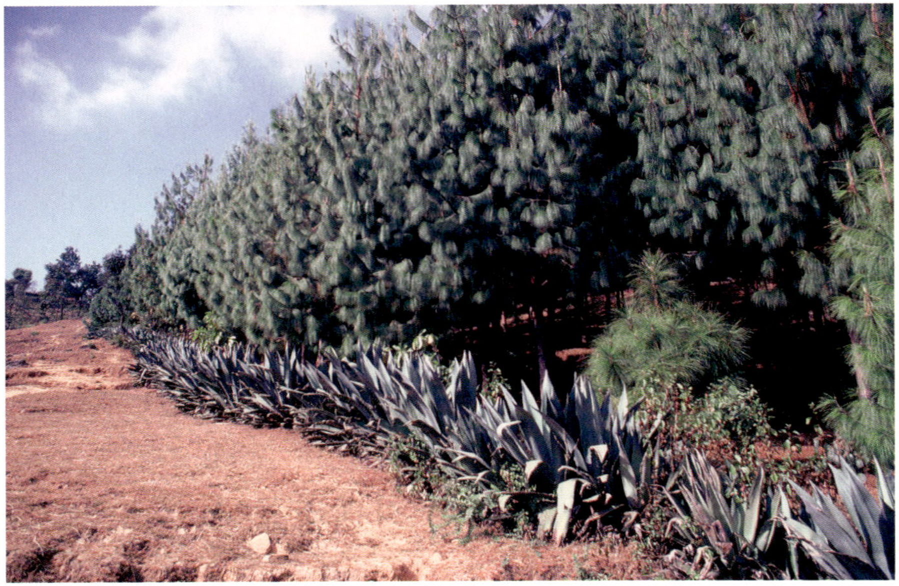

A living windbreak fence is created in Nepal by bunching and tying together the upper third of rice plants along the outer edge of the field in an attempt to reduce the force of wind and potential for blowdown of the crop.

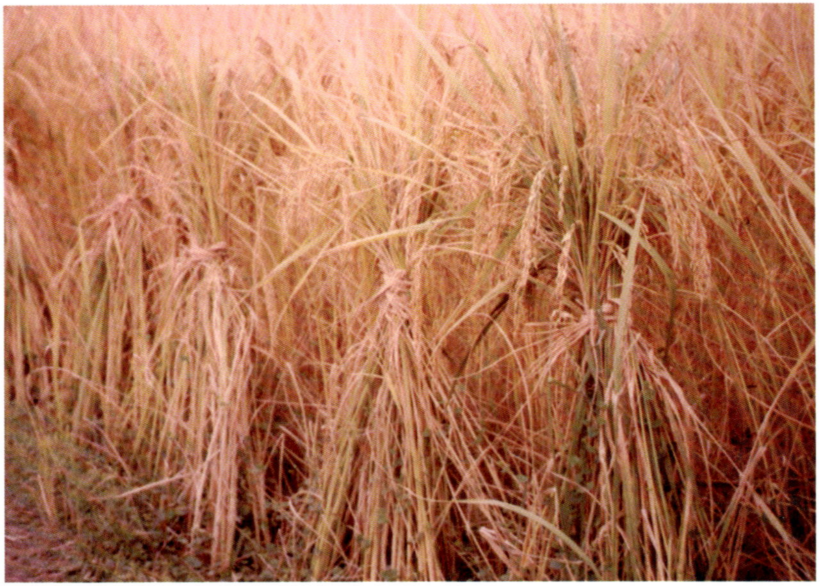

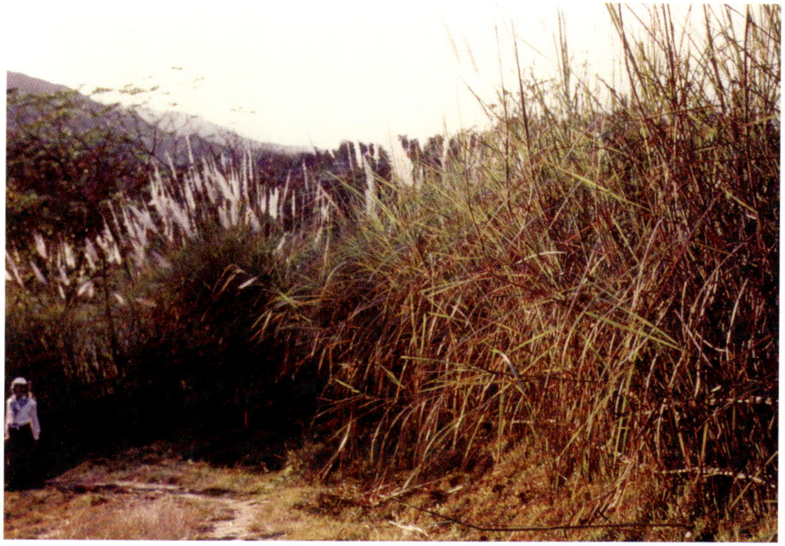

A much taller and sturdier windbreak is provided by some grasses and by sugarcane, also in Nepal.

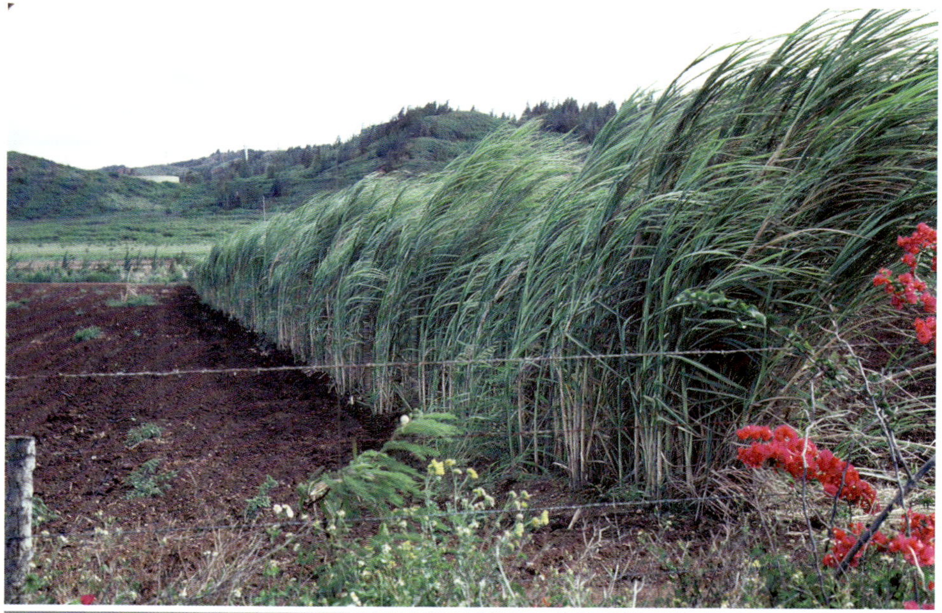

And here near Kahuku O`ahu, Hawai`i, USA, living sugarcane fences slow down the movement of windblown soil across the field.

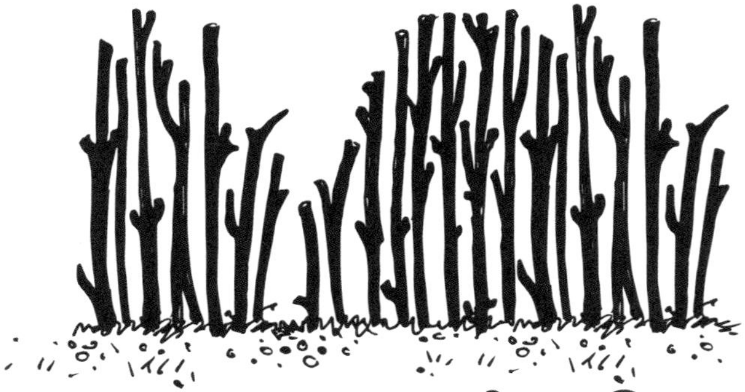

Fences made from DRY VEGETATION

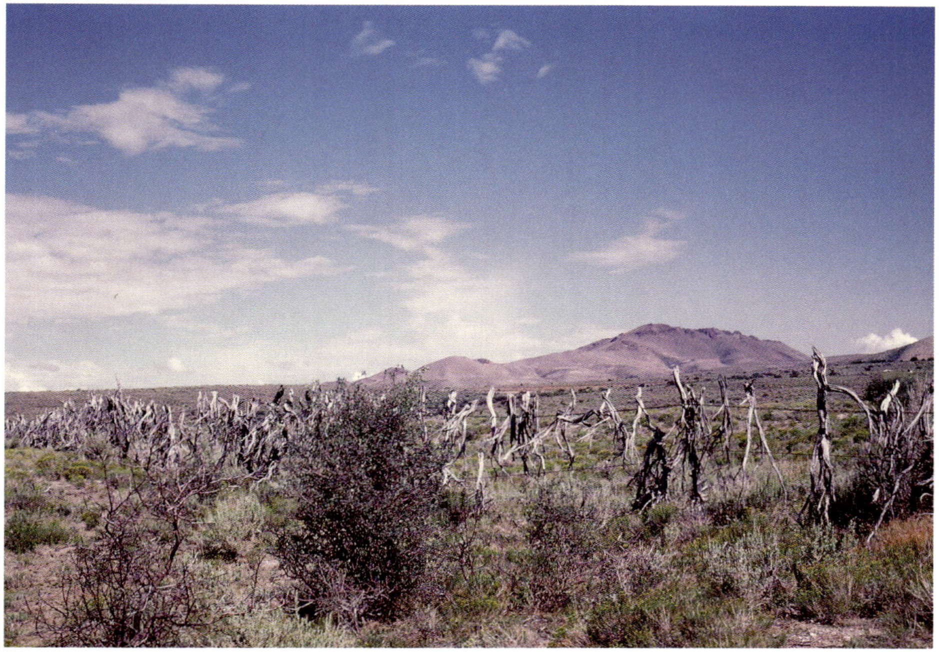

Barbed wire strung across the open range, as here in Nevada, USA, would be a bad accident waiting to happen if not hung with sagebrush to make it visible to fast moving steers or riding cowboys. This, in effect, becomes a sagebrush fence.

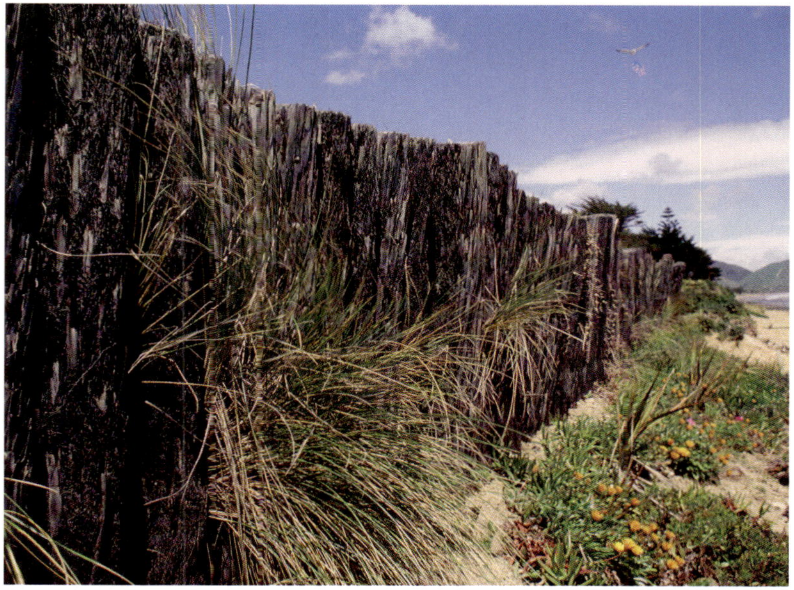

I was told that this solid fence composed of tree fern trunks in New Zealand was a "punga fence," to keep the pungas from coming inland from the beach. In Mäori mythology, punga is a supernatural being, the ancestor of sharks, lizards, rays, and generally unwanted things. Maybe it is a contemporary attempt to keep unwanted people from coming up from the beach onto private property? Or maybe it is a futile attempt to keep beach sand dunes from eroding?

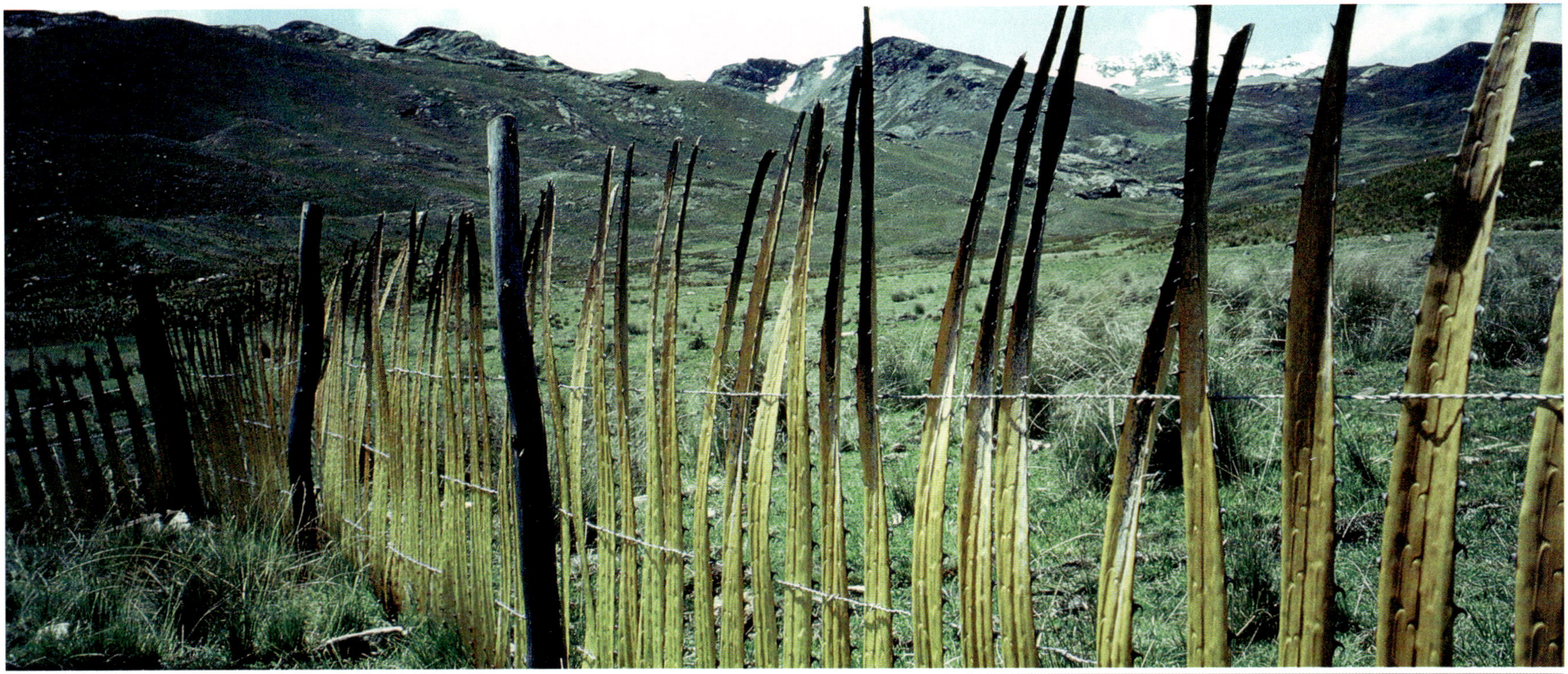

Another example of fence builders making good use of materials close at hand: In the Huascarán area of northern Perú, there are few trees for wood but there are plenty of the largest bromeliad in the world, the Queen of the Andes (*Puya raimondii*). This dramatic plant is only found in the Andes, and is best known for its spectacular flower spike, which can reach up to 33 feet in height, bearing over 8,000 whitish-green blooms which turn purplish with age. The spike may take as long as 80-150 years to flower! Meanwhile, at its base, the plant produces a dense cluster of bayonet-like leaves, each of which is edged with fishhook-worthy spines. What excellent fencing material!

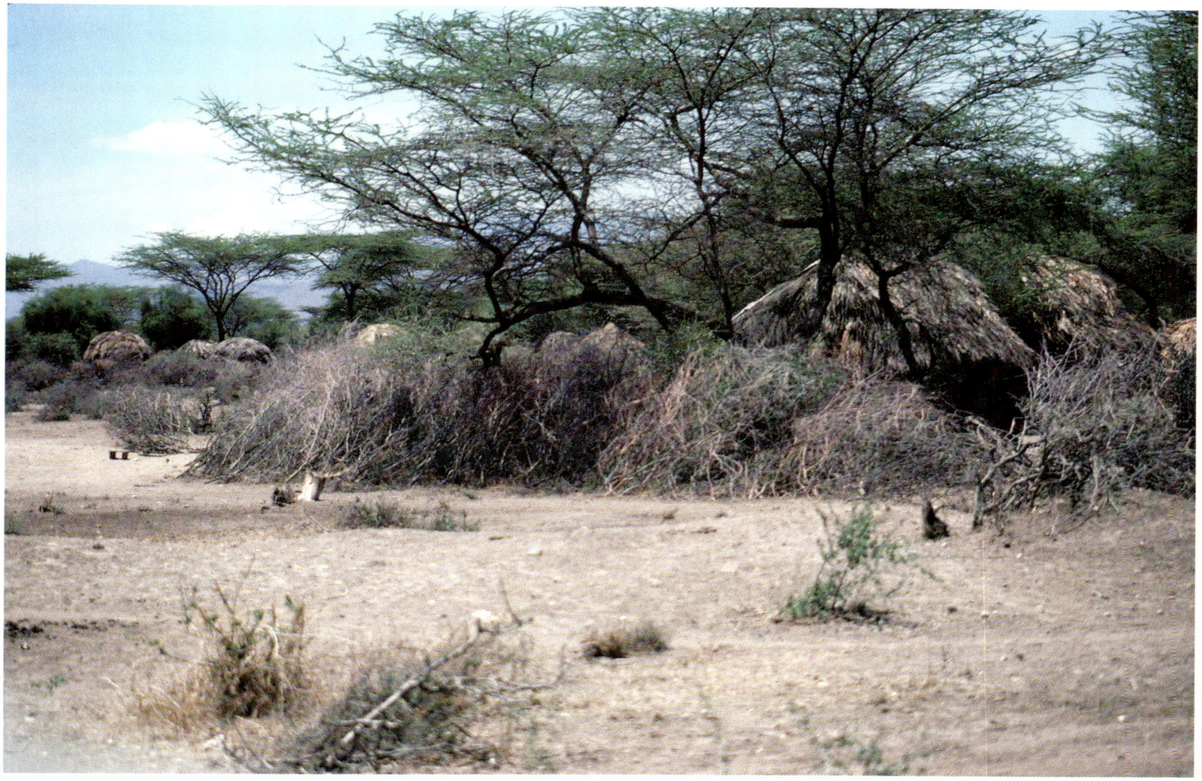

This stand-alone brush fence in Samburu National Park in Kenya is made of thorny acacia branches. It is a diurnal fence, pulled into place around the thatched hut dwellings and the livestock in the evening to give protection to humans and animals from big cats such as leopards and lions. In the morning, it will be disassembled.

Cocoons mean survival.
Frowsy, fenced-in closeness, for the soft African darkness invites
fangs and claws—
which too spell survival for
the fiercer and
the more desperate.
The semi-arid plains provide
brush burrows
and decide who is in fact
the fittest.

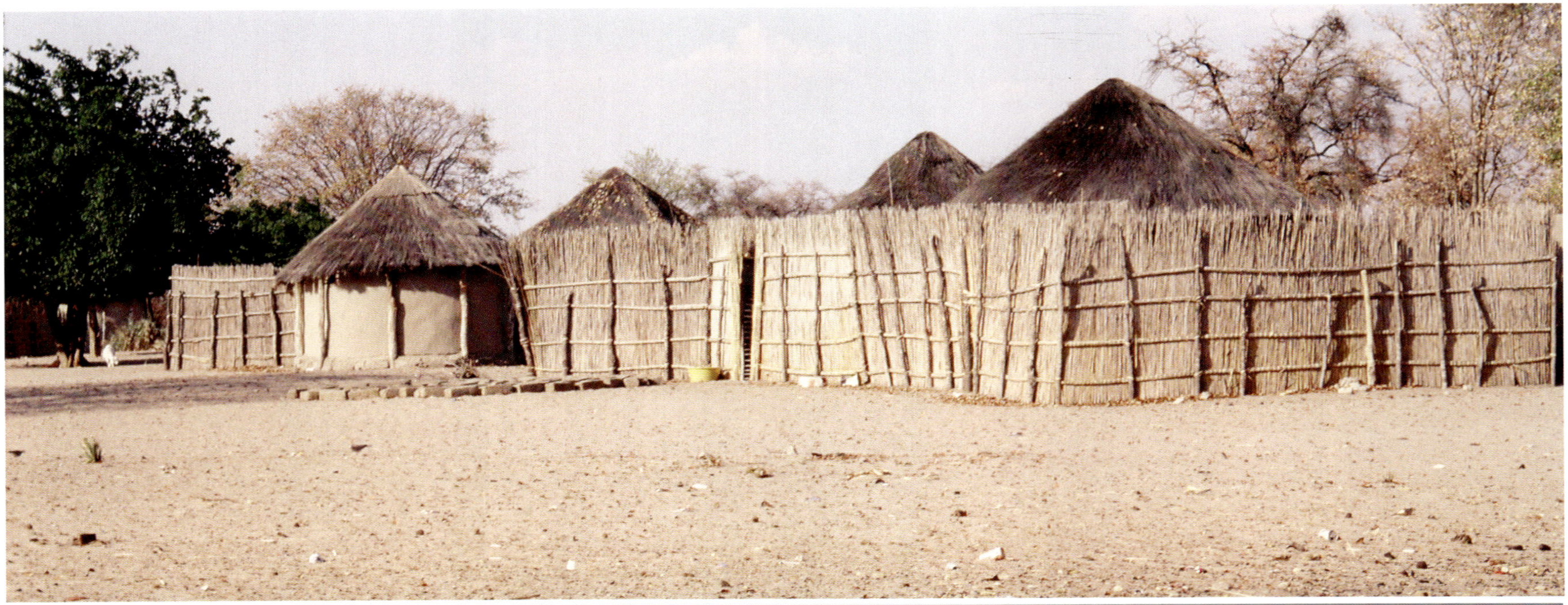

This fence in Botswana serves the same purpose, but is made to stay up day and night to protect the compound where people and animals live.

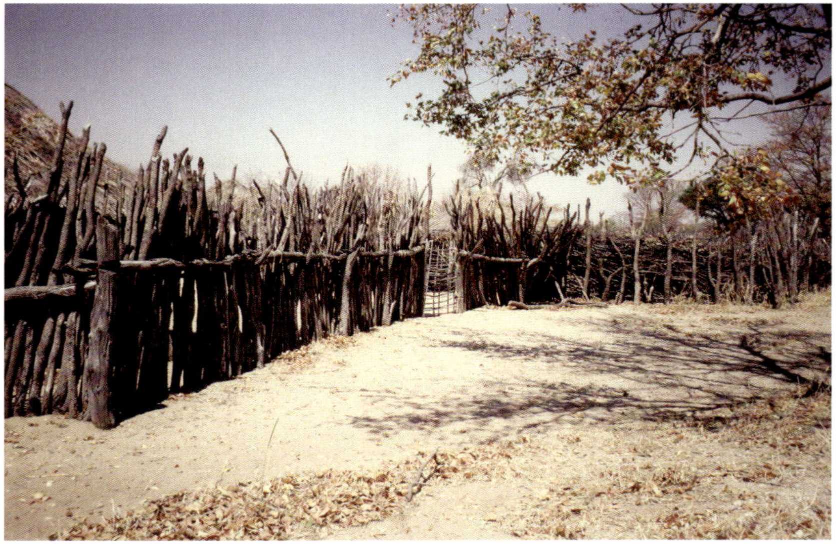

Other Botswana families build impressively sturdy protection around their compounds.

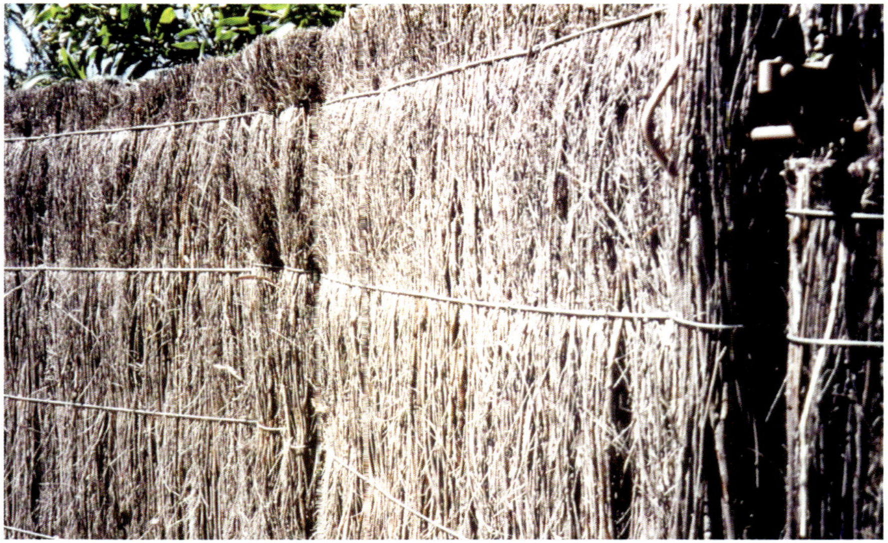

A thick barrier fence in Australian Capital Territory is made of reeds secured tightly with wire. This also was a big investment, and its purpose is not clear.

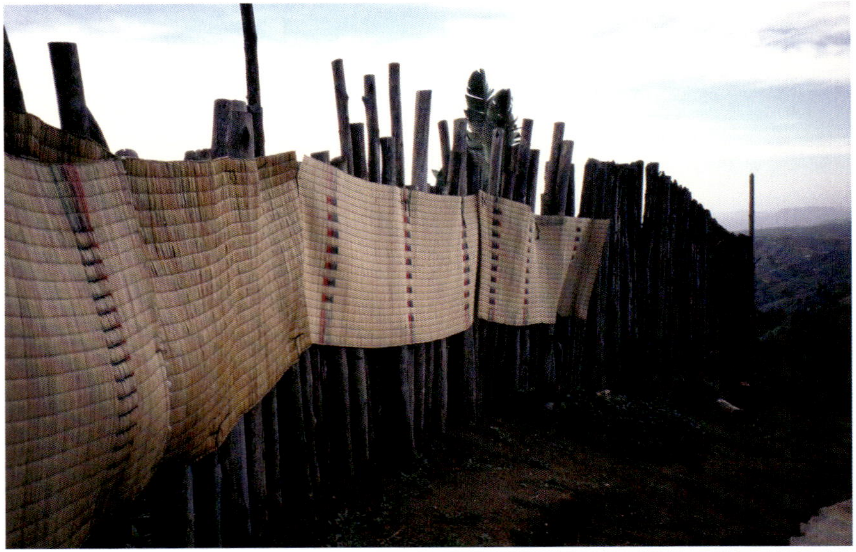

Here is another curious situation, found in South Africa. This is a very sturdy fence, and a big investment of time and effort. Why add woven reed mats? Is it an important windbreak perhaps? If so, the wind must be very strong in this area.

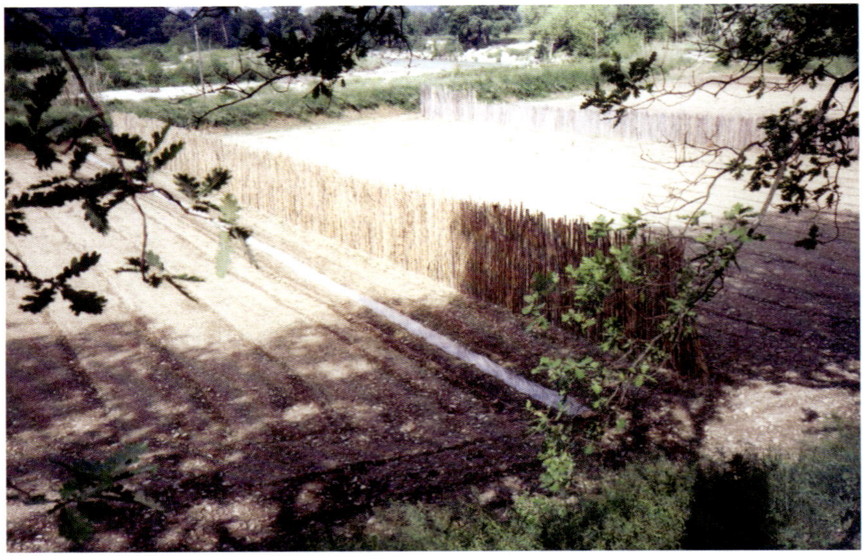

Here, the windbreak role of the fence is clear. It is made of bamboo near Vaison-la-Romaine, Provence, France. Whatever this farmer is growing, it must be a valuable crop.

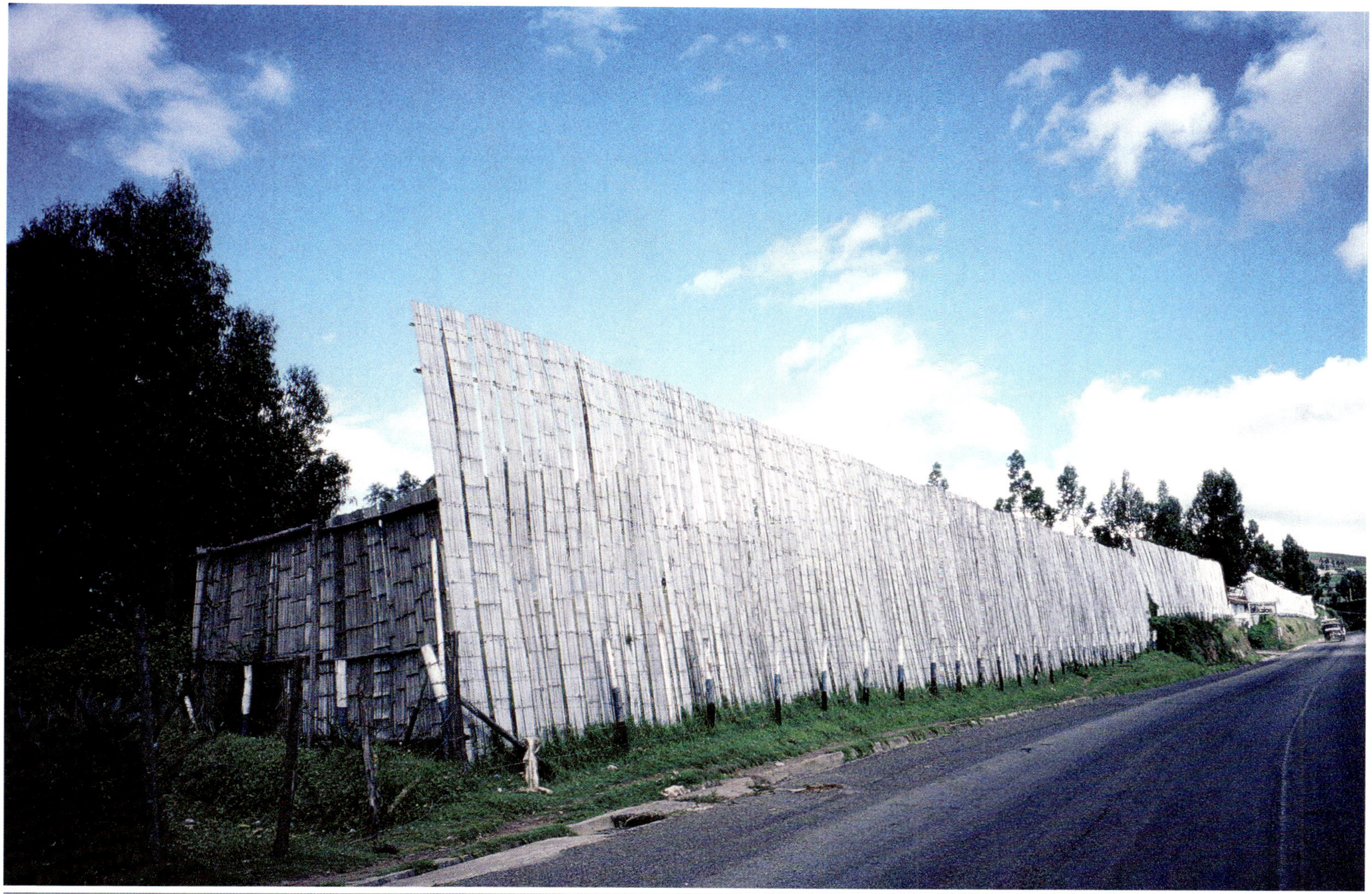

This fence in Ecuador utilizes split bamboo to create a windbreak around roses being carefully grown for the export market.

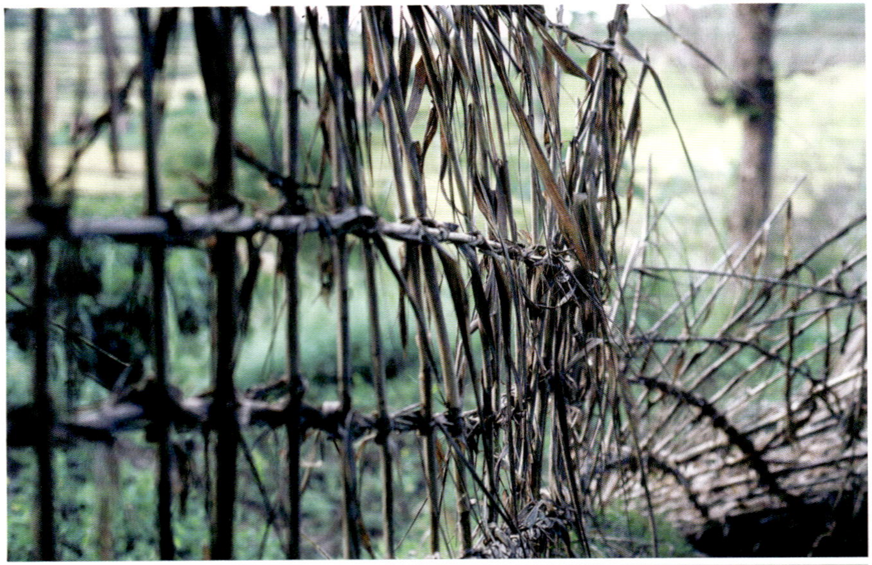

This cornstalk and cane fence in Nepal seems too flimsy to contain any animals, except perhaps chickens or small game birds?

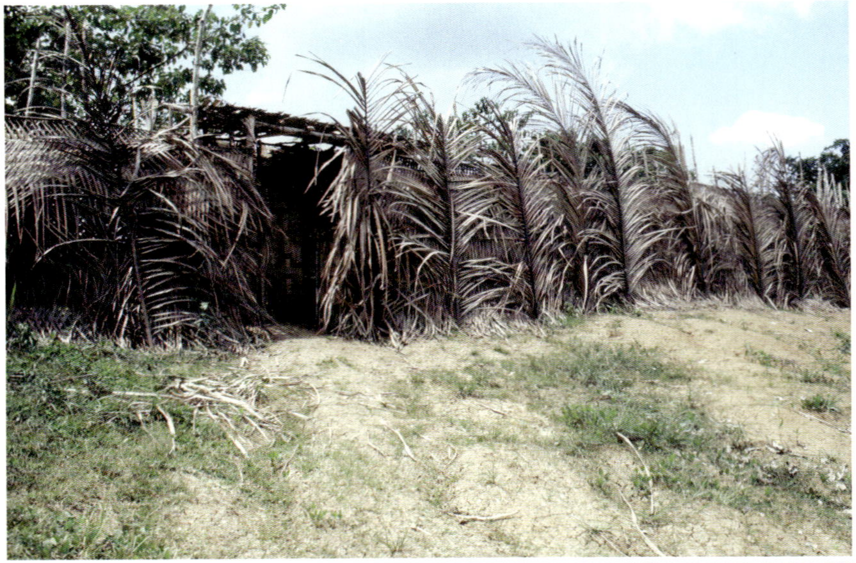

This rather gay coconut frond fence in Papua New Guinea is actually not meant to contain anything. Fronds are set up from time to time to create a party space inside, and they announce that the festivities will soon begin!

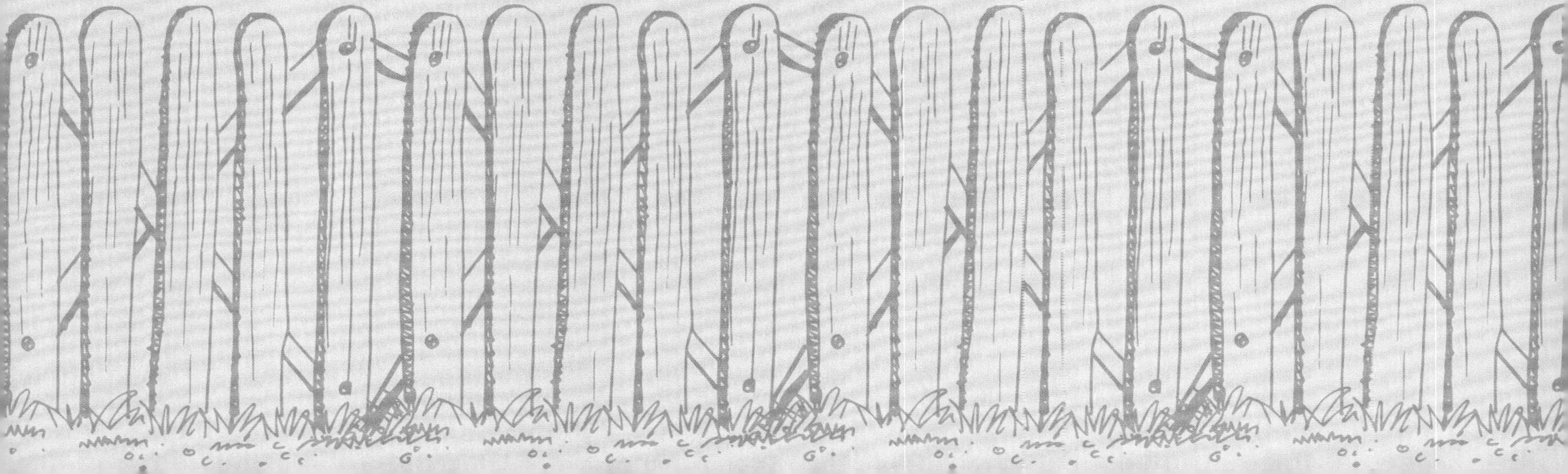

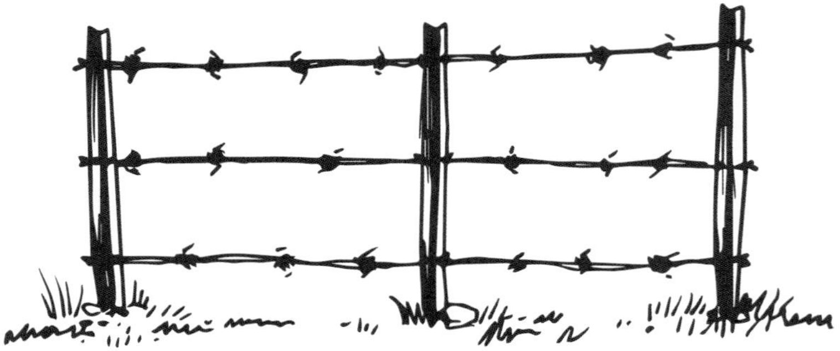

MOSTLY WIRE

Offering strands from light-weight to cable strength, with or without barbs, stiff woven or flexible mesh, the availability of wire has allowed fence-builders to go places and do things only dreamed of before.

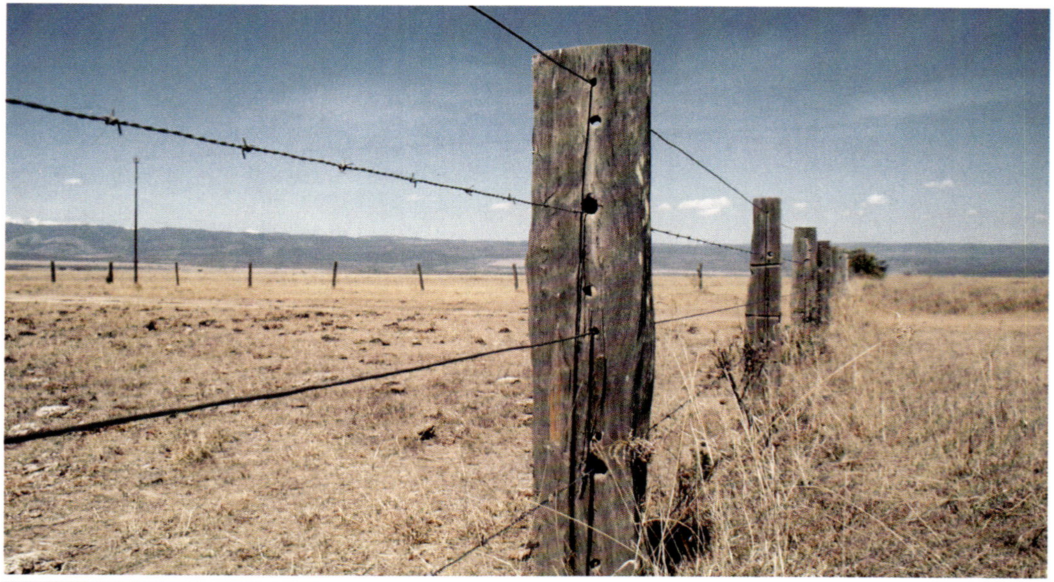

Sometimes a little wire can make a big difference. Here in the Rift Valley of Kenya, where wood and other fencing materials are scarce, wire makes a fence possible. I wonder if they are keeping things in or keeping things out? Notice how the wire is painstakingly threaded through holes in the wooden posts. Why not just attach the wire to the posts with screw-in hooks, for example?

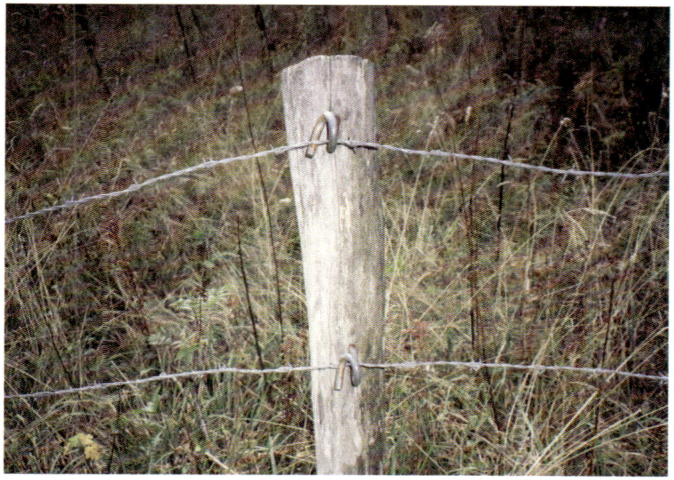

This special S-hook not only easily attaches wire (barbed or otherwise) to the wooden post, it also allows the farmer to take the wire off temporarily and lower it enough so he/she can pass through the fence. Here it is in use in the high summer pastures of the Jura, Switzerland.

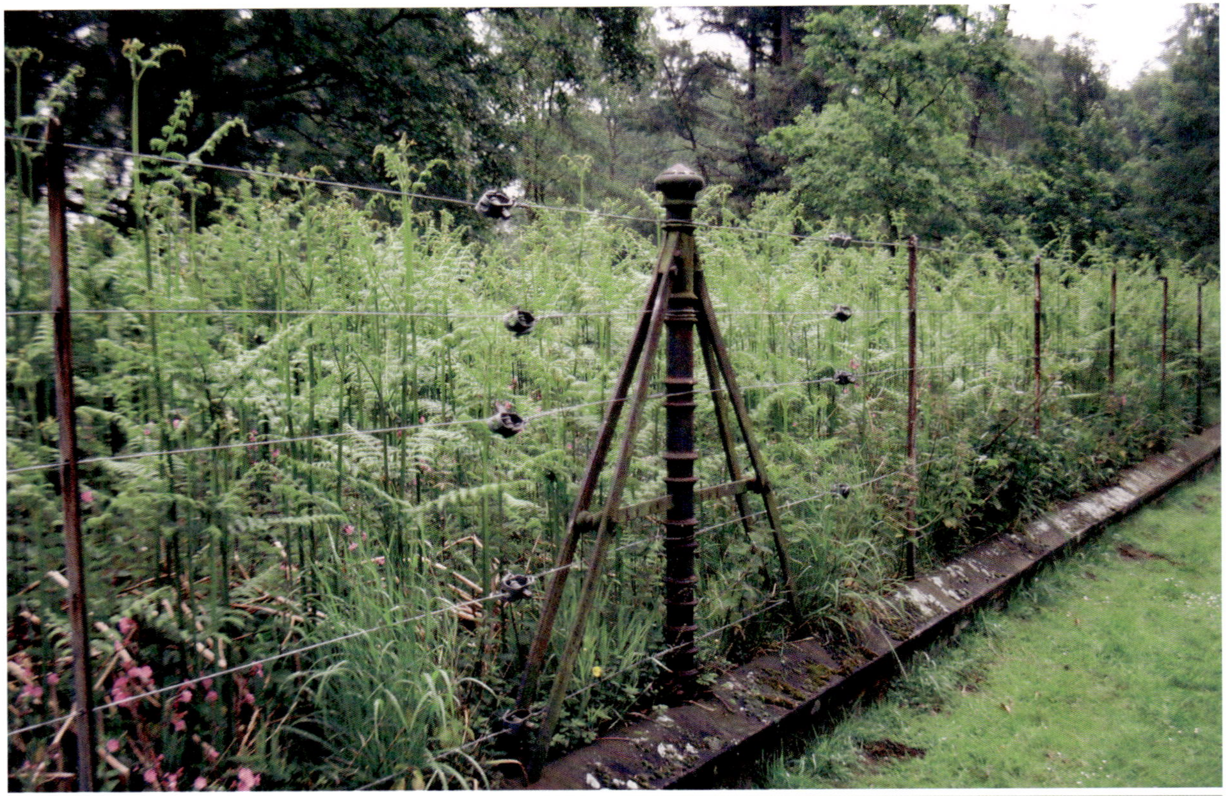

The naturally "wild" is still visible through the wire here, but someone wants to keep those invasive plants and animals from crossing over into their domesticated space at Sandringham Palace in Norfolk, England. Security seems particularly tight, doesn't it?

Sometimes, fences are meant to keep out, or at least deter, people, as with this electrified wire fence protecting a colony of nesting terns on the beach at Jervis Bay, New South Wales, Australia.

This multi-strand barbed wire fence, reinforced with metal chain spreaders, is likely an effective deterrent, at least for humans, if the USA Department of Energy "No Trespassing" sign is not enough. It is around the Los Alamos, New Mexico, USA site of the Manhattan Project which developed nuclear weapons during World War II.

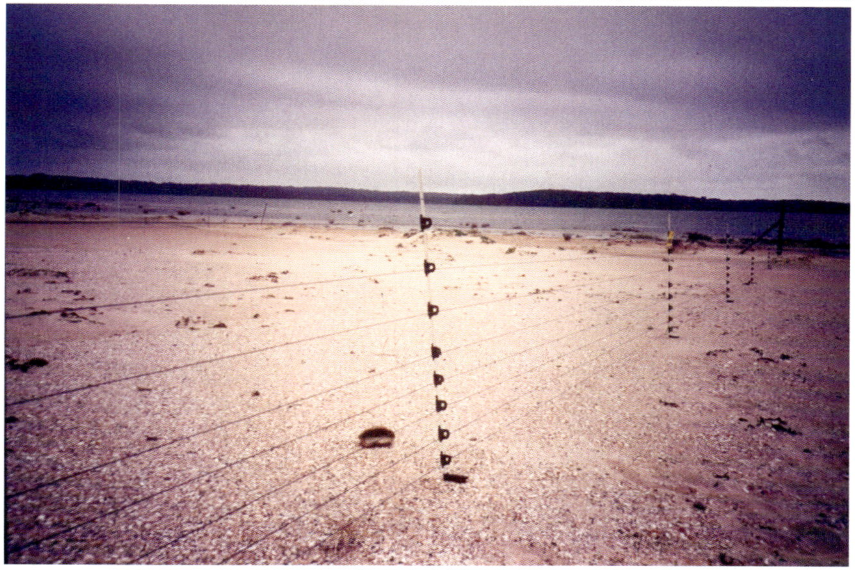

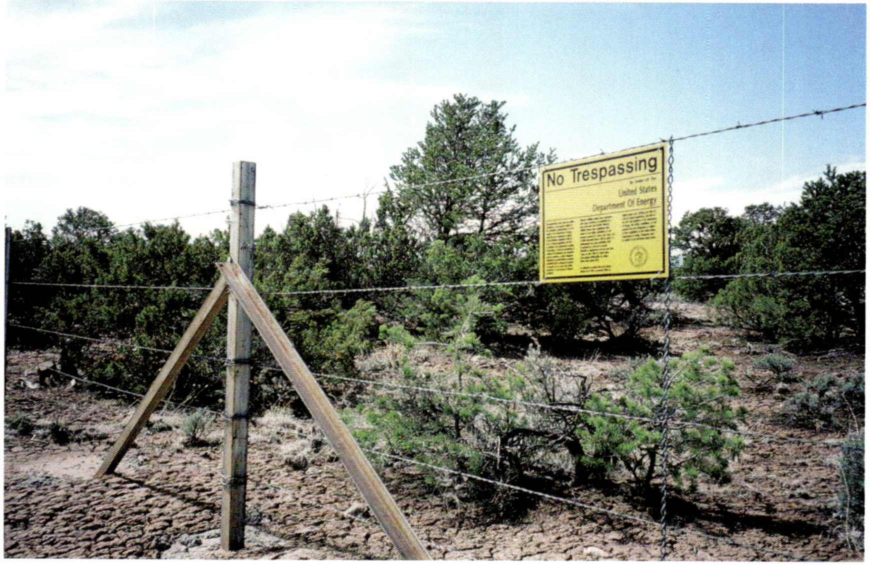

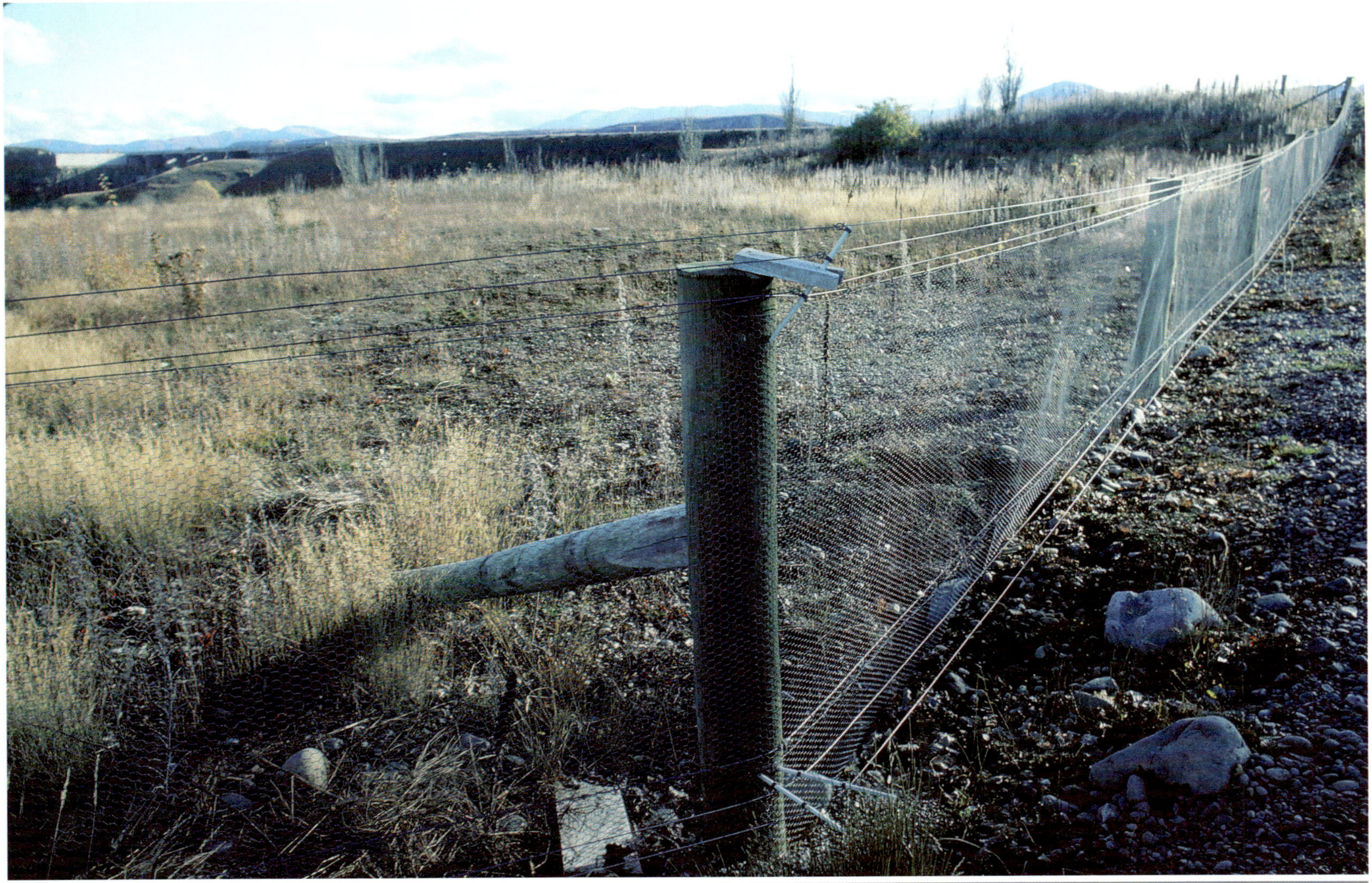

And sometimes a fence is an attempt to keep everything out, as with this buried mesh topped with electrified barbed wire, protecting the nesting area of the endangered black stilt near Twizel, New Zealand.

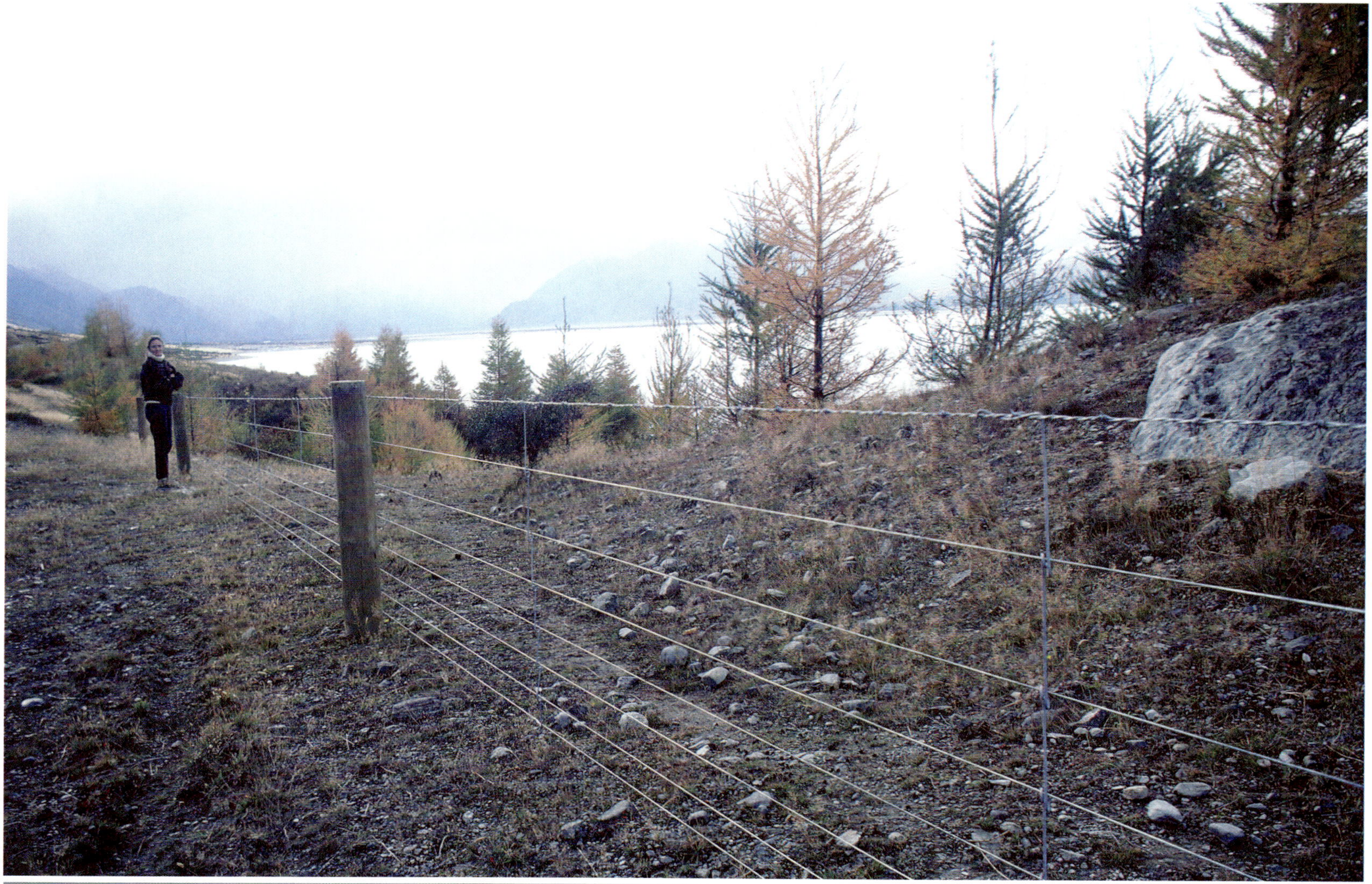

The size of wire mesh can be varied in the same structure, as here in New Zealand, where 'close together low down' protects against wandering sheep and 'wider spacing higher up' keeps cattle out. Note the addition of wire spreaders at regular intervals to add strength between posts.

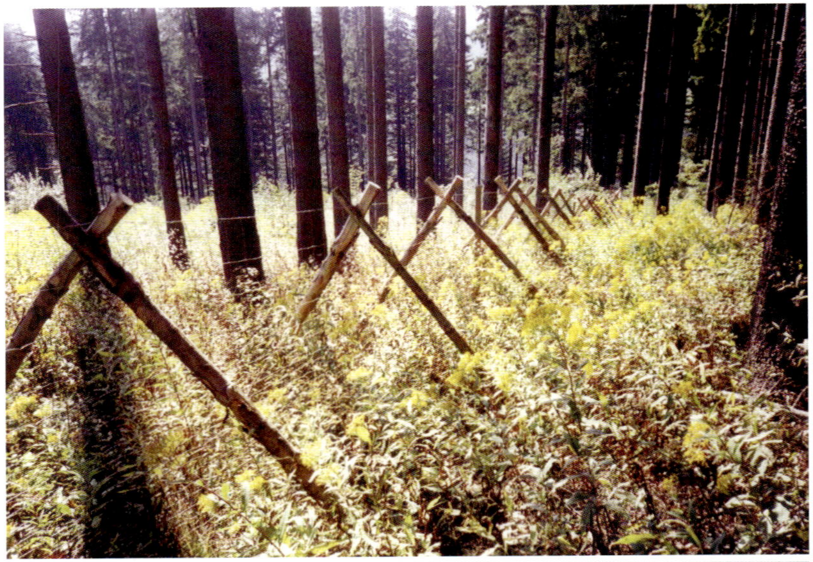

This is an example of the stake and rider approach being a practical fence for controlling deer in Germany's Black Forest area.

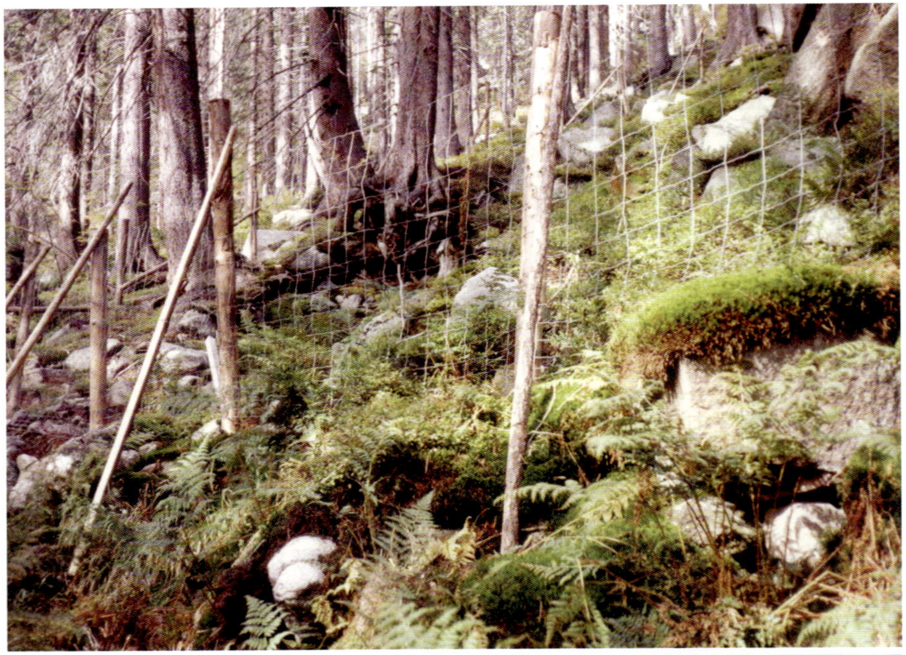

Posts could not be set very deep in this forest either because of the rocky terrain. But the builders of this deer fence in Krkonoše National Park, Czech Republic chose to use well-braced posts, especially where the slope is steep.

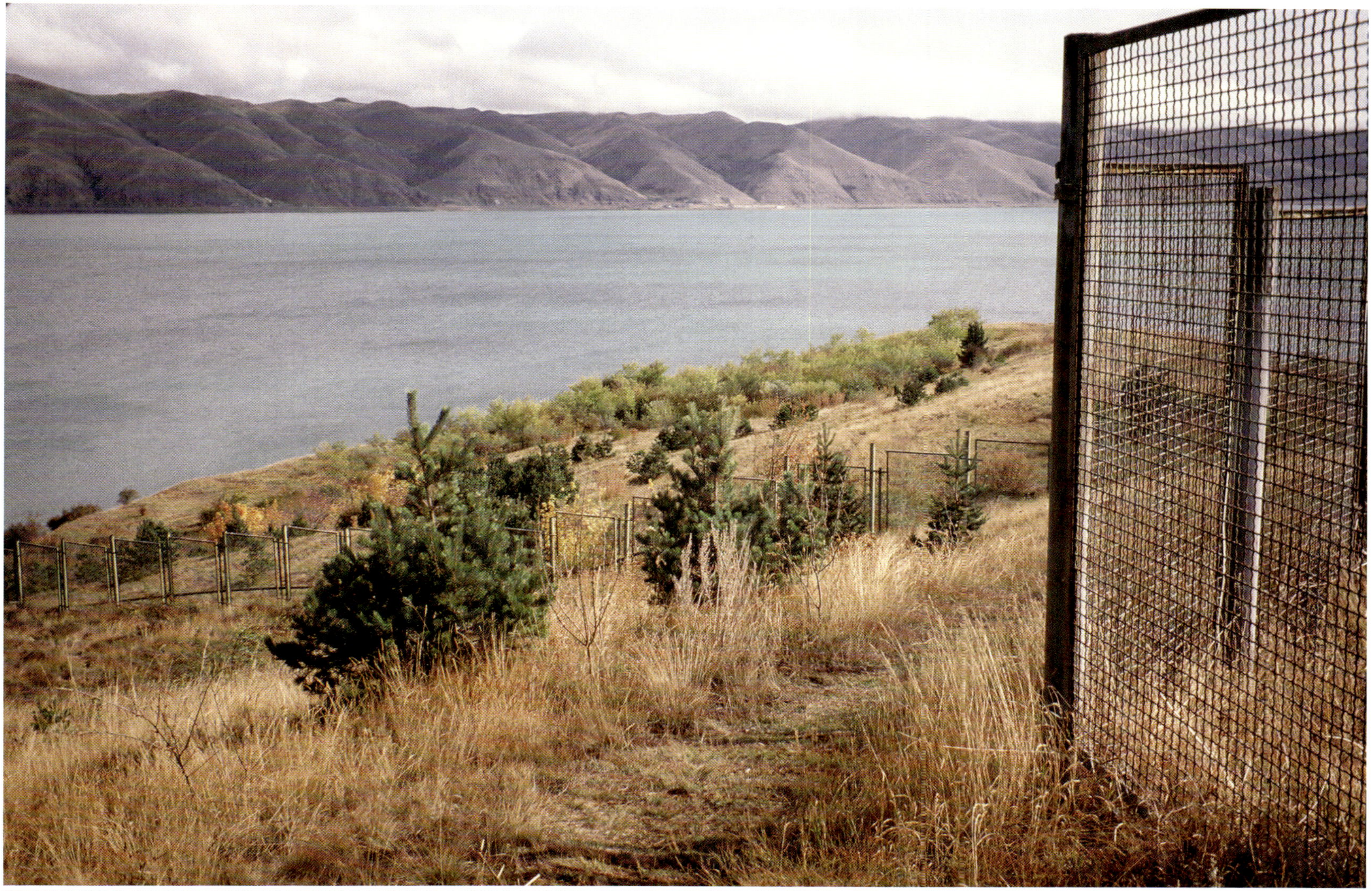

This too is a deer fence. But this one, near Lake Sevan National Park in Armenia, is keeping raised deer inside a game shooting park. It is high and sturdy.

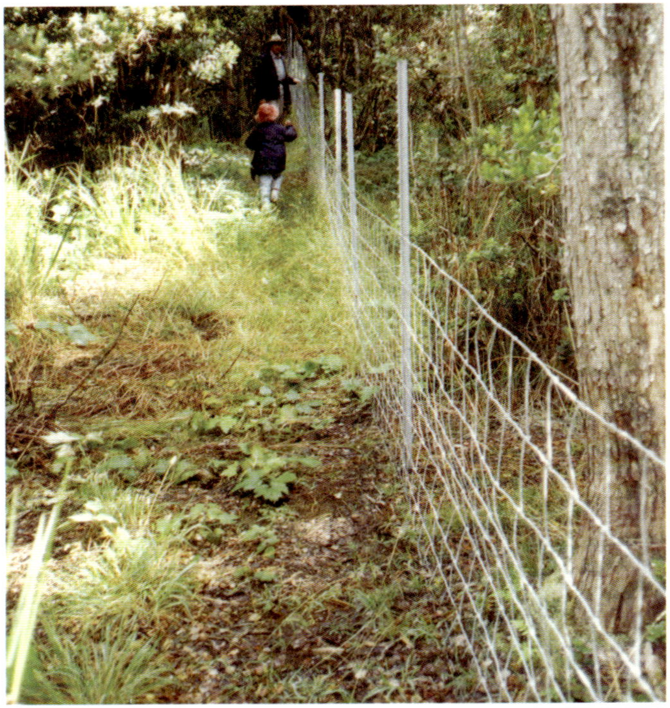

If it is feral pigs that you are managing for, you need to go not only strong, but also deep, burying a heavy-duty woven wire fence as has been done here in Hawai`i Volcanoes on the Big Island and other National Parks in Hawai`i. Even though installing pig fence in this rough terrain can cost $40,000 or more per mile (!), the biologically-rich forest it protects from devastating pig damage is considered worth it.

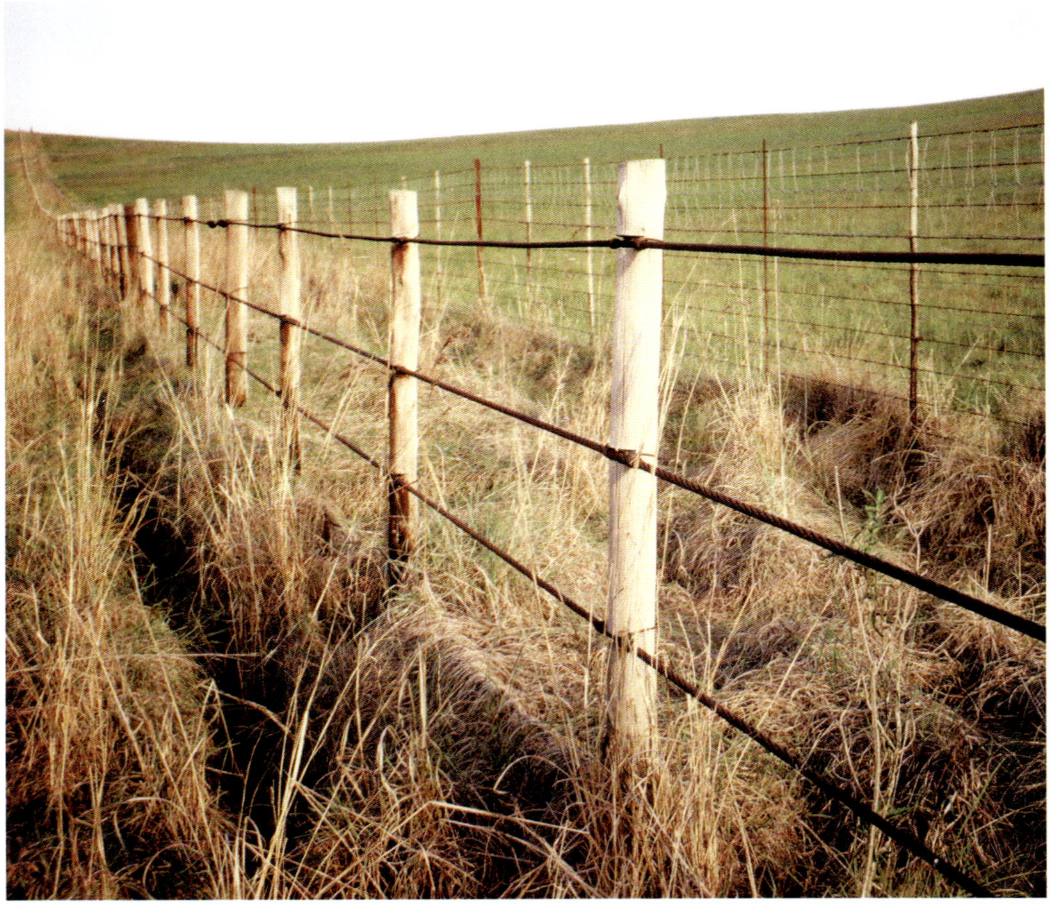

This is the Natal area of South Africa's approach to wild rhino fencing. Those heavy wire cables make it seem very sturdy. But rhinos are pretty sturdy themselves, and I'm not sure I would like to see this fence tested.

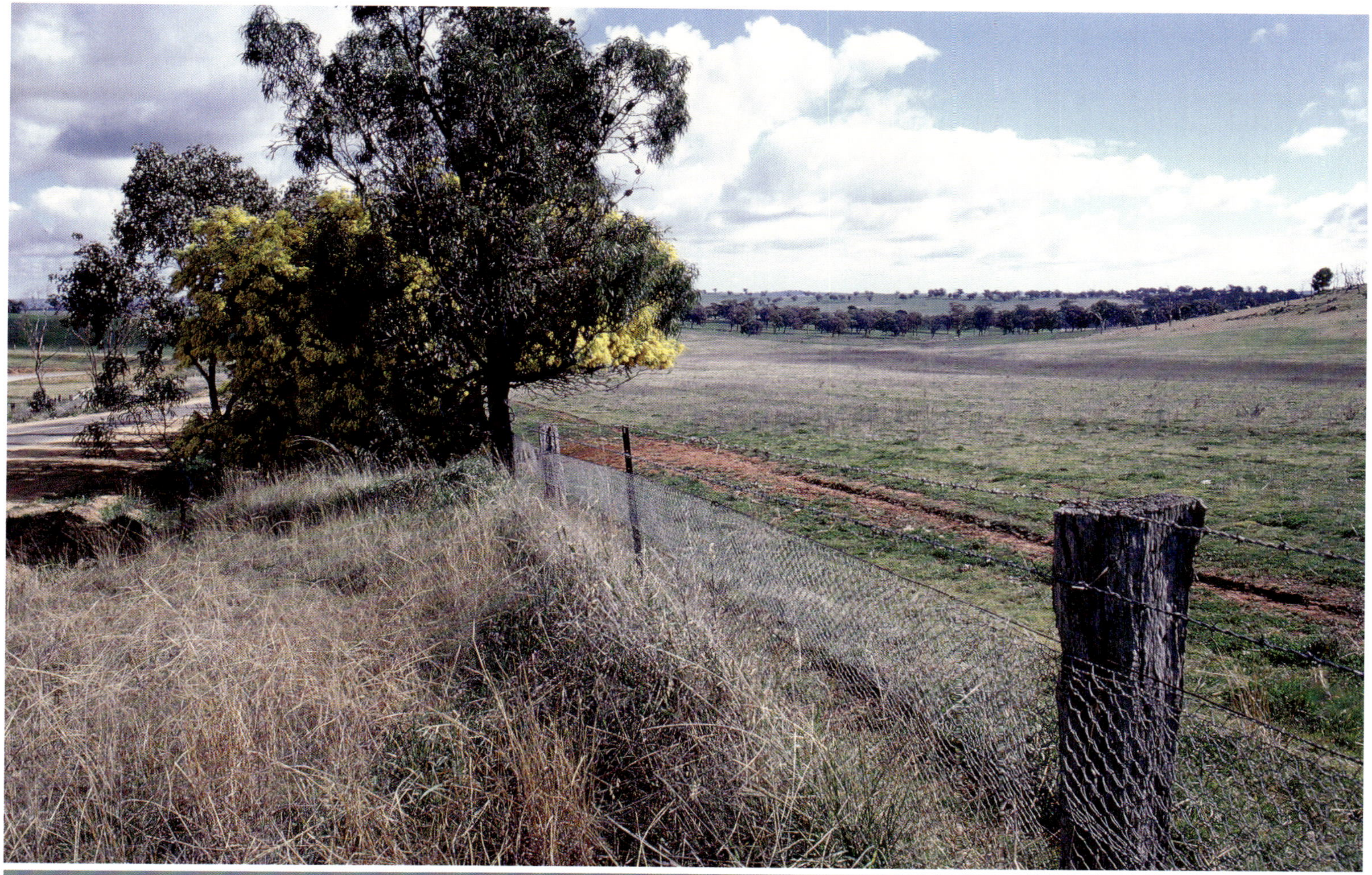

Most often, wire fencing is used to manage farm animals. Like this woven wire fence in New South Wales, Australia, around a large sheep paddock. Note the double strand of barbed wire on top as an extra precaution.

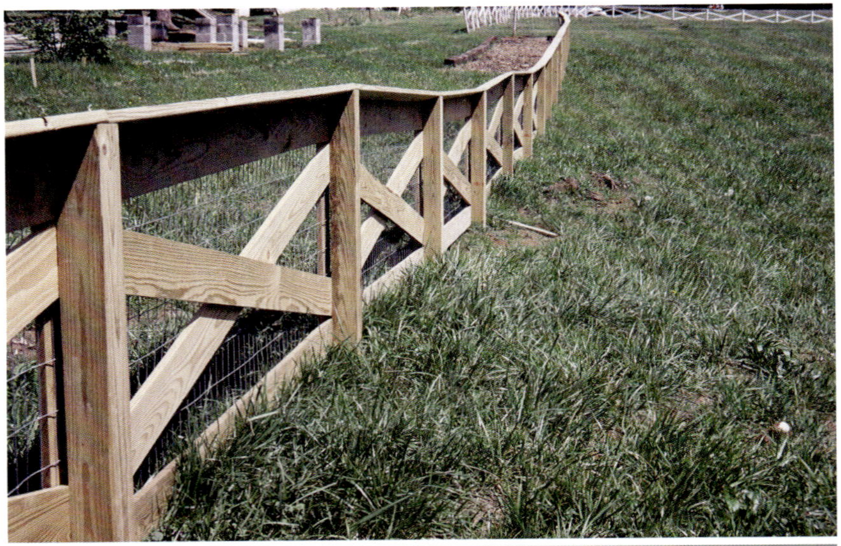

This showy fence in North Carolina, USA, uses lots of treated pine boards, but the builder did not stop there. He/she added a woven wire interior which should make it effective against a range of small animals. Or maybe this is a woven wire fence abundantly supported and reinforced with wood? In either case, if there are bears in this area, I don't believe this fence (or much else) will keep them away from the bee hives visible in the background!

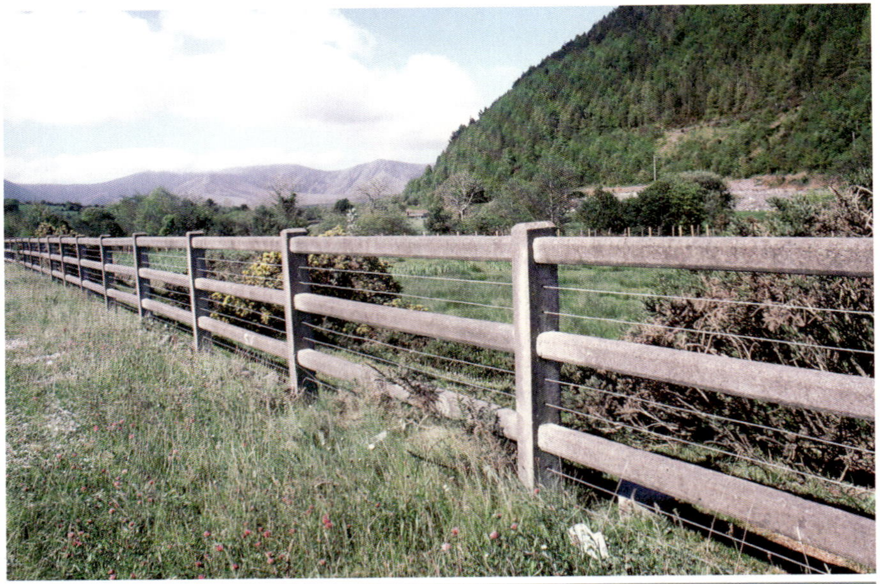

This farm fence on the Iveragh Peninsula, County Kerry, Ireland was described to me as "pig tight and bull strong." It certainly has a lot going for it, being made of cast concrete and very heavy wire. Notice again the practice of threading the wire through holes in the upright posts. You would not want to make a mistake and have to re-do even a short section, would you?

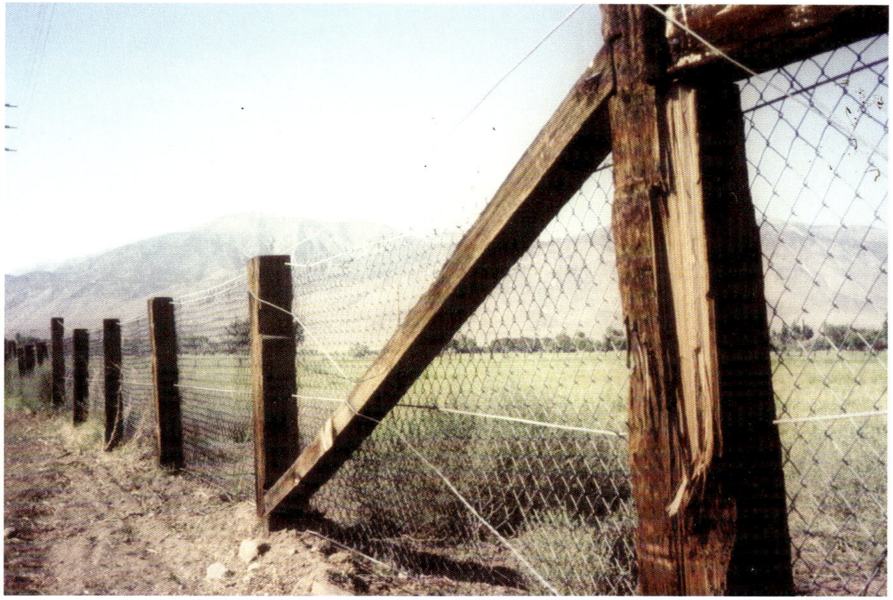

In Owens Valley, California, USA, this fence is considered "bull tight."

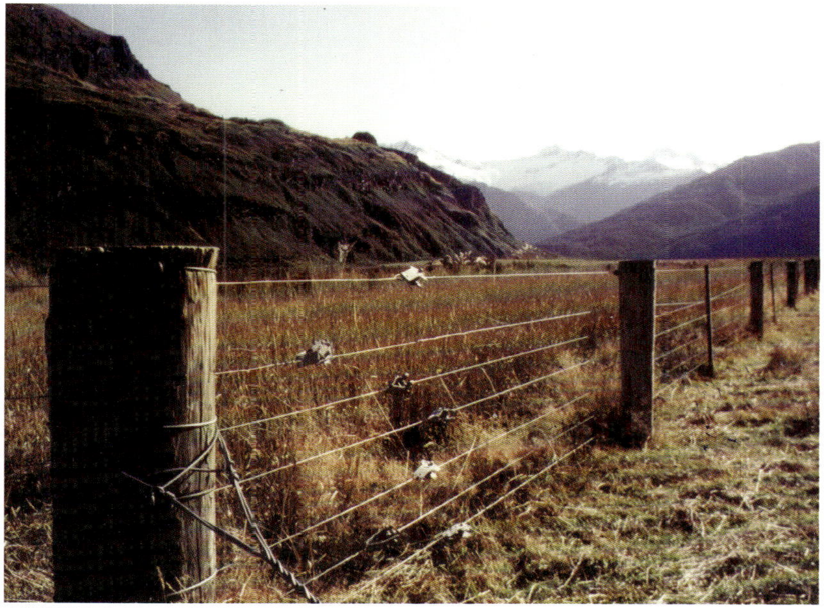

But this one around a sheep paddock in the high country near Mount Aspiring on the South Island of New Zealand seems impressively strong as well, even though it is meant for smaller animals. Note the wire tighteners to maintain the tension.

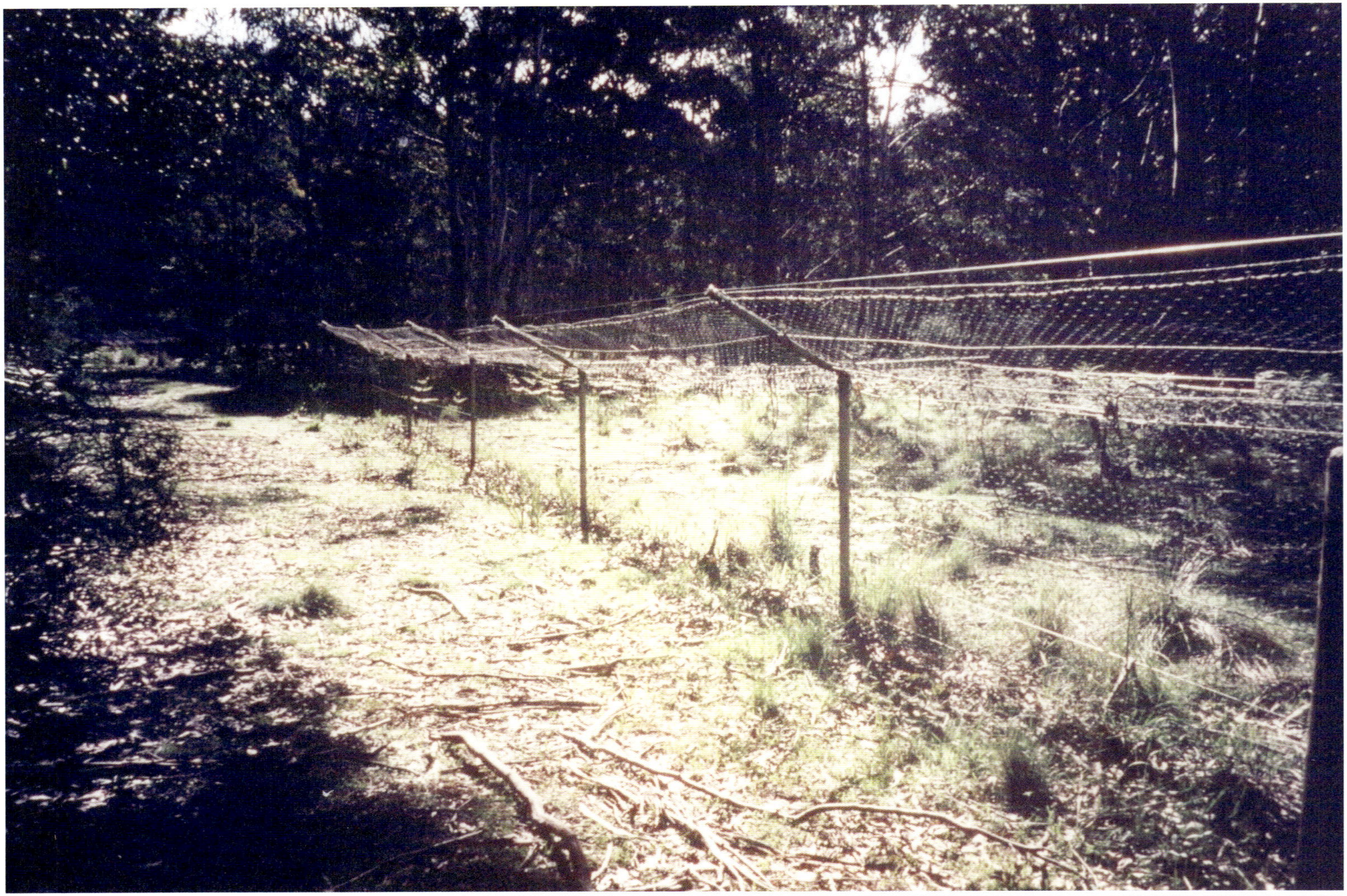

Shape can be even more important than strength in some situations, like this fence around a nature reserve in Tidbinbilla, Australian Capital Territory designed to protect ground-nesting lyre birds and koala from predators.

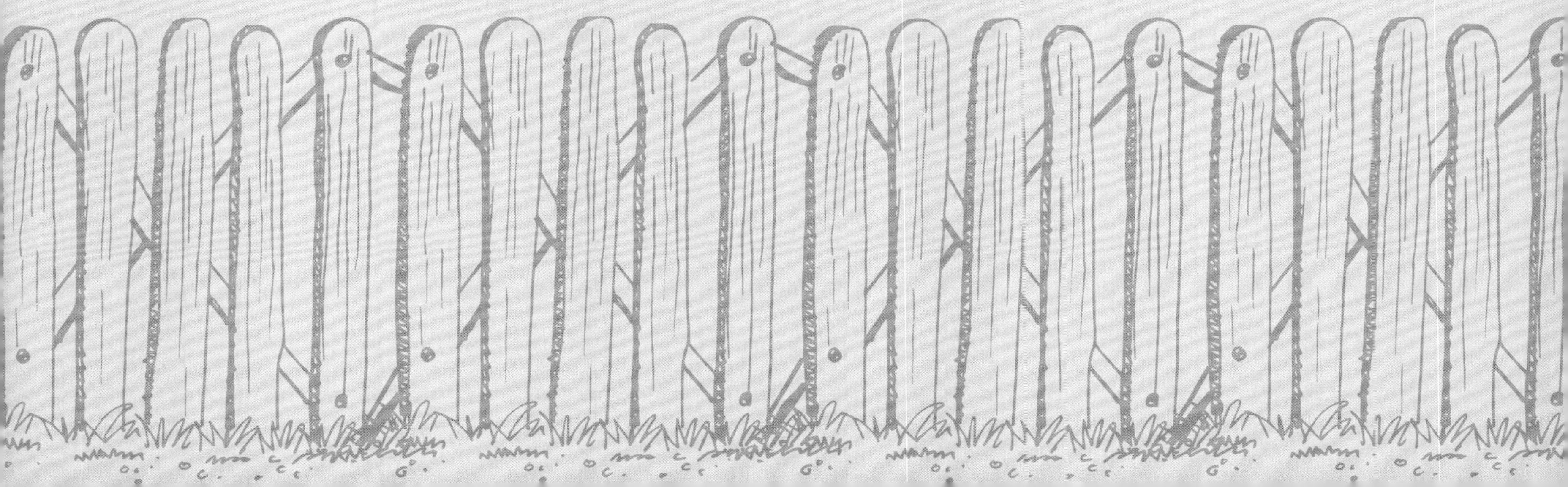

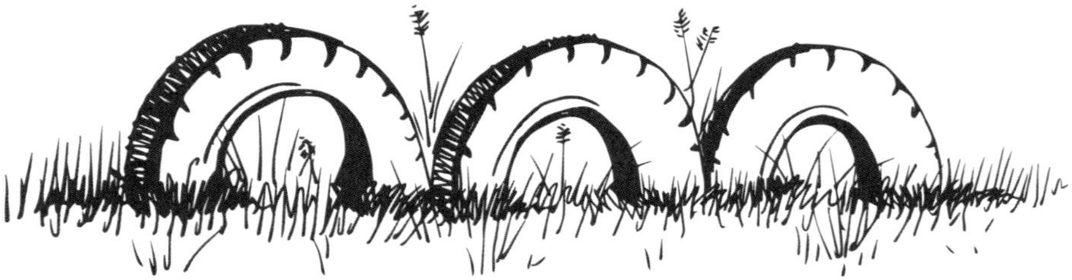

Fences made of STRANGE STUFF

Fence builders are often innovative and creative out of necessity, but they can also be whimsical just for the pleasure of it. If they do not have access to traditional materials, do not wish to use them for some reason, or are simply feeling their sense of humor, they may choose building materials or combinations of materials ranging from the wonderful to the downright strange.

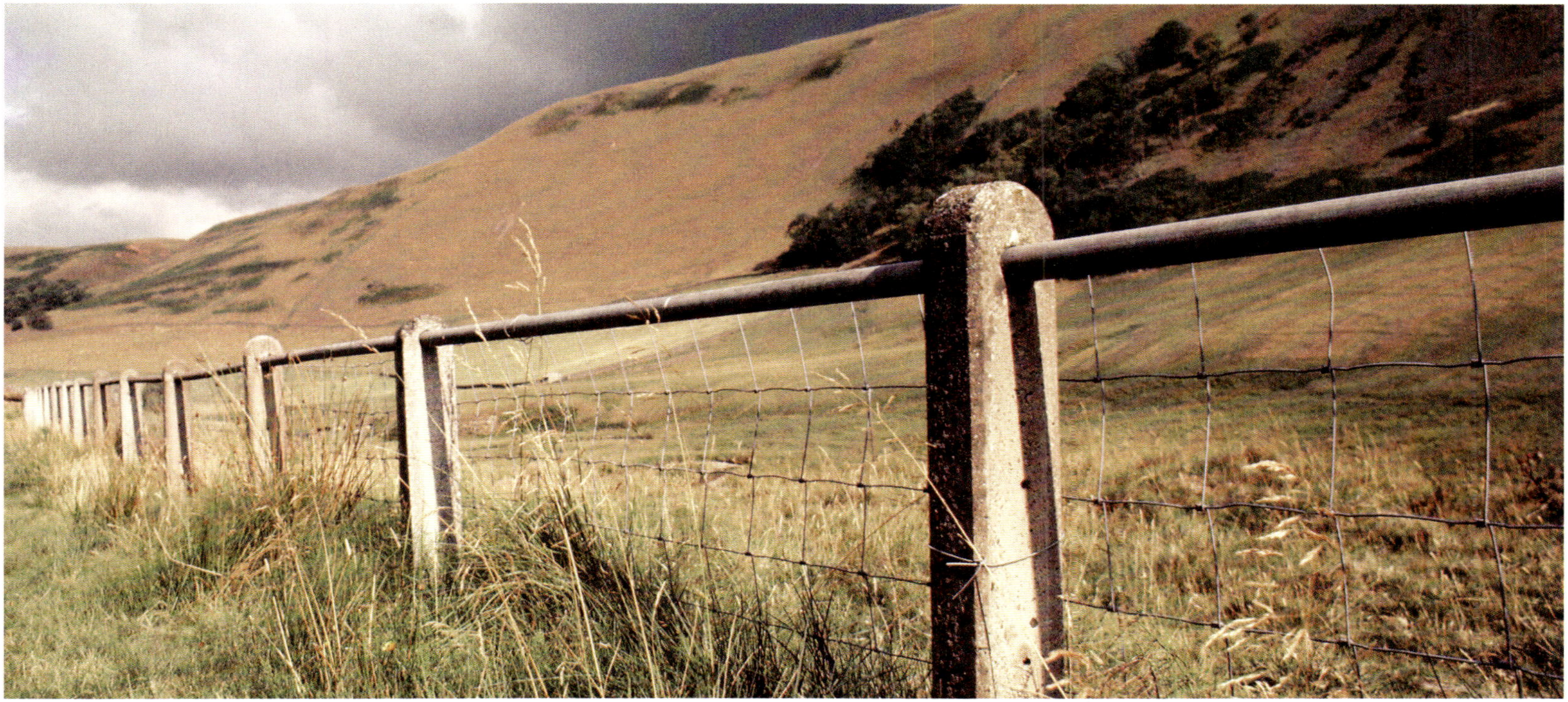

Here is a strong fence using concrete posts and metal pipe (!) threaded through drilled holes. It was erected by the government at the request of the Northern Ireland landowner as replacement for the original (possibly a gorse or blackthorn hedge fence) which was removed during a road improvement project. Expensive compensation. He might have assumed the new fence would last forever, but actually, due to water and frost action, much concrete does not outlast durable wood.

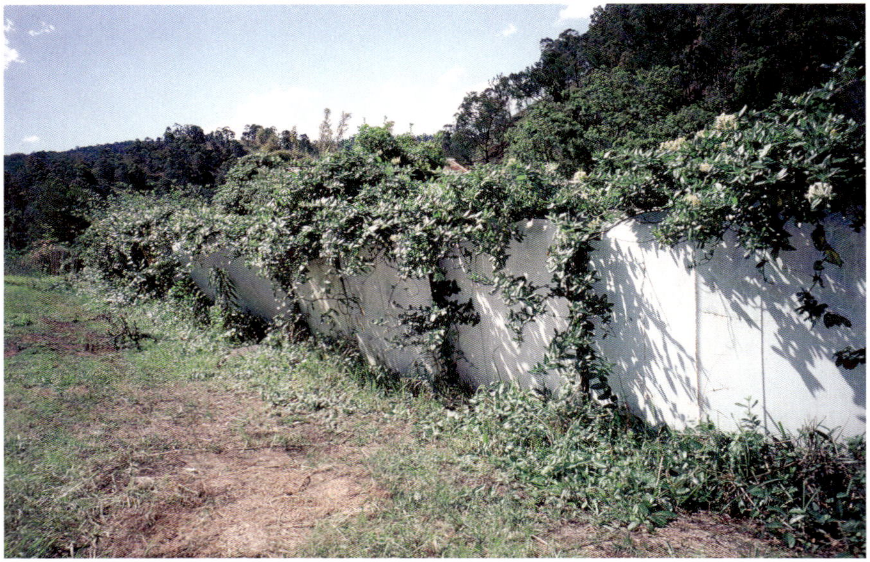

Here, a "panel-beater" (car body repair specialist) in New South Wales, Australia finds a use for old auto body parts and achieves privacy as well. The scars of grisly accidents past are being softened by flowering vines.

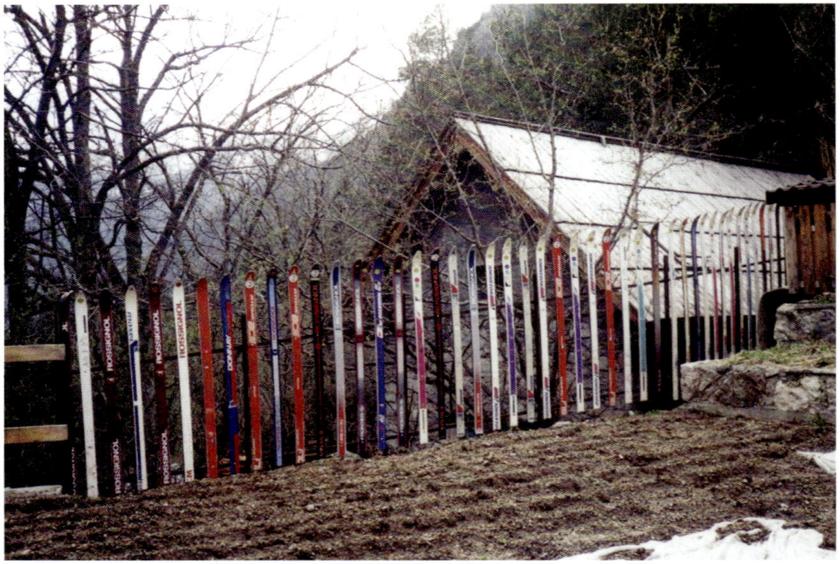

A closed picket fence is often used around a home for visual privacy, to block headlight glare, or to reduce noise from the neighborhood. This suburban homeowner in New Hampshire, USA presumably was a skiing enthusiast, with friends who either gave up the sport or cast off older equipment. (Some of these remind me of my own outdated pair.)

Having once given wings
Admitted the glaring rush of noon
And chanced the evening pearl among the sticks
We now stand rooted, transfixed in service to some
Lower lord.
We have no heroes, no legend of glory to come
Relentless serious strict austere caustic cold
Disappointed we.

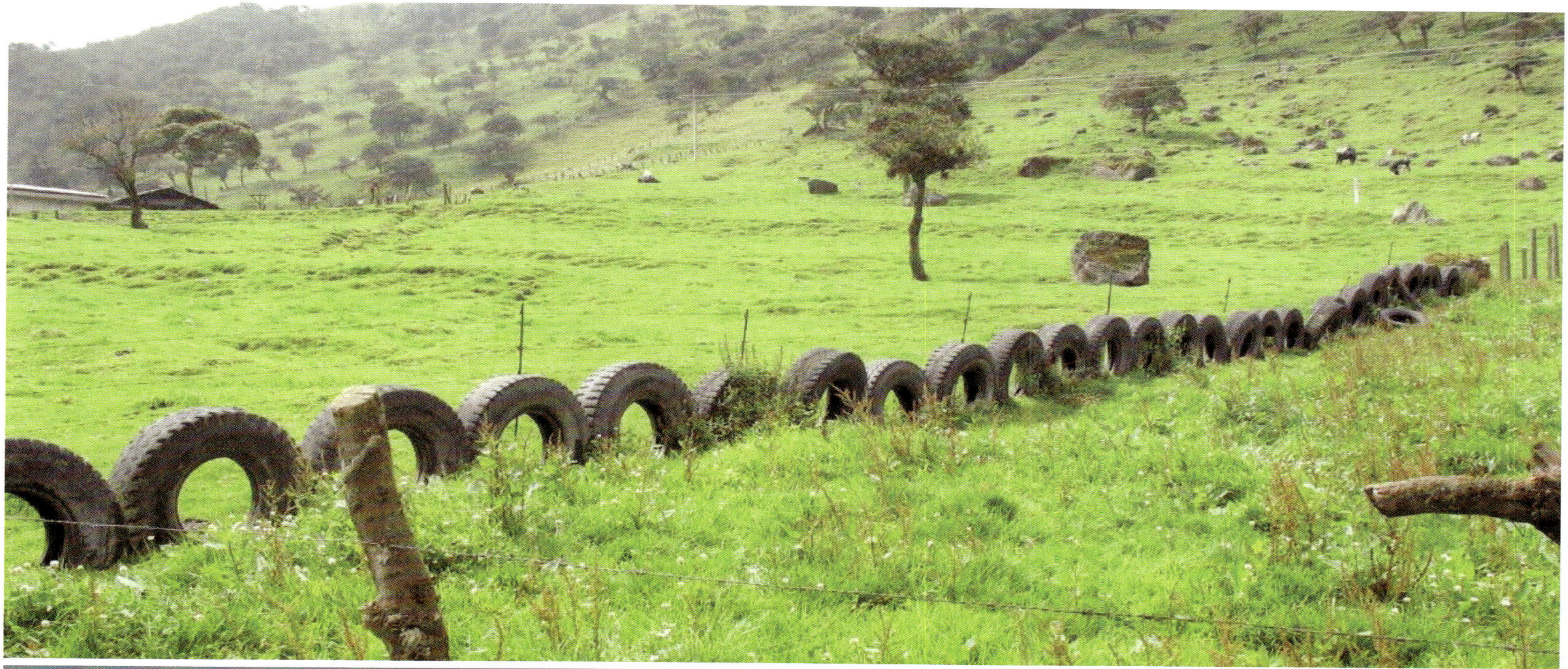

If what your friends have to offer are not used skis, but worn out rubber tires, then that's what you use. This Ecuadorian farmer in the Andean foothills near Papallacta seems to have made a sturdy fence by augmenting his wire on metal and wooden posts with old tires. When resources are scarce, use what comes to hand.

Then there is plastic.......

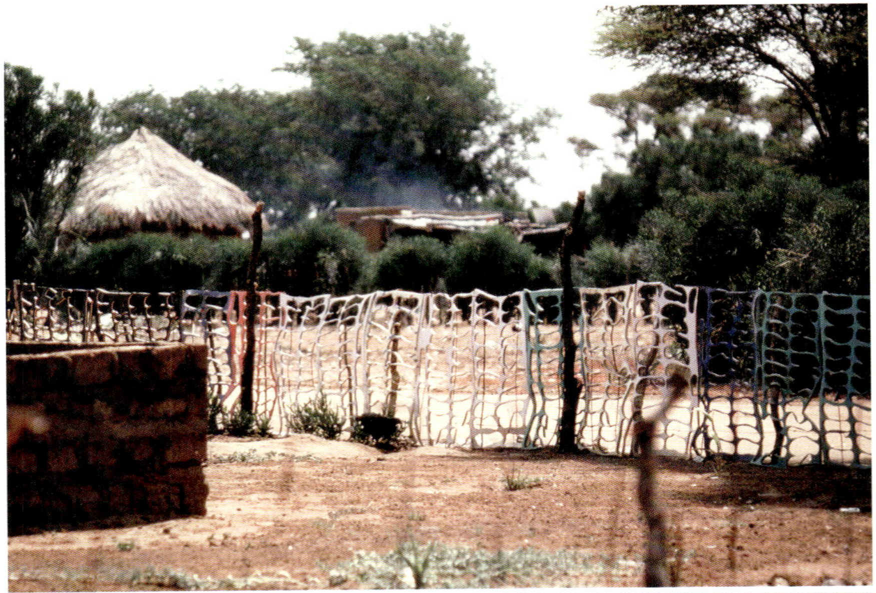

An ingenious way to recycle/repurpose the "waste" from a Botswanan shoe factory which produces flip-flops. The sandals are cut/punched out of sheets of durable rubberized material, leaving behind what someone recognized as potential flexible and durable fencing material. Why not use it?

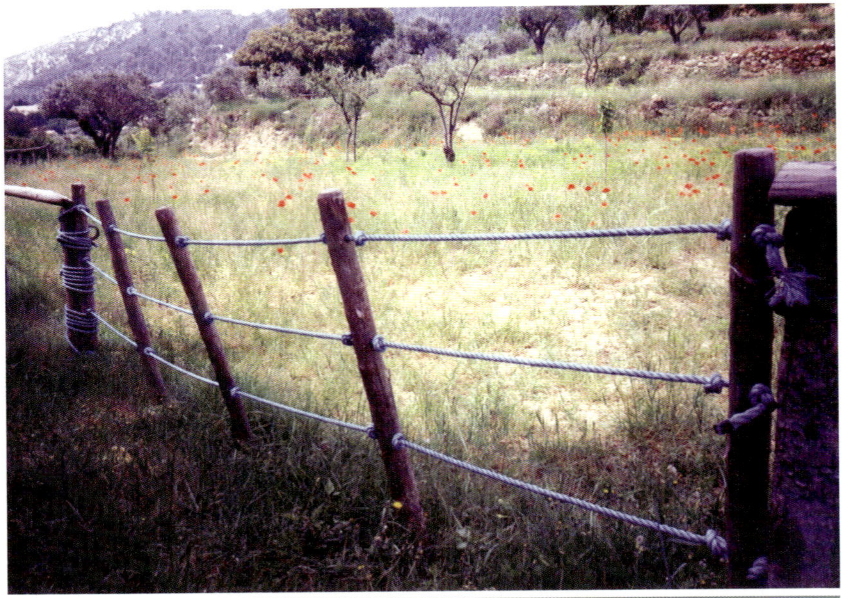

Thick plastic rope makes this fence gate in Provence, France conveniently flexible and easy to open and close.

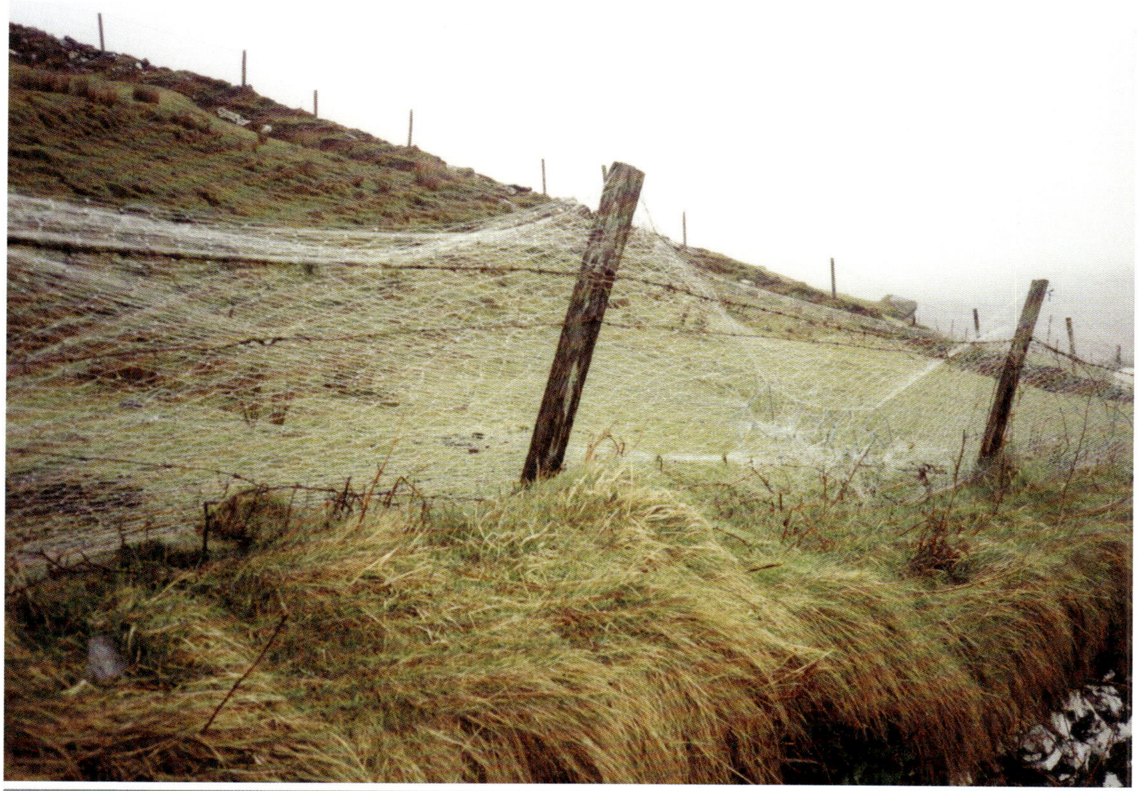

Plastic fishing net makes a floppy but apparently serviceable fence along the coast of Donegal, Ireland.

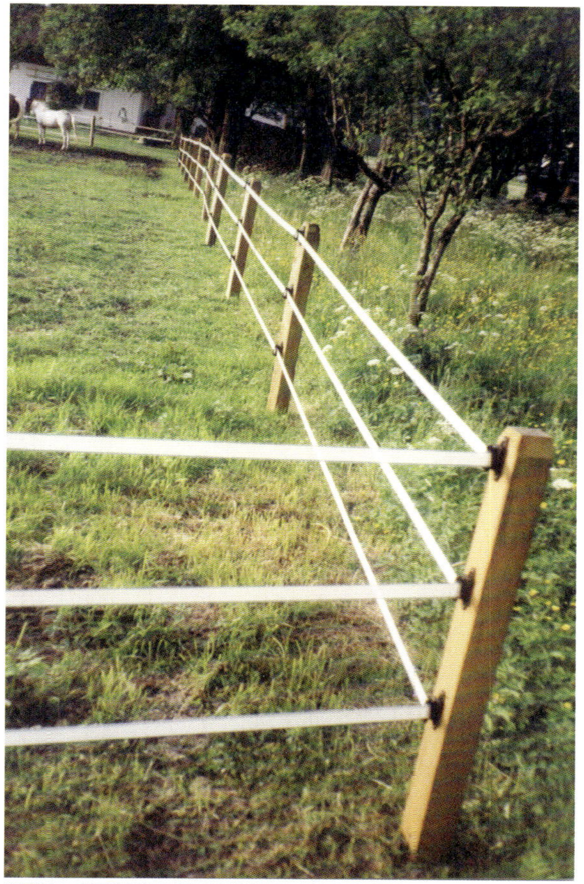

Wide plastic tape makes a snappy presentation and does well as a horse fence. It can even be electrified if necessary.

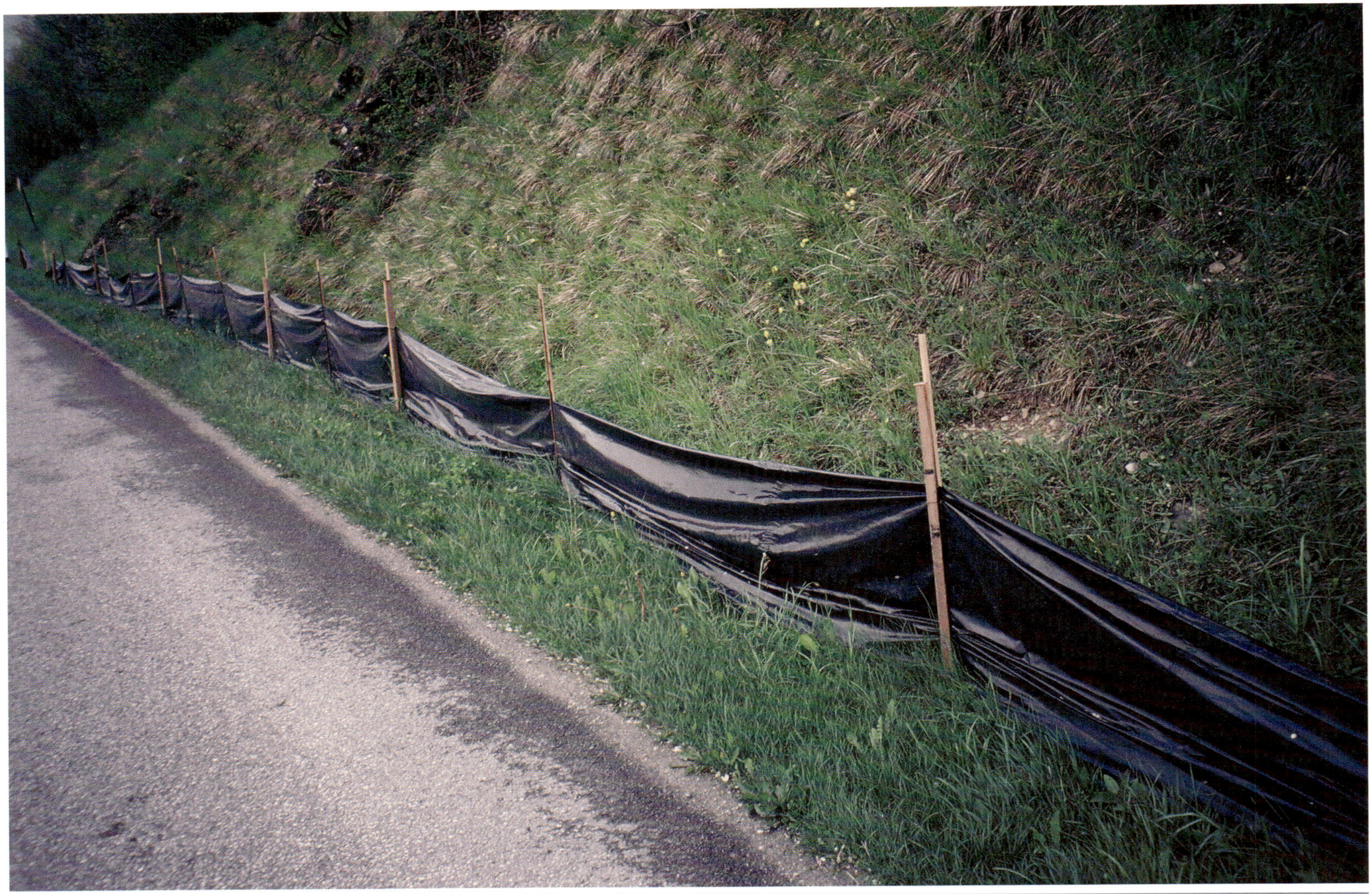

You have got to love this frog fence in Alpi Marittime National Park, Italy. It is temporary, quick and easy to put in and take down, inexpensive, and effective in guiding frogs and other amphibians to underpasses or other safe road crossings during spring migration.

Fences made of stone?

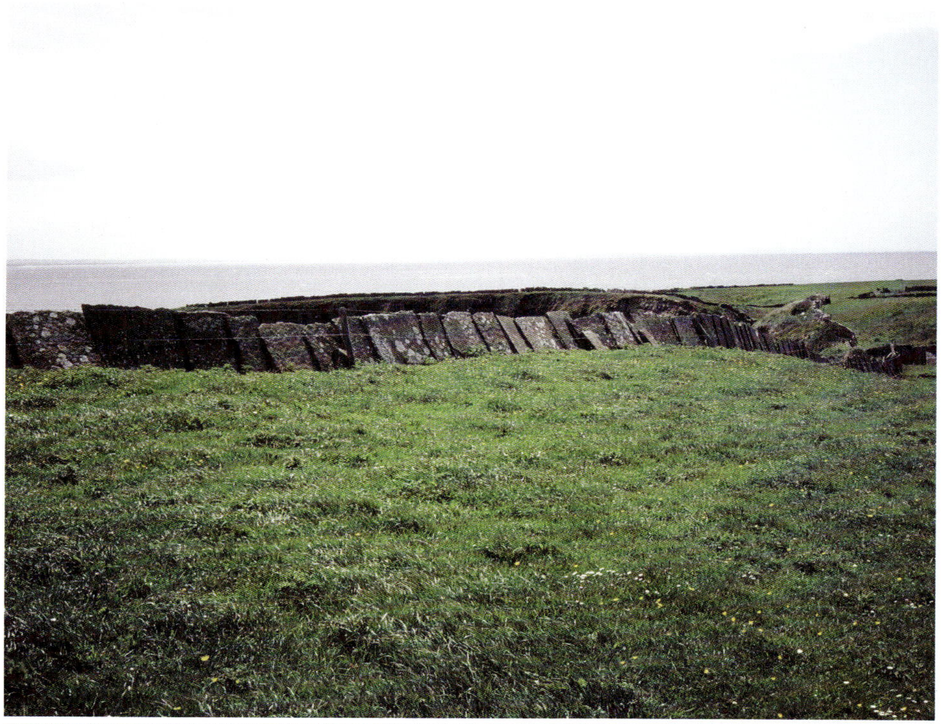

This is a fence in County Claire, Ireland near the Cliffs of Moher, and yes, it is made of thin slabs of stone called flags, about 3 feet high and about 1/4 inch thick. Work with what you have is a fine approach, but doesn't this seem like a LOT of just work?

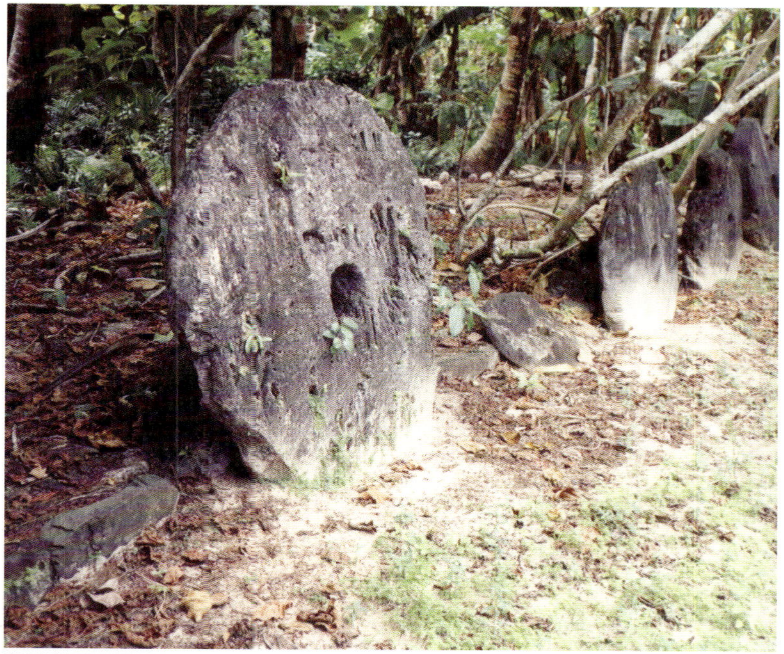

Here is the best stone fence of all. It is made of traditional Pacific Island money. Wheels are carved from stone mined on neighboring islands and transported in dug-out canoes to Yap, where it is still revered and used as a boundary marker indicating wealth and prestige.

Watery fences...

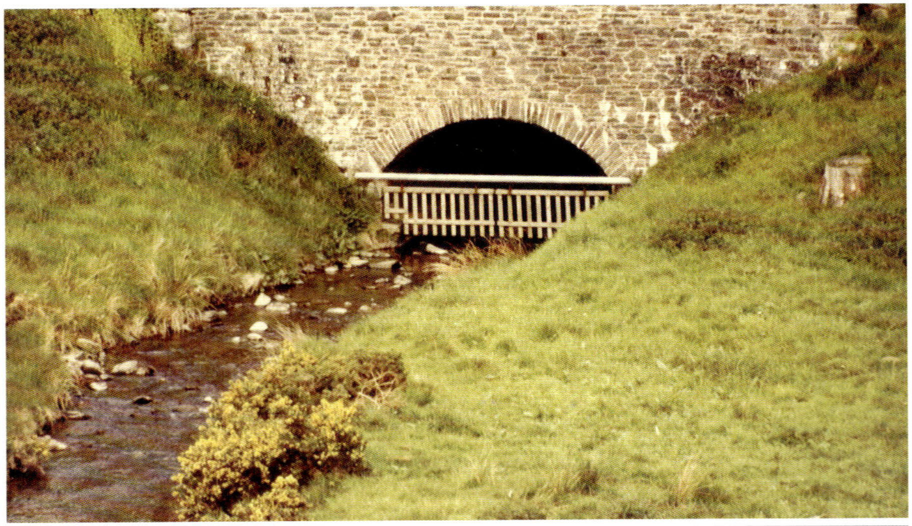

In the lowlands of Scotland, this fence prevents sheep from getting into the stream culvert and escaping beyond.

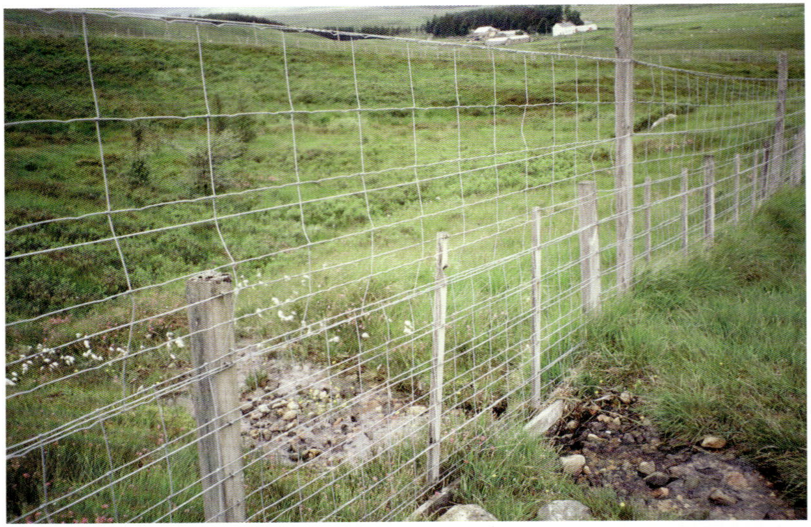

Here in Scotland, near Glenmoriston, a strong high fence for keeping in farmed red deer also lets the burn (stream) flow freely through it.

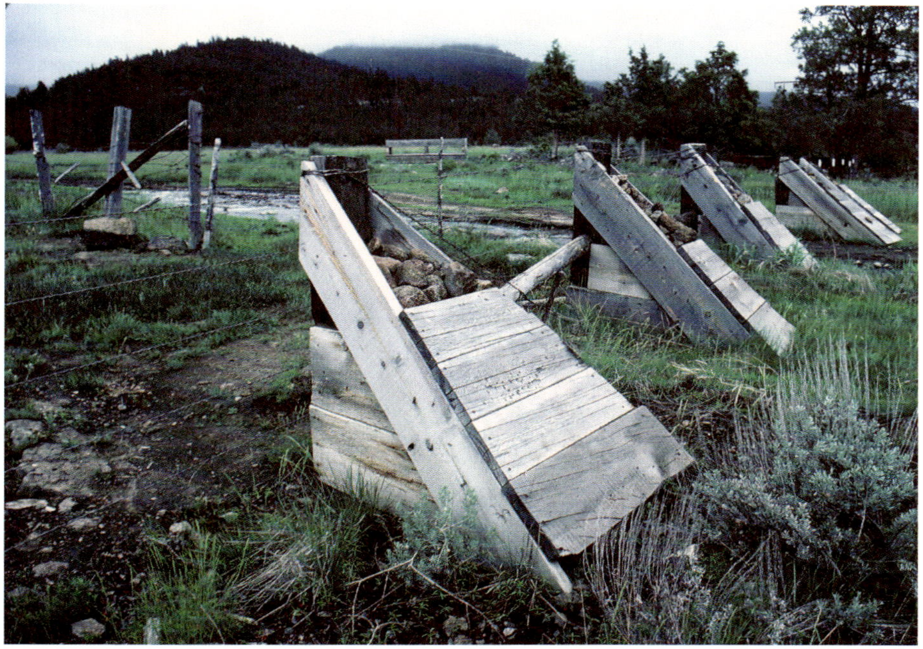

This fence in rainy Oregon, USA must deal with a different water issue. Upright posts must be anchored and heavily weighed down with cribs filled with stone to keep ground frost from heaving them akilter each spring.

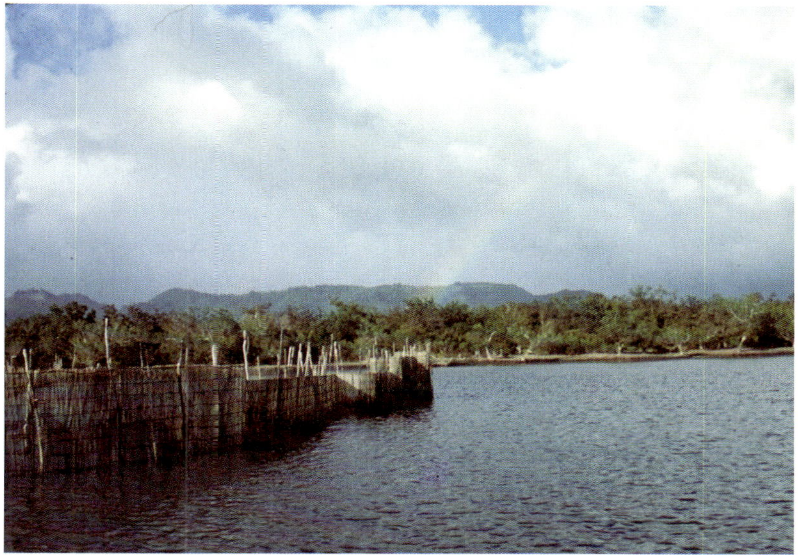

Aquaculture in the Philippines requires fish fences.

Metal fences...

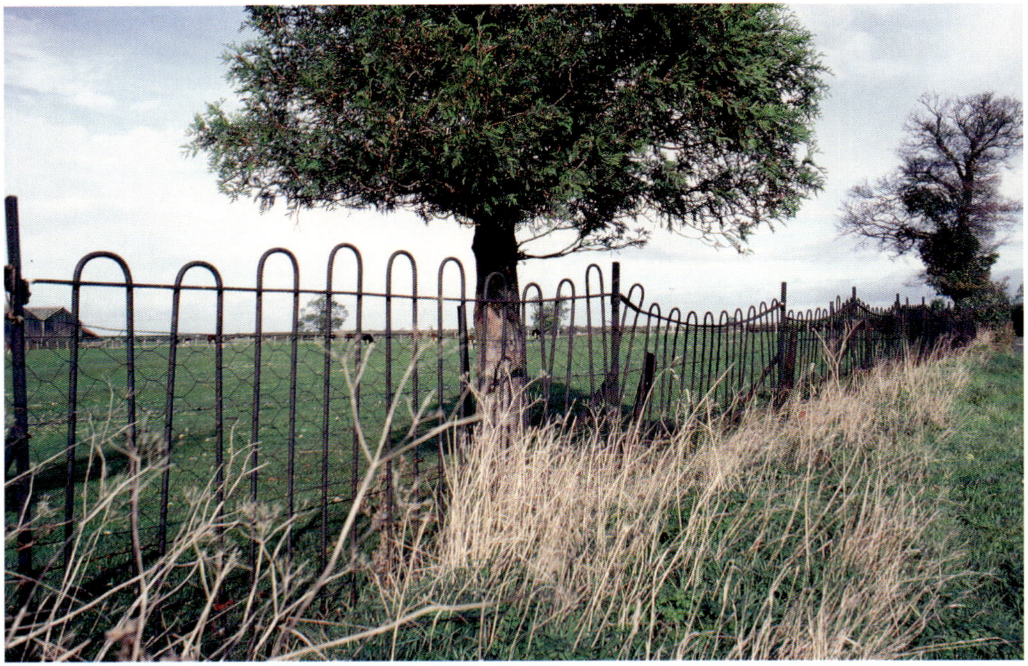

A rather unusual metal fence-building material is being used here near Middle Littleton, England. Was it re-purposed from something else? Built to order from long metal rods?

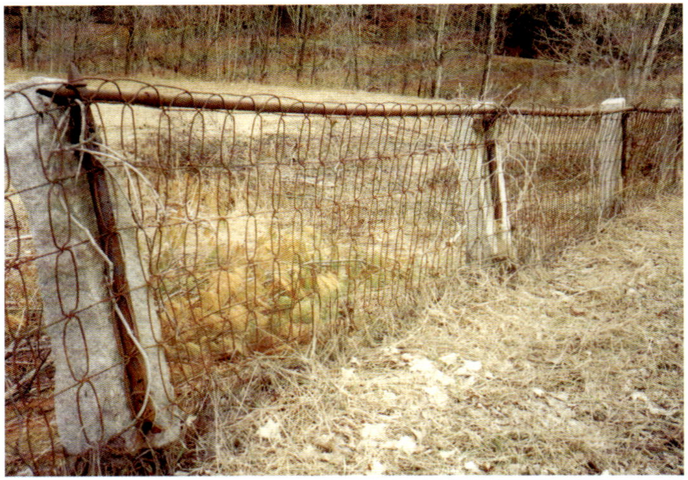

Is there a factory making beds/ bedsprings nearby? Or is this just a Slovenian style of heavy woven wire mesh?

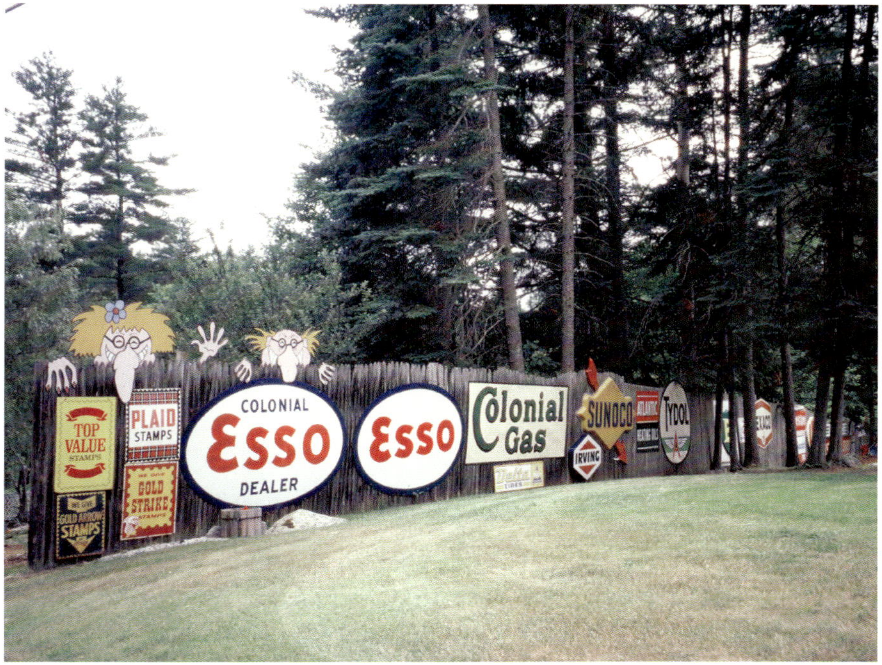

One New Hampshire, USA property owner amuses passersby with this plain wooden privacy fence turned garish with old gas station signs.

And invisible fences.

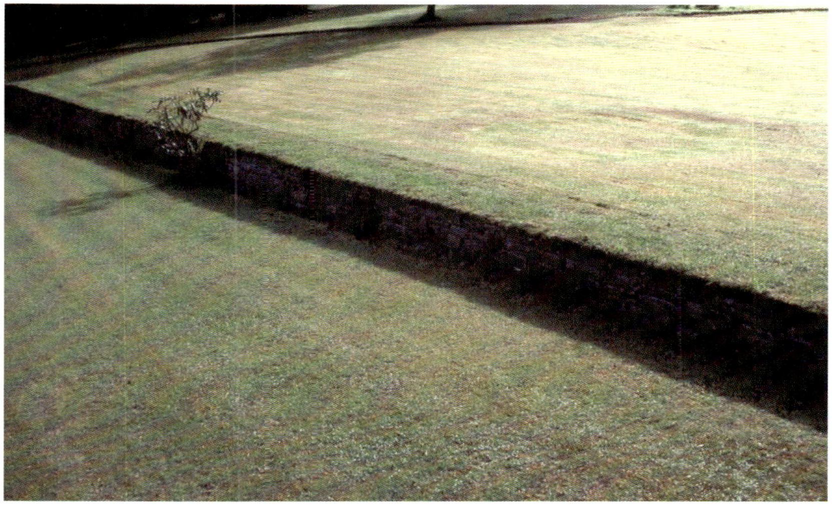

Here is what you could call an invisible fence. The well-known landscape architect Lancelot (Capability) Brown, was much in demand in England in the 1700s to design pleasant pastoral landscapes as viewed from an estate's castle or country home. One of his trademarks was the construction of what he called a "hoo ha." It was actually a ditch or terrace, not visible from the dwelling upslope, but deep enough to be an effective barrier to keep grazing animals in their pasture downslope. I count this English hoo ha as a fence, of sorts.

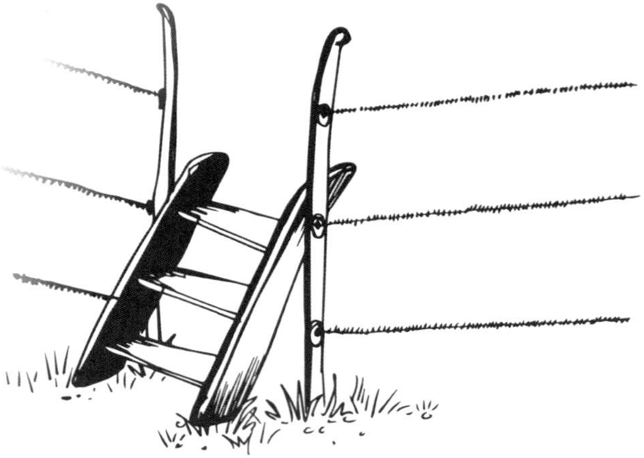

GETTING BEYOND THE BARRIER

Often stiles or step-overs are built into fences for people to go through or over the barrier.

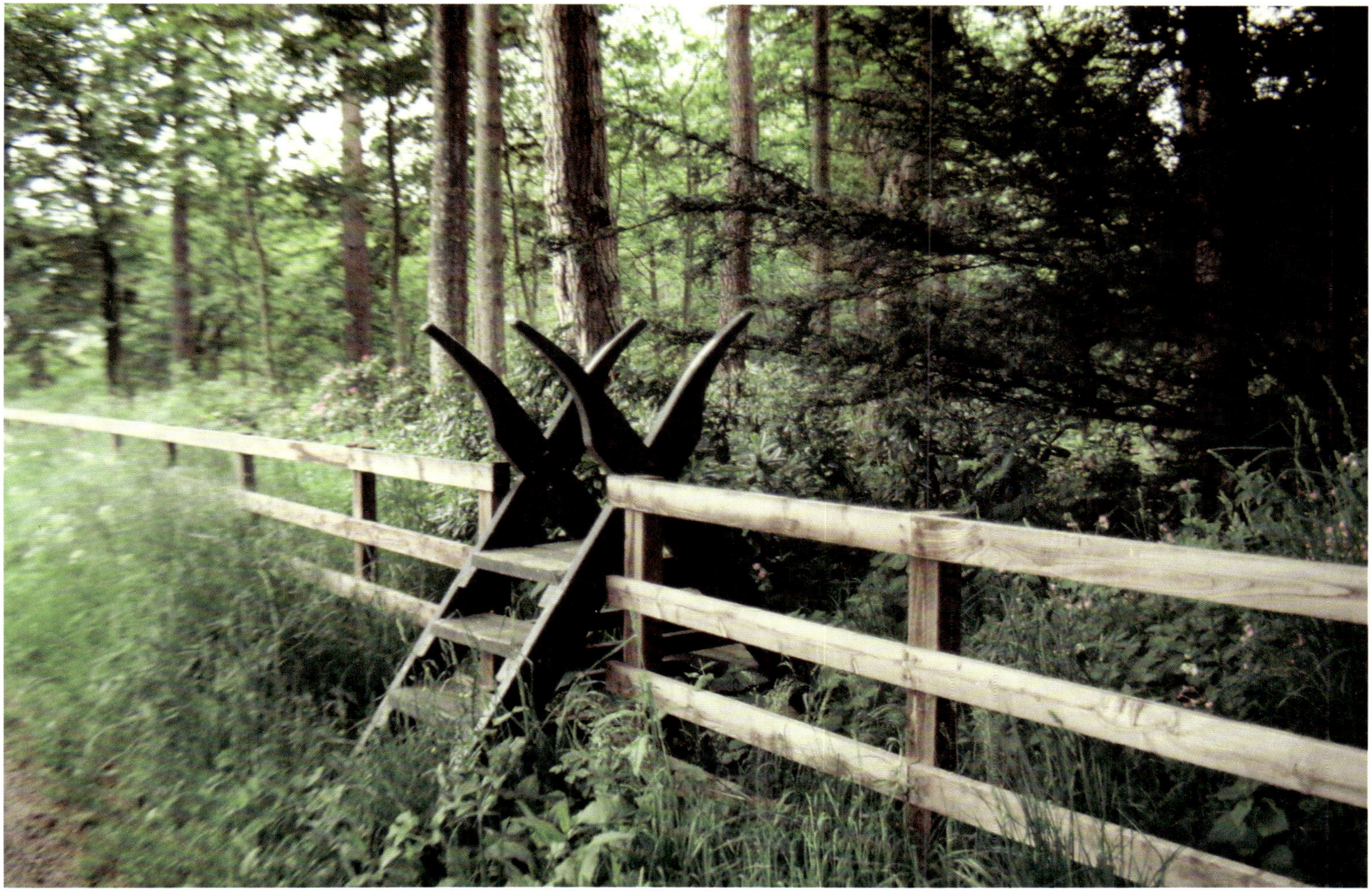

Elegant European style stop-over.

Simple notched pole design step-over in Nepal.

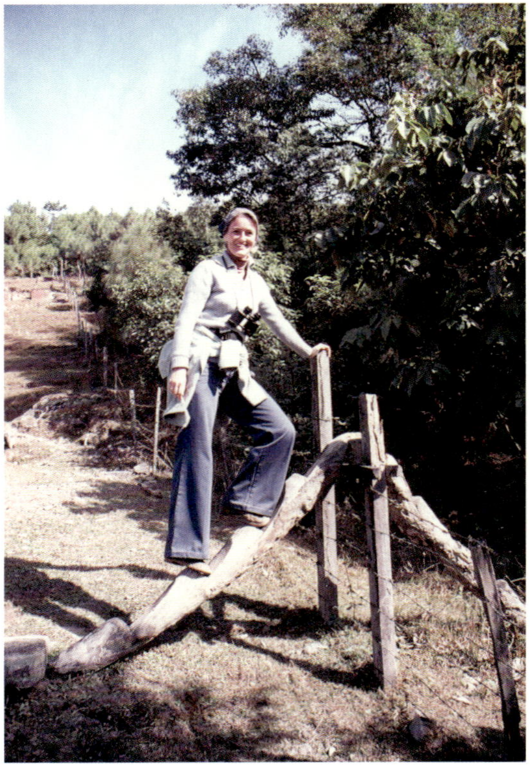

Sure-footed step-over for recreational trails in New Zealand.

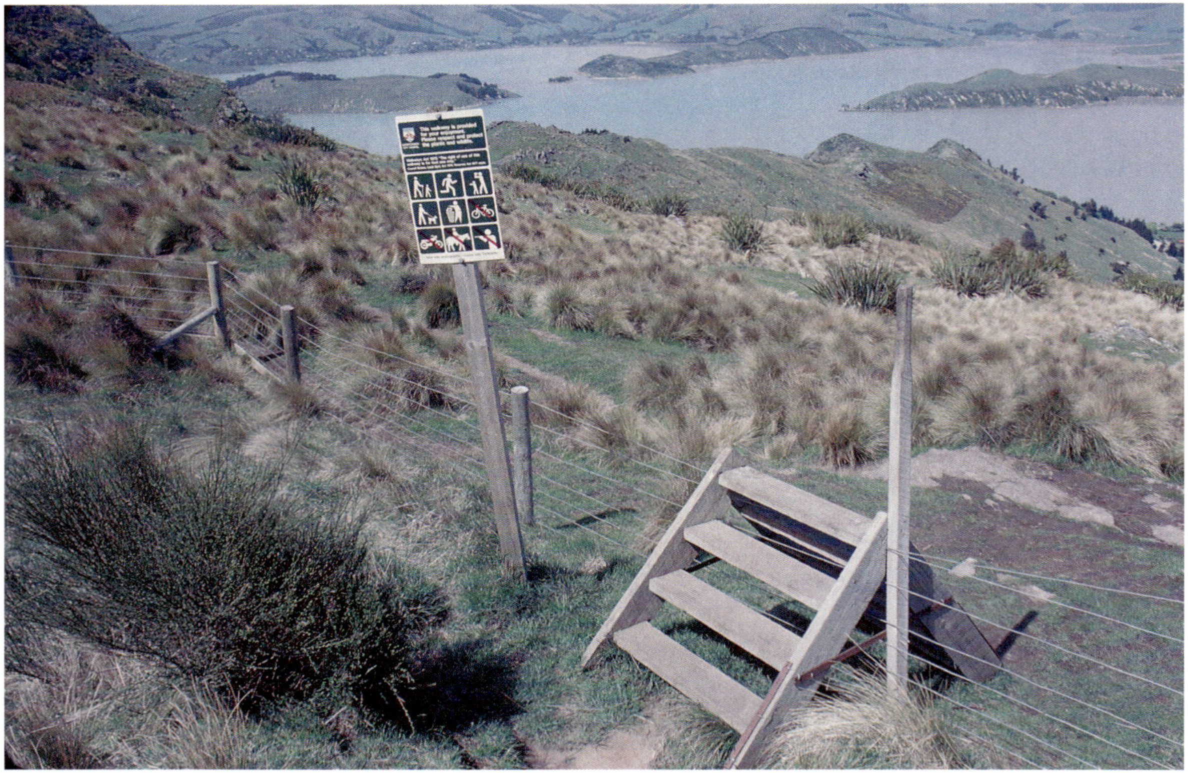

A zigzag pass-through like this one in the Austrian Alps, works as easily as a gate for people, but most large animals will not enter it.

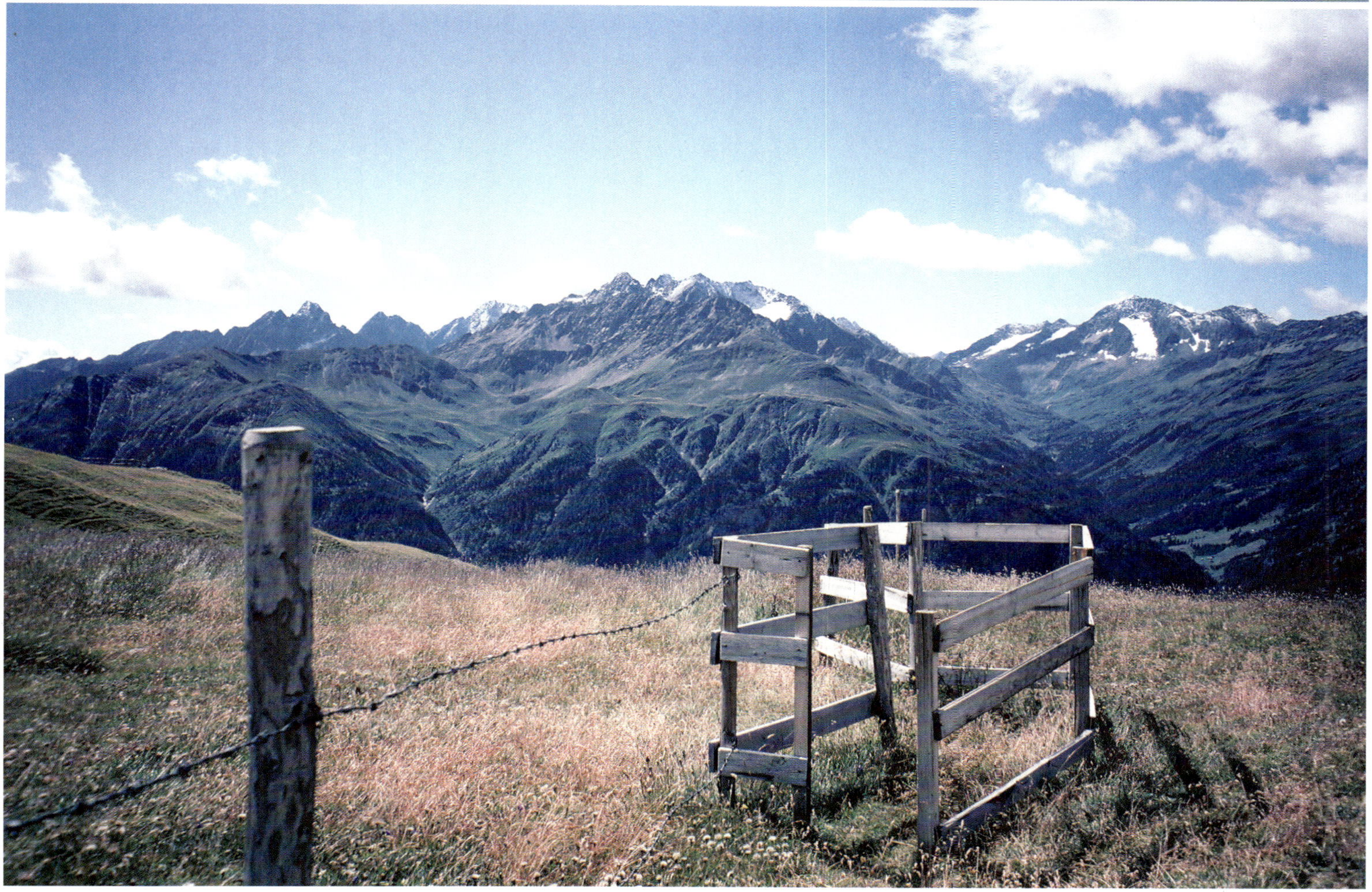

Most often, fences have gates built into them. These are often lockable for "controlled" access. Here's one on a cattle ranch near Kona, Hawai`i, USA.

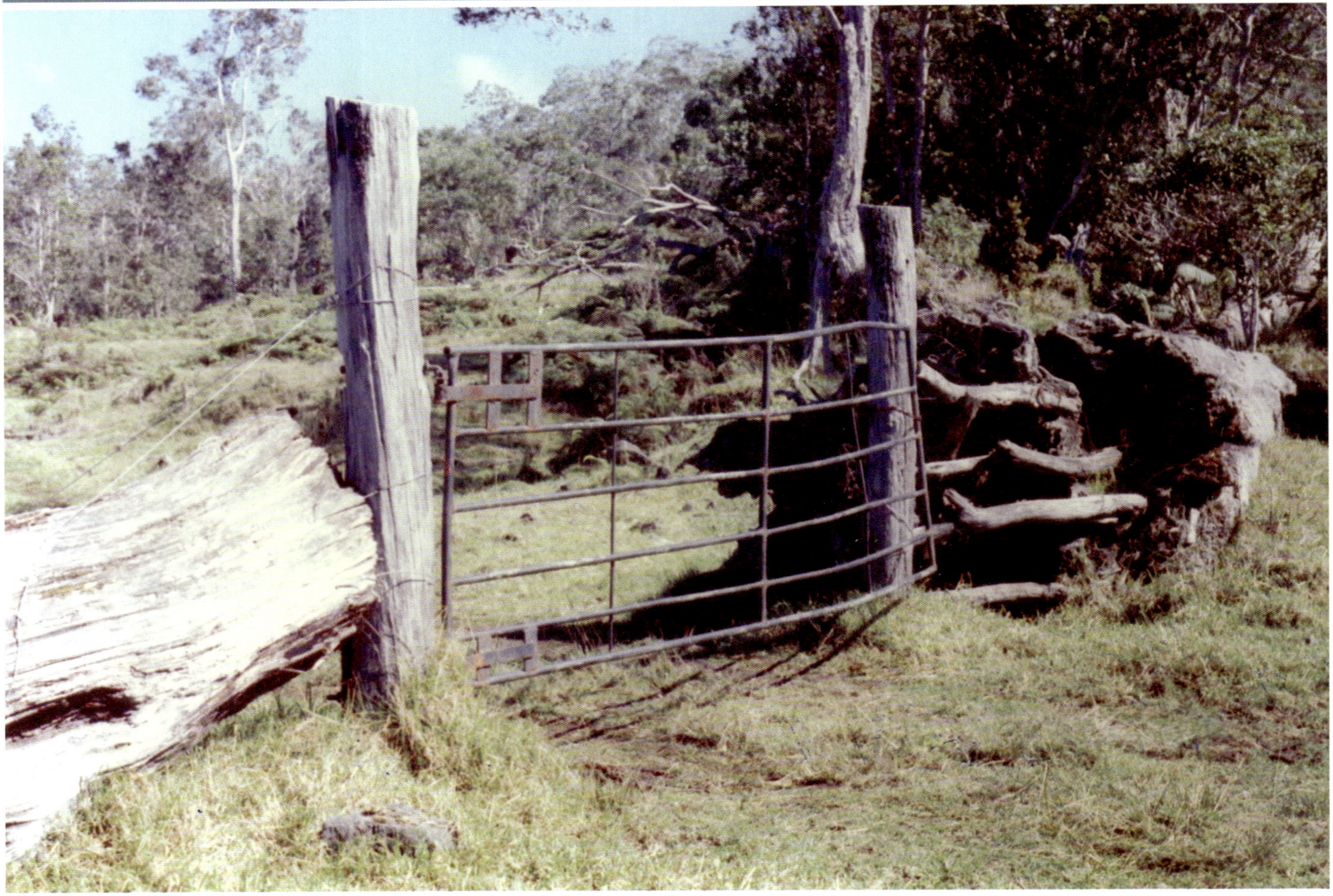

And one in New Zealand with specialized control through the use of cattle bars in the opening (also known as judder bars or a cattle grid), which hooved animals are reluctant to walk across.

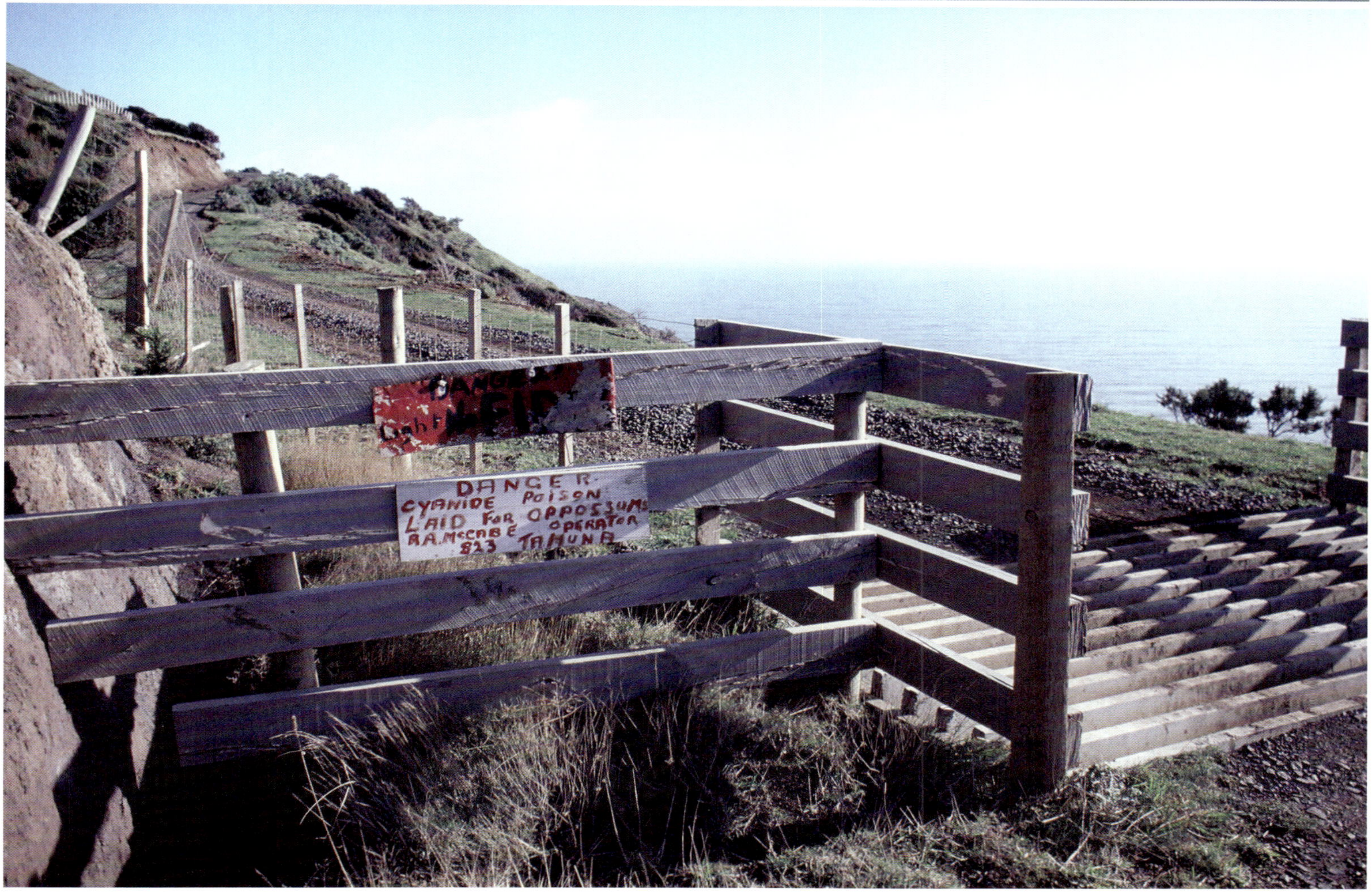

And here is another New Zealand story waiting to be told, just outside Mount Egmont National Park which protects Mount Taranaki on the North Island. It's a wide gate. Was the fence up before the forest was clearcut and converted to pasture?

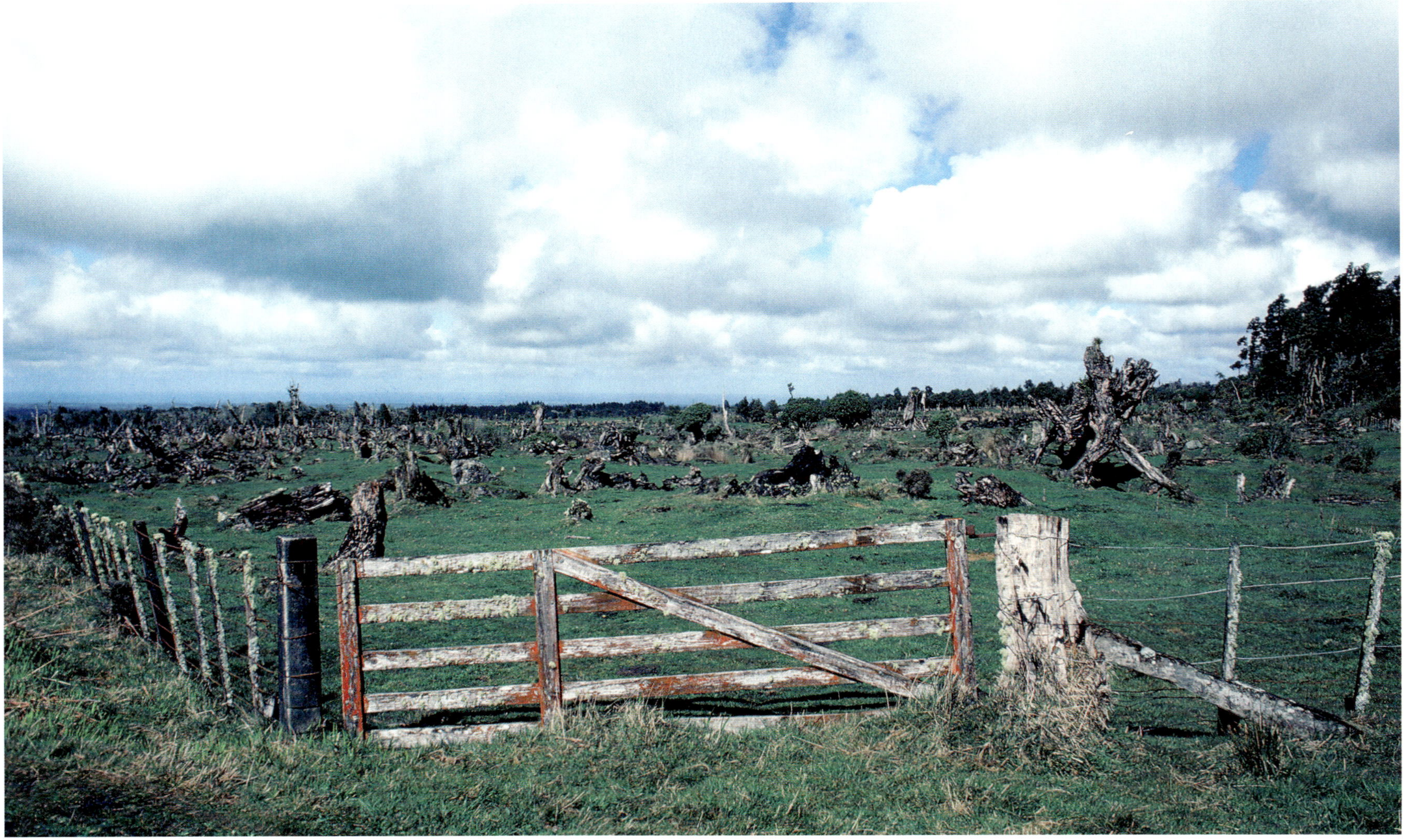

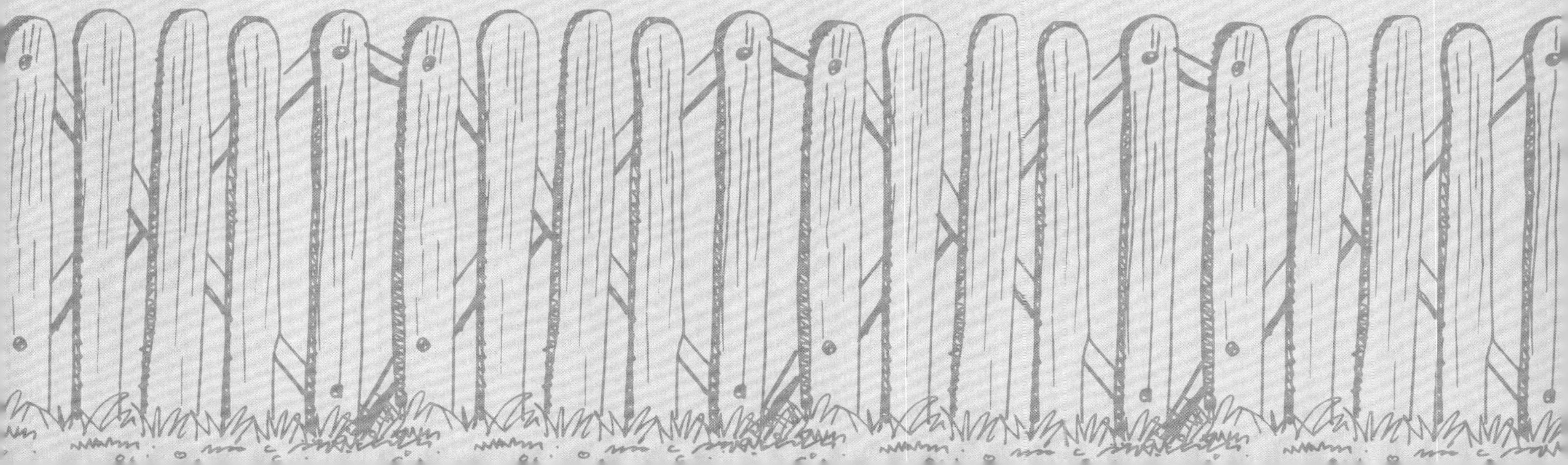

Fences, even with gates, are physical and/or psychological barriers. They may effectively influence behavior for a time, but like so many other "walls" we humans put up around our possessions and ourselves, others (and Nature) will find ways to overcome them. In time, barriers break down—as well-known American poet Robert Frost wrote in his poem Mending Wall, "Something there is that doesn't love a wall." That something is a natural desire for freedom and access which will have its way, no matter how sturdy or fearsome the wall or fence.

We know this historically. Hadrian's Wall only briefly kept the Picts from invading Roman England, as ultimately the Great Wall of China did not keep out invaders. The Iron Curtain (a fence built not of physical material but of government policy) was created by the Soviet Union in an effort to block itself and its satellite states from open contact with Western Europe and non-Soviet-controlled areas after World War II; policy changed with the end of the Cold War in 1991 and now that boundary is returning to open Nature as the European Greenbelt. Australia's Rabbit-proof Fence failed in its mission to contain an animal considered a pest. Many historic wooden fences, as well as stone walls, in New England now run without function through reforested land, attesting to the ability of Nature to reclaim natural habitat after humans' efforts to domesticate it.

Nevertheless, we keep building fences.

Increasingly, I hope we recognize the need to make these barriers porous as much as we can so that cooperation, rather than confrontation, is promoted. International Peace Parks on national borders are a good example. The first in the world paired Glacier and Waterton National Parks (in Montana, USA and Alberta, Canada), and this has been working well since established in 1932. The international boundary runs through heavy forest and is marked simply as a modest swath cut through the trees.

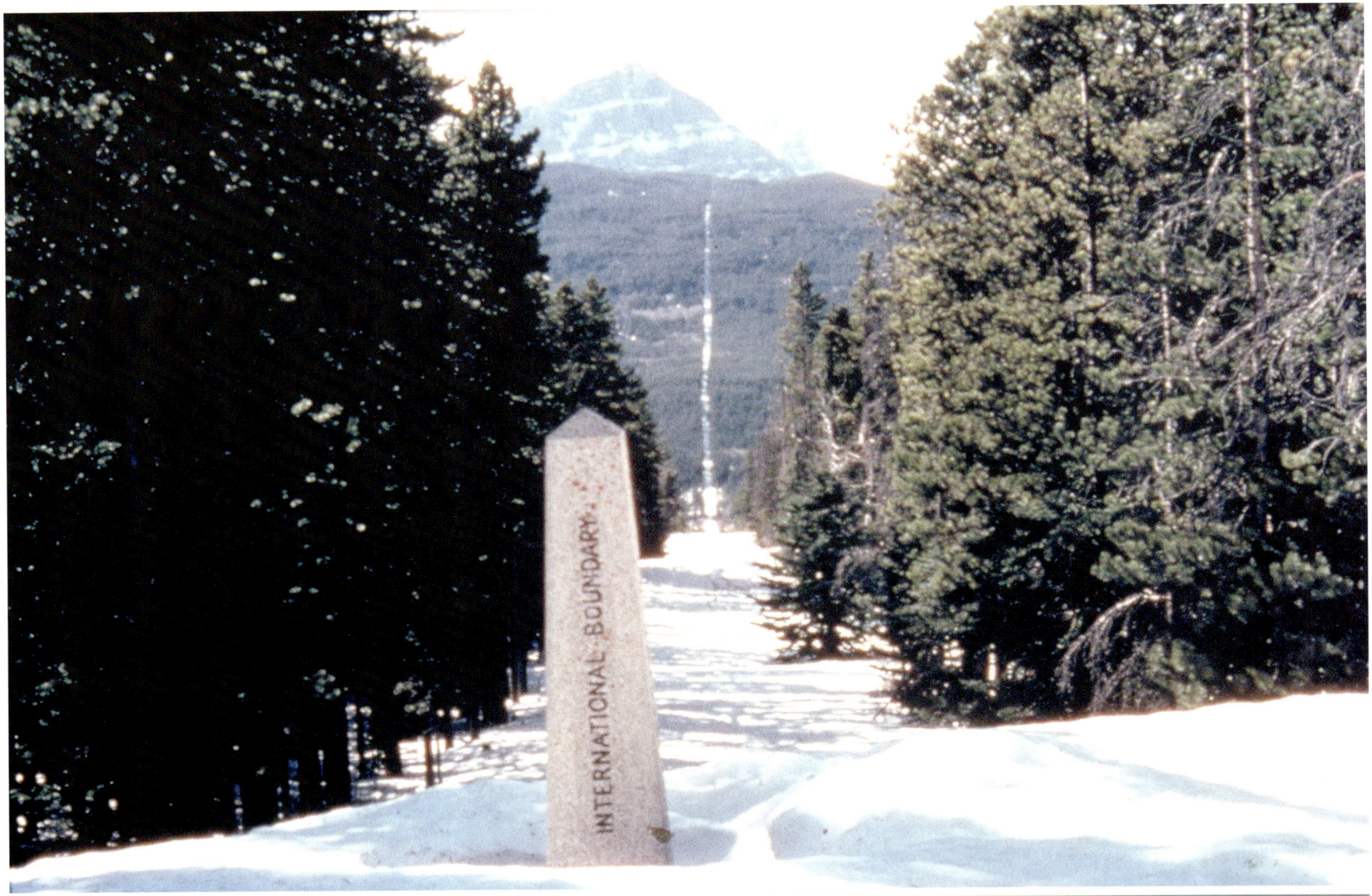

Glacier – Waterton International Peace Park between the USA and Canada.

Is it unthinkable to establish a Korean Demilitarized Zone Peace Park? And one for the more than 30-year conflict between India and Pakistan over ice and snow on the Siachen Glacier? Others? Can we make these border fences porous at least to Nature, not blocking the free flow of wild plant and animal life through them?

At the societal level, I earnestly hope that at least some of our old fences and barriers between people are coming down. Are we not learning to resist building cultural fences to keep "us" in and "them" out? Fortunately, in academia long-standing rigid disciplinary boundaries have yielded to interdisciplinary programs in recognition of the interconnectedness of both life and knowledge.

I believe barriers to compassion and understanding need to be dismantled wherever we recognize them. As we view fences in the landscape and fences in society, let us remember that they have historic reasons for being there, and also that their stories change over time. Fences are not permanent. Let us strive as my late Vermont colleague and friend Carl Reidel wrote … *to understand the meaning of old fences, maintain the best of them, take down those which divide us, and create new limits that ensure justice for all.*[2]

About the AUTHORS

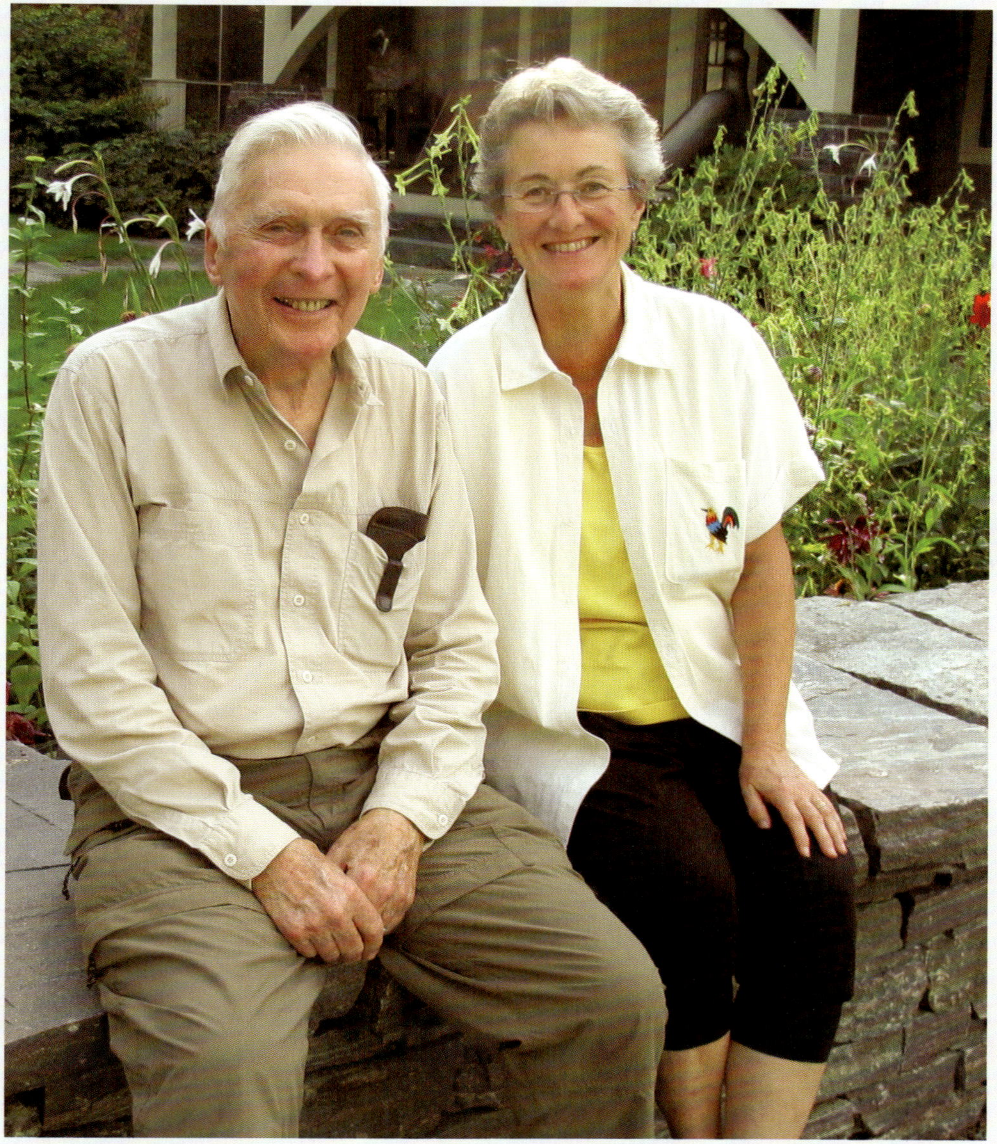

Larry and Linda Hamilton, in their hometown of Charlotte, Vermont. (Photo credit: Kitt)

Lawrence S. Hamilton (1925-2016) was Professor Emeritus at Cornell University. Grounded in love of Nature and a strong sense of fairness, Larry was a much-loved educator, environmental conservation leader, and peace activist. This book is a testament to his curiosity and good cheer, the love in his heart, plans in his head, and mud on his boots.

Linda S. Hamilton, Larry's wife of 36 years, is a conservation planner and Nature advocate. Completing this fence book project for him, based on his annotated photos and initial draft, was a privilege and a labor of love after his death.

About the POET

Marie Riley is an educator and lawyer. She met Larry and Linda on the Big Island of Hawai'i, on a hike from Kipuka Nene down to a coastal campsite lit only by star-shine on the Pacific Ocean. Larry's enthusiasm for fences and their stories led her to pen these poems.

Endnotes

1. MacCleery, Douglas W. *American Forests, A History of Resiliency and Recovery*. Forest History Society Issues Series, 2011. p. 9.

2. Reidel, C. *The Fence Viewer*, Vermont Quarterly, Spring 2012.

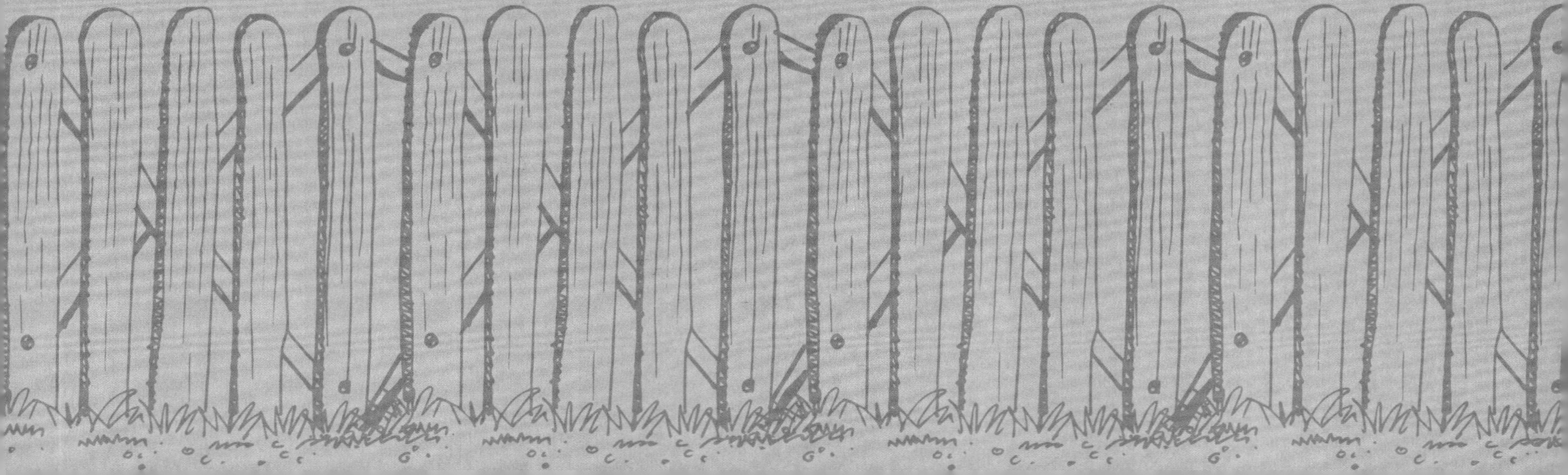

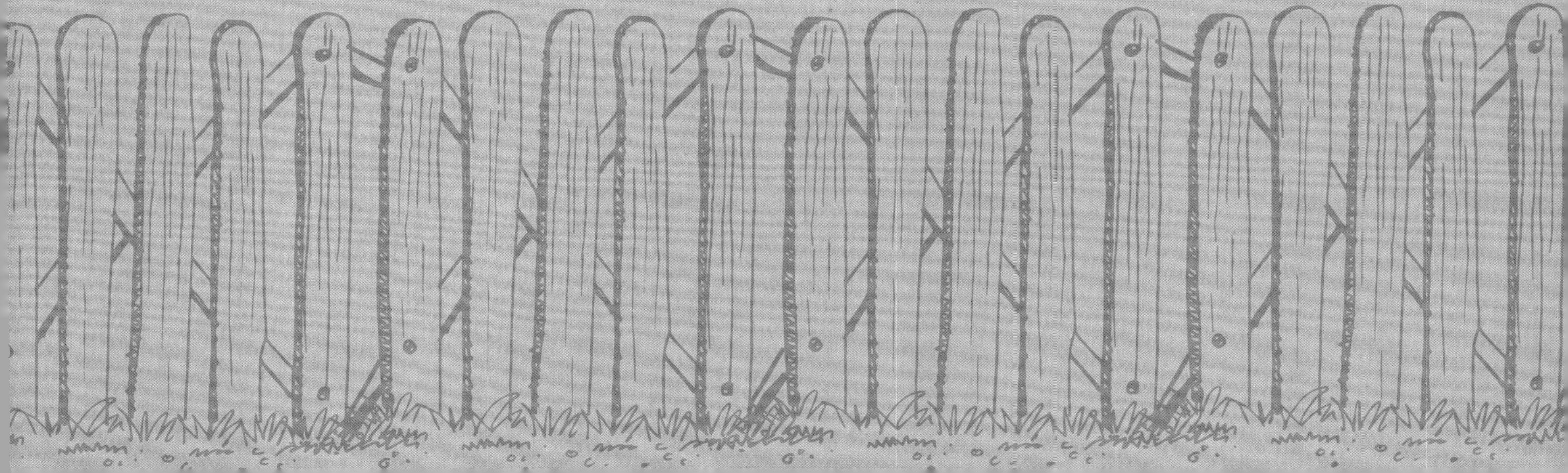